More Curious than Cautious

A Survivor's Adventure Travel through Paradise
1955-1957

By
Peter Fraser

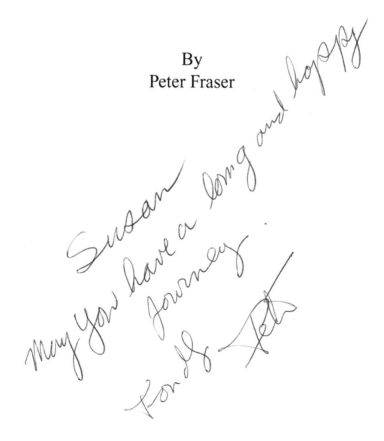

Susan
May you have a long and happy journey.
Fondly, Peter

First published by Dog Ear Publishing
4010 W. 86th Street, Ste H
Indianapolis, IN 46268
www.dogearpublishing.net

ISBN: 978-159858-770-8

This book is printed on acid-free paper.

Printed in the United States of America

Dedication

This book is dedicated to
my very patient family
who never understood
my need
to see the world.

Acknowledgements

Generous help from several people got this struggle through a very lengthy process. I praise my Editor, Peggy Emard for the amount of patience she demonstrated in getting the text ready. Several computer-savvy friends at my retirement place kindly helped out, including Rick and Joyce Tullis, whose enthusiasm pulled me through a period of doldrums. Florence Temko kept pushing to get the job done. Ruth Lawson (computer preparation, cartography and research) and her family were there to offer a friendly hand. Don Robinson suggested a great idea that turned the narrative into a real adventure story. Young and brilliant staff members lent a willing hand when they could, along with endless encouragement from many others. I thank them all. Above all, I thank those who listened, and listened, and listened, without complaint. Are they ready to go through it again with the second half of the adventure?

Appreciation

I want to thank the following dance teachers and their indispensable assisting spouses, among many others, for their knowledge, enthusiasm, and patience that made such a difference in my life: Bill and Carrie Kattke, Cliff and Joan Wormell, Ralph Page, and Don Armstrong for Squares and Contras; Mary Ann and Michael Herman, Rae and George Nemovicher, Kenny Speers, Estelle and Bill Birnbaum for International Folk; Richard Powers, Hannah Roberts, Patri Pugliesi and Joan Walton for Vintage; Ann Smith for Scottish Country; Christine Helwig, and George Fogg for English Country; all were such good friends and fine teachers. I loved you all, and long live the memories. "To live is to dance, to dance is to live." (From the wisdom of "Snoopy," in "Peanuts," by Carl Schultz.)

Introduction

This is not a tourist guide book. This is a collection of my memoirs, from my photos, my journals, my watercolors, and from extensive letters that I wrote home. The text was basically copied from a skeletal document I typed upon my return to New York a half century ago. I have done considerable editing to make things clearer to those readers who may be unfamiliar with the subject areas or the events. I have tried not to update anything but the most essential facts. Everything mentioned was true as stated.

I relied on www.history.navy.mil/faqs/faq.67-3htm-48K for "Seabee History: Formation of the Seabees and World War II"

I did resort to using the *Encyclopedia Britannica* for the early history of Samoa.

The information about The Missionary Period of the mid-1800s to the mid-1900s was taken from *The Blue Laws of Rarotonga*, a small booklet written in 1879 by The Council of Arikis (Arikis, island chiefs), most kindly donated by Jean Mason, Coordinator of the Cook Islands Library-Museum Society, Rarotonga, Cook Islands.

I used various contemporary periodicals for the stories of the lives of the first few years of two boys in Fiji.

The rest of the text is based either on my own observations and notes or things that I was told by people I met.

I call the residents of these islands "The People of the Coconut Culture." In describing each cultural group with whom I visited, I take time to discuss their homes. The word "house" implies something familiar and different to the reader. The traditional huts found in the various island groups were distinctive. Therefore, in Tahiti I use their word *fare*, pronounced (FAH ray), to describe their traditional bamboo and thatch homes. In Samoa I use their word *fale* (FAH lay), in Fiji I use their word *mbure* (MBOO ray), and in New Zealand I use the Maori word *whare* (WHA ray). I have used a lot of local words for local color. I urge the reader to try to accept the local vocabulary as the text progresses for a better understanding of the story.

I have always been curious about the world around me. I never got into trouble with this attitude until I started to travel on my own. Then, as I was gaining experience, I began to be less cautious. The chances I took may seem mild to the readers of the early years of the 21st century. Some of my exploits were risky, but I wasn't aware of it at the time. I took chances with transportation because there was no other way to get to where I wanted to go.

My personal adventure hero was Richard Halliburton, author of several travel books in the early 1900s. He opened travel doors for my generation. He owed his daring exploits to those intrepid Victorians who endured great personal hardships as they blazed trails to unknown parts of the world. There have always been adventurers.

Contemporary adventure travelers go for luxury or excitement, with "extreme" activities. These sports, like conquering Mount Everest or jumping from high bridges, were unheard of when my generation was exploring exotic places. The thrills of climbing among treetops or roughing it in ATVs in the deserts were still in the future. So look closely, your predecessor's footprints are already in the sand.

The main purpose of writing this book at this time was to preserve what I saw and my experiences. Many of these ways of life are disappearing with the passage of time and the homogenization of the world's cultures. At some point, all humans may be living similar lives. The differences in our cultures that made us interesting will have been forgotten. How dull it will all become.

Modern forms of transportation have made every place on earth readily accessible. Past generations of adventurers led the way to the places where the luxury resorts are located now. Yet there is more to travel than planes and resorts. I ask you, the modern traveler, to make an opportunity to meet the people who live on the other side of the fence surrounding the resort of your choice. But like you, they too have busy lives, trying to survive the modernization that has changed their cultures so radically. They may have little time for strangers. An open mind adds so much to the travel experience.

Come with me and get acquainted with the People of the Coconut Culture.

TABLE OF CONTENTS

PART THREE
The Islands of Fiji
A Bit of Grammar
Fijian Words Used in the Text and Their meanings

PART FOUR
New Zealand and the Maoris
November 1956

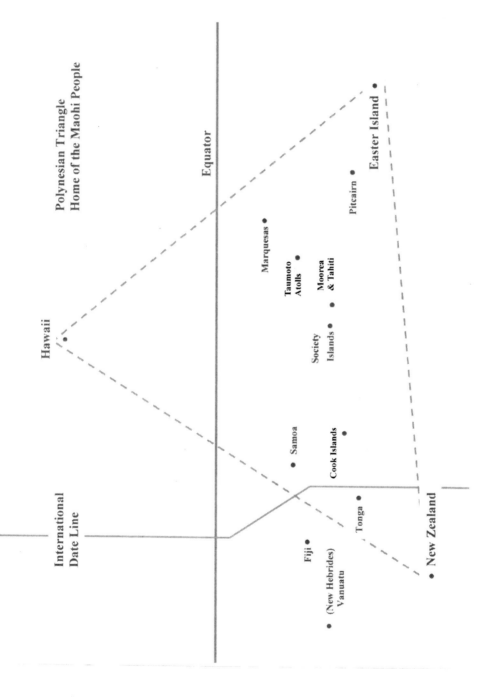

Polynesian Triangle
Home of the Maohi People

Equator

International
Date Line

Hawaii

Marquesas

Taumoto
Atolls

Moorea
& Tahiti

Society
Islands

Pitcairn

Easter Island

Samoa

Cook Islands

Tonga

New Zealand

Fiji

Vanuatu
(New Hebrides)

PART ONE

Chapter 1
A CRUISE TO TAHITI

What a day to be alive! A brisk breeze helped to relieve the tropic heat. Lively sparkles of sunlight danced on the broad shoulders of the sea's swells. Each wave seemed to be playing a spirited game with our schooner, urging her onward, drawing her further across the vast expanse of the Pacific Ocean. Our goal, Tahiti, was 2000 miles to the south. For the two weeks that were to follow, I knew that I would be fulfilling most men's dreams of a lifetime. I was at the helm of the *Te Vega*, one of the world's most beautiful sailing vessels. Her 134 feet of ocean-going splendor churned up a wake of white and turquoise foam in brilliant contrast to the deep royal blue of the sea and the paler hue of the cloudless sky.

All around me was the activity of pleasure. Several blue-and-white-clad sailors checked gear or made splices. A group in the shade on the starboard side painted everything white. One seaman was high aloft in the rigging, swaying rhythmically in his tiny bo's'n chair. On deck, a few of the passengers lounged in canvas chairs, deep in books or conversation. Two men leaned on the railing and stared at the endless horizon. For everyone aboard, this was one of the nicest days of their lives.

I laughed at myself as I stood at the wheel. We were cruising out of Hawaii to the fabled South Seas with me, a committed landlubber for three decades, in physical charge. To me, the casual chain of events that put me into this position was still a source of wonder.

I began my reverie. In 1948 I graduated from Cornell University with a B. A. degree in Anthropology. I hadn't realized it at the time but the courses I had selected at random became the basis for my life-long fascination for travel. I had studied the histories of many cultures, arts and architecture, foreign languages and Geology. I rewarded this achievement with a solo trip around Western Europe from war-obliterated Rotterdam to Pompeii. While earning a M. S. in Education, I had taken every opportunity to explore sites of Greek Mythology, Medieval splendors and Renaissance creativity. In 1953 an ill-conceived hitch-hiking trip from Venezuela down the western spine of South America to Bolivia and back combined danger, terror and incredible good fortune for my safe return. 1955 was the year to "See America First" with a circuitous route from New York to California that enlightened me about our own national differences. I was soon in Honolulu with Japan as my next goal, when Lady Luck waved her magic wand and changed any further whimsical plan.

A day or so later, on a bright October Sunday afternoon, I was in the midst of a large cheering crowd gathered on Waikiki Beach. We anxiously awaited the end of an outrigger canoe race that had started off of the island of Molokai several hours before. It was the opening event of Hawaii's Aloha Week, and the people were in a happy mood. A lead-off event was a surfing contest, which had attracted the huge crowd.

When the first canoe appeared, the cheering started in earnest. Later, during the award ceremonies, another loud cheer arose. Coming around the point of Diamond Head, we saw a magnificent schooner under full sail. It was the *Te Vega* returning from its recently scheduled luxury cruise to Tahiti and its nearby isles.

With my feet planted firmly in the warm sand, I chatted with my companion, Bob Dohlman, a fellow Long Islander. Bob had sailed his own boat single-handedly from California to Honolulu. I mumbled something about how much fun it would be to sail on that schooner. "I would like to go on that beauty someplace, anyplace."

It was too much to try to suppress a nautical urge rising within me. At that moment, I envied all those who had been born with a love of the sea and had taken a chance to go on voyages that only such a craft could offer. No longer did crewmen suffer the conditions of long-distance sailing as in the days of Magellan (1500s), Tasman the Dutchman (1600s), Wallis or Captain Cook (1700s), and other Pacific explorers. The romance had not been diminished with modern conveniences and comforts, or so I thought.

There on the beach that day, I indulged in a series of daydreams that led me step-by-step to the very crew on the deck of the vessel arriving in her home port. The crew and I were separated by a mile of water and decades of experience. The nearest I'd ever come to onboard life was while I was staying with Bob as a guest on his little sloop moored at the marina. That teased my imagination into believing that I was already developing sea legs and a taste for life at sea.

At home in New York, I'd been a clumsy sailor at best and a nervous trans-Atlantic traveler by steamer, in spite of my family background. My parents and my older brother were avid sailors who raced 30-foot sailboats around triangles on Long Island Sound every weekend. I preferred bicycling around New England and staying at youth hostels. As a young teenager, I'd been put in sailing class, but to the best of my memory, I was never a captain of the little two-person craft. I had never soloed. In spite of all this, sailing on the *Te Vega* seemed possible and tropically adventurous, at least from the sands of Waikiki.

Bob was no help when he suggested, "Why don't you go see the captain? Maybe you could go as a work-away."

I turned and stared at him. "Me? Don't be silly."

He shot back, "No kidding. If you want to go to the Islands, this may be your chance. They often take guys like you. Go see him tomorrow."

I gave it serious thought but was afraid to take the first step. The marina was full of far more experienced sailors who would give anything to go. I waited for a week so that I could honestly have the excuse, "I asked, but there was no place for me." Besides, I had arrived in Hawaii fully intending to go to Japan and see as much of Asia as I could before returning home. I even had maps of Japan in my backpack.

The following Monday afternoon at about 4:30, I got off of the bus in front of the dock and walked tentatively towards the great schooner. Up to that moment, I had no idea how big she really was. In fact, it was beginning to look to me as if she might really be large enough to carry passengers comfortably on the open sea. I had worn my Levi's and Topsiders, rubber-soled deck shoes that I knew would be acceptable, even if I wasn't. Properly shod and hoping that I would create a most favorable first impression, I climbed up the gangplank. I noted that the entire deck was covered with fiber matting and was shaded from the tropical sun by huge canvas awnings. The gleaming white paint and the brilliant brasswork sparkled and punctured the half light.

To the left was a cluster of very un-nautical looking men. Had they also been looking for a work-away job? As they left, I realized that they were local merchants of food, laundry, and ship stores. Suddenly they were gone, and I was left alone, facing two men at a card table. Before I realized it, I heard myself asking if there was any possibility of shipping out as a work-away.

"Have you any experience?" asked the man sitting at the table.

"Not much," I admitted. "I've sailed on some small boats at home, on Long Island Sound."

I was asked, "Do you know the difference between a sheet and a halyard?"

"Yes, and I know which is port and which is starboard," I heard myself volunteering as I pointed vaguely to the two sides of the boat. "But don't ask me anything more."

"Just a second," he said as he turned to the man standing next to him, "What do you think?"

The two of them rapidly looked me over, from the top of my crew cut hair, down my trim 75 inches of height, to my Topsiders. Without more than a nod to each other, the captain turned back to face me and said, "There might be a chance for you. Come back tomorrow morning at eight. We'll see how you shape up until we sail Thursday. It's understood that you are going only one way. You do not expect to come back, is that right?"

"Yes, it is."

"All right. Be here tomorrow ready for work."

It may not be true that "clothes make the man," but maybe "Topsiders make the sailor."

The news I took back to my friends at the marina shocked them. Until then, I didn't know that some of them had gone to the *Te Vega* and had asked for work but had been refused, even though they were experienced sailors. They told me that one of the regular crew had become ill in Tahiti and had been left there to recover. The *Te Vega* would have sailed short-handed if they could not find a one-way crewman.

During the next few days before departure, there was plenty to do. The crew's quarters had to be painted. The officer's quarters had to be painted. The lifeboats had to be painted. The passenger's quarters had just been painted. The only activity that did not involve painting was stowing away the supplies for the trip. This was a deluxe boat on a deluxe cruise, and the supplies that came aboard emphasized just that. The meals had been planned to be the best of international cuisine, including a wide choice from the boat's wine locker. In the lounge was a well-stocked library, including the very latest periodicals available in Honolulu. The furnishings were done in the very best of good taste. The passenger's cabins were connected with private baths. This was really traveling, I thought.

At the end of the two-day trial period, I had apparently passed my competency and compatibility tests, as Captain Darr came up to me and asked if I still wanted to go on the voyage. I answered that I did. We shook hands, and he said, "Welcome aboard, lad."

My last hours ashore were spent sitting in the office of the French consul waiting for a visa that would permit me to get off of the boat and stay in the islands around Tahiti for a period of up to four months. Along with the application, I was able to prove that I had onward passage to some other port as I had purchased an open ticket on Pan American Airways for a distance equal to half way around the world with unlimited stopovers allowed. I also had to prove that I could post a $200 bond in the only Tahitian bank, against the day I might become destitute and have to be shipped out at their expense.

This sort of thing had happened in the islands before, so the authorities no longer admitted anyone of doubtful financial status. In Tahiti, foreigners were welcome only as long as their money held out. When their money went, so did they. It was (and is) expensive to visit there, as it is so far from any other place. Perhaps it is these very safeguards that have kept it so isolated and have made it more of an attraction to the otherwise jaded traveler.

I was not piped aboard as a dignitary. Instead, I was greeted with the Articles of War that I had to sign, indicating that I understood the conditions of shipping out. Because I was not a paid hand, I requested two amendments. The first amendment guaranteed that I could not be ordered to go aloft into the rigging. The second amendment guaranteed that I could not be ordered to do anything that required I go beyond the confines of the railing around the deck. I didn't want to risk falling overboard. Thus signed on, I saddled myself with my backpack and went below to the crew's quarter, the fo'c's'le, to stow my gear.

Along the converging sloping walls of the triangular cabin in the bow of the boat were eight pairs of double-decked bunks called sacks that hung by chains from the steel hull. Each sack was a rectangle of pipe with a two-foot wide by six-foot long strip of canvas laced to the pipe frame. On each sack were a folded blanket, a set of linen, and a pillow. This was to be my home for the rest of the voyage, come Hell, or high water...and it did!

Occupying part of the meager open space in the middle of the fo'c'sle was a stack of small lockers for the crew's gear, which at this point was still stacked on the sacks and every other available surface. The fo'c'sle had the look of a sea-going attic. It was hot and stuffy, but this I knew would clear out when we were underway. There was only one vacant sack, an upper. Fortunately, it was near the ventilator that opened out into the fresh air of the deck above. Now I knew that at least I would have some fresh air while sleeping. In fact, the question casually crossed my mind why no one else had grabbed it first, since all the rest of the crew had at least one trip of experience. That, I decided, was my good fortune.

I changed into Levi's and a white tee shirt, which was the closest my wardrobe from the backpack could come to match the uniform of the crew, and reported to the first mate. "Nothing to do until we sail," he said.

I joined those already at the railing making their last minute feathery farewell conversations with friends on the dock. A small Aloha band of two portly Hawaiian grandmothers draped in muumuus, plunked on ukuleles as they accompanied a spirited grass-skirted trio who swished and swayed to every treacley sweet island tune. The seven passengers consisted of two couples. One of the couples brought along their teenaged son. One of the men was a medical doctor, a necessity for such a trip as this. Captain Darr's wife and pre-teenage son completed the guest list. All of the guests, and most of the crew, had flower leis around their necks. The leis had each been given with a kiss, an island custom wishing the wearer "Aloha," meaning both "happy trip," "speedy return," and "love." It was sad for me to be leiless at departure time, as it meant there was no one on the pier to wish me "Aloha." I had no fragrant memories to comfort my thoughts in the lonely hours that lay ahead.

Suddenly I heard "three bells." It was 5:30, and it was the boat's signal for "All ashore." The few visitors departed, and the gangplank was raised. All hands were at their stations. The lines that had connected the *Te Vega* to the pier were cast ashore. The motor, which had been idling, was speeded up. This caused the propeller to spew forth foam, which slopped around the pilings of the wharf. The widening pool of bubbling turquoise water separated us more and more from the shore.

Edward, a full-blooded Polynesian crewman, balanced easily on the bowsprit as he hung onto the forestay. He could have been the cover picture hero of any South Seas novel. He was silhouetted against a pale blue liquid sky with a few streaky clouds underlined with crimson. The whole scene was gilded with the golden rays of the sinking sun. Edward was dressed in faded blue denims and a white and blue striped tee shirt that broadened his already massive chest. Cocked jauntily on his thick black wavy hair was a spotlessly white sailor's cap. His smile bared perfect white teeth in a dark-skinned mouth that would have been too broad in any face with features less magnificently hewed. This huge Polynesian, a perfect example of the rare male elegance of his race, was waving enthusiastically to a slim, bronzed Hawaiian *wahini* standing on the dock.

Under a collar of flower leis, she wore a dress of yellow and white *pareu* (PAH ray oh, or *pareau,)* the brightly patterned material made in Britain exclusively for the tropical islanders. It was surely her latest gift from the departing sailor. She put her hands to her mouth, and as she sent him a kiss, she appeared to say a soft "Aloha."

Edward responded with a hearty Tahitian "*Aroha*" that was more like a cheer, "ah ROWW HAA!" One by one, he used his free hand to remove three leis from around his neck. One was of yellow frangipani, one was of purple orchids, and one was of white *tiare* (tee AH ray), a small, star-shaped, very fragrant blossom. He tossed them into the sea as a pledge to return to the lovely *wahine* he was leaving behind. He undoubtedly had done the same when he left the last port of call.

The cheers and alohas from those on the pier became weaker and weaker. We were on our way.

As soon as we were shipshape, the order was given to hoist sails. The seamen all jumped to their posts, and with the aid of mechanical winches, only the final tightening had to be done by manpower. The "Yo ho heave ho" that I expected to hear turned out to be just grunts. With the increasing canvas sucking in the slight sighing puffs, we pointed towards the open water.

To keep me out from underfoot, the mate told me to coil and stow away the gaskets, the canvas straps used to keep the furled sail neatly secured to the boom. I'd learned my first lesson. I was beginning to hear the new nautical vocabulary being used from stem to stern.

The wind was not strong enough to push us forward without the motor, but the effect of being under sail was wonderful. On deck, there was the joyous chatter of happy voices. From the shore and nearby water, we heard the whistles and horns of other craft wishing us well. Diamond Head was dusted with the purple hues of dusk and stood out sharply against the pale arc of Waikiki Beach. As we watched, the lights of Honolulu came on one by one. The darkness of the tropical night wastes no time in absorbing the brightness of the dying day. Within a few moments, the stars overhead began to shine and competed with the dazzle along the shore.

This, I thought, was going to be my last sight of land for a long time to come, and I felt that that if I was really in my right mind, I might better jump off now and swim for shore.

Less than three hours out to sea, the wind had died down to such an extent that all hands were called on deck to drop the sails. We were only carrying about three-quarters of the total sail area, but it was a tremendous amount of canvas as it began to collapse around us like a circus tent. Fortunately, there was no wind to make it unmanageable. In a remarkably short time the sails were furled, and I was right on the job of tying the gaskets around the sail and the boom.

One of the very most important things my father had made me learn in childhood was how to tie a square knot. I glowed with pride that I had so quickly become a member of the crew in good standing. All that was left for me to do now was to coil the lines and replace the equipment. But coiling a line was not to be as easy as I had thought. It seemed to me that each line had an individual whim twisted into every fiber, giving it its own peculiarity. Indeed, most of my coils had turned out to be figure eights rather than stacks of zeros. Both the line and I were new at this game, and it was to be a challenge between us.

At two bells, or nine o'clock, I was called for my first watch, or nautical guard duty. I was stationed on the bow and told to watch for things that could go wrong, such as loose rigging, floating objects in our way, or an uncharted reef. "What does a reef look like?" I asked.

"You'll know when you see it," was the unhelpful answer that I received from Don, my watch companion. Thus the fate of the boat was resting squarely in my hands.

As I stared off into the night, it became a matter of great concern to me that we were heading off into the nothingness that lay ahead. Was it going to be anything more than mere chance that would direct us to some tiny speck of land sticking itself above the surface of this vast ocean? As I continued to look out at nothing, I wondered if there really might be a chance to slip right off the edge of the earth into the huge empty void ahead with only the stars above to witness our disaster. I pinched myself and tried to laugh it off. Of course the world is a globe, and we will always be on the top of it … or so I tried to believe. But just maybe.…

A half hour later, I was summoned to the wheel. This was my first chance to be helmsman, a position that had looked very nice to me while I was on watch at the bow. I was no longer going to stare off into the unknown. I was now going to steer into it. In front of the great wheel was a large brass binnacle that was lighted up inside. A thin black vertical line was painted on the far side of the white interior. The line was in permanent relation to the bow and, hence, was our direction. The entire central horizontal portion was a floating disk with a compass painted on it. The disk was free to swing one way or the other as the great wheel was turned. The compass had a multipointed star pattern painted on it, including one very fancy point that always pointed towards magnetic north.

Around the extreme outer edge of the disk was a circle of 360 numbers. Any number pointing at the painted line was our course at any given moment. The course was set when Captain Darr decided which number on the disk would guide us towards the harbor of Papeete, Tahiti. When the line and the number were not together, we were off course. This sounded easy enough.

When I took over, we were right on course. I had been watching Captain Darr for several minutes and had seen only the slightest movements to the right and to the left, appearing to be casual efforts to keep a balance. Once at the wheel, I was able to hold it there for almost a full minute. Then the disk began slowly to slip off to one side. This I compensated for by turning the wheel slightly, as I had watched the captain do. If I had turned it correctly, and if I had a bit of luck, the course would have been regained. However, in split seconds I saw us falling off further and further. I turned the wheel the other way and watched the number approach the line and then slide right past it again. The more I concentrated on the little lighted area in front of me, the harder it became.

At first the disk would go one way, and I would turn the wheel the opposite way. Then the disk would go the other way, and I would swing the wheel around again. My entire body was gripped with a tenseness I had never known before. I suffered from embarrassment, from anger, and from fear of having to walk the plank and swim for home. The wheel had to be swung one way, then the other, harder and harder, faster and faster. It was almost spinning in circles. Of course being a novice, I was compensating too much. We were hardly out of sight of land and already I had put the great yacht almost beyond control. We were winding through the night, leaving a phosphorescent wake that resembled the track of a frightened serpent.

Captain Darr, whose close and watchful eye had not wandered from my wheeling, took over and soon righted the vessel back on the course to Tahiti. With a simple "It'll take a little time, lad," he handed it back to me. It was not long before the antagonistic parts were racing past each other again. My face, reflected in the light of the binnacle, must have been terror-stricken. I did not stand watch alone that night.

Our watches were alternated every half hour between the wheel and the bow. While I was up forward, I could hear the happy off-duty Edward as he strummed contentedly on his ukulele. As he sang the melodious tunes of his homeland, he was accompanied by the rhythmic slapping of the rigging against the spars and the seas sloshing against the hull. Edward, the music, and the night were all made for each other. All he needed was his *vahine*.

I stared at the bowsprit as it sliced at the endless horizon. The ocean was gently alive, each wave giving a lift and a fall to the bow. The boat and the sea seemed to be partners in a watery waltz. It was a beautiful night.

Just before eight bells the midnight watch appeared, and so I went below. Going from fresh air to fo'c'sle was a shock. A dozen men lay snoring in their stifling, tossing, smoke-filled quarters. Fortunately, I was able to grab my sleeping bag from the top of my backpack, and I headed for the deck. I found shelter under a lifeboat on the lee side of the cabin. My last thoughts were that it had been a long and exciting day. I was proudly satisfied with my wonderful adjustment to shipboard life.

I hadn't been asleep very long when I woke with a start to find the sleeping bag soaked. The wind had picked up and was flinging salt spray around the corner of the cabin, where it formed into little rivulets that drained right under the lifeboat. Gathering up my gear, I reluctantly returned below, defeated in my attempt to camp out at sea, wetter and wiser. Above the night noises of the sleeping crew, I heard the splashing of water against the steel hull six inches from my ear. Overhead, the rigging slapped and banged against the mast that came through the deck and into the fo'c'sle, making our cabin into a sound box of nocturnal nautical noises.

"All hands," someone shouted down the hatchway. Momentarily dazed, I could hardly recollect where I was. A glance around at the clock, and I recalled all too vividly that I was at sea. It was 2:30 in the morning. What a start to the second day.

When I got on deck, everyone was at their post ready to hoist sail. The wind had freshened enough to attempt sailing. Up, then down, then up again! My God! "What a life this is going to be," I groaned quietly, as I reported for duty. Since I had so successfully tied on the gaskets, I busied myself in taking them off. I had automatically promoted myself. With the gaskets off and the lines cleared, the sails were hoisted, only to find that I had also methodically gone about untying the mainsail from the boom. This was immediately obvious. The crew grabbed the flapping mainsail and secured it to the boom again. There were few cheers of praise.

Sailing to Tahiti, or to Hell, was of little consequence to me at this point. Sea life was quickly losing any glamour attached to it by novelists and nauticalists alike. I returned below and collapsed onto my sack with sheer fatigue and self-annoyance for ever even thinking of attempting such a foolish adventure. It soon became apparent that under sail, we were not going to maintain an even keel. A rock and roll had been added to our dip and dive.

I found that my crosswise sack now slanted downhill towards the side of the hull, and with each rise and fall I was constantly slipping headlong towards the cold, sweating, steel wall. Long moments of agonizing thought went into the solution of the problem of how to make a change. Finally I got up and reversed the head and the foot. At first it seemed satisfactory. Then I found myself bracing my feet against the cold damp hull. It was something like standing up on the diagonal. A relaxed knee could suddenly cause me to slip into a crumpled heap. It was only then revealed to me why this, of all the sacks, had remained vacant to the last. By the clock it was almost four, the halfway point until morning watch.

Dawn was welcome and the call for chow even more so. At the wheel again, I was surprised to see the shadowy form of land to port. It was the huge volcanic mountain mass of Mount Haleakala of Maui. Perhaps I was not alone in my first thought that sparkling bright morning: Maybe I could make it if I jumped overboard and swam for it now.

Though surely not forgotten, the mishaps of the night before were never brought up again. I was assigned a regular watch, eight to twelve, night and day. In the morning it was one hour on and one hour off. The "on" was spent at the wheel. Soon after I began my watch, the captain's young son came up on deck. He spotted me where he had seen me the night before and asked with wonder, "Have you been driving all night?" It certainly seemed like it.

The daylight hours at the wheel were very pleasant, though the struggle to line up the compass was no easier. On the plus side, there was the bright sunlight, the agreeable stiff breeze, and the sight of the billowing cream-colored canvas contrasting so wonderfully with the matchless blues of the sea and the sky. The easy pitch of the boat through the rolling swells, the general feeling that all was well, combined into a feeling of plain delight about being aboard.

The "off" hour was occupied by brightening up the many brass fixtures all over the vast area of the deck. I was told specifically not to spill any of the cleaning fluid on the teak planking. I rubbed. I buffed. I polished. I shined cleats, plates, winches, and knobs. Finally, I succeeded in knocking over the can. And so it was that I bumbled my way through each watch.

By late afternoon, I could look back on certain accomplishments of a personal nature. I had washed, dried, and darned some clothing. I had managed to shower and shave in a "head" with both the dimensions and motions of a revolving door. I had been asked to help "serve a cable," which was merely neatening up the rough edges of a splice. The remainder of the free hours was spent in the sun on the lee side reading a paperback copy of *War and Peace* and observing crystalline azure waves, each crest laced with snow white suds. Life indeed was looking up.

By the fourth day out we had raised and lowered the sails many times. The coquetry of the winds proved to be mere temptations that enticed us to capture them and harness their fickle power to pull us onward towards the legendary islands. Once up, the huge white lungs flapped and fluttered momentarily until they drew their first full breath of the breeze. Swelling with pride, they drove us southward with some vigor until, with some contrary whimsy, the wind would die. Then flapping helplessly on their skeletal spars, they seemed to be begging to be taken down. Thus they rested until another Aeolian puff would lure us into trying again.

At night, the massive shadowy forms of the sails contrasted beautifully against the star-sprinkled, endless black heavens. Whenever I looked aloft, it seemed as if the tips of the masts were slicing the night sky wide open, releasing a trail of brilliant star dust, a milky wake in the heavens as glorious as the phosphorescent trail we dragged through the ink-black, trackless ocean. We were truly sailing amongst the lights of the universe.

As the steering became easier, I took time to have thoughts beyond the wheel. I stared at the easy-to-find constellation of Orion, The Hunter, a favorite from my own homeland. With only the naked eye, three stars in a short straight line can be seen that indicate the jewels of his belt, and another two or three mark his dangling sword. Other stars form his bow and the arrowhead, but they are harder to locate in the usual urban, light-polluted, night sky.

Another cluster with which I wanted to become friends was the simple but significant Southern Cross, which can be seen when the viewer is south of the Tropic of Cancer. This is a sure sign of being in the tropics. Its base star points directly south. I have heard that it is the most obvious major constellation for the southern hemisphere. There is belief that the voyaging Polynesian explorers made sky charts by which to navigate the vast ocean wastes. Some of these charts indicated known islands and wind or sea currents. But as they sailed north or south, as we were doing, they would lose familiar stars and gain new ones. I wondered if these intrepid ancient navigators knew they were sailing on the watery surface of a sphere, and not in some huge flat dish with a drop-off edge at the next horizon.

I became aware that the sky was also giving us a warning. Around the moon, a magnificent luminous rainbow had developed. This was a sure sign of foul weather ahead, but at the moment it was another phase of nocturnal beauty.

While I was at the helm, I should have been concentrating on the compass. Instead, I mused on the ancient mariners who first challenged these waters by navigating their sailing canoes on their voyages of exploration. They probably began about a thousand years BCE (Before Common Era) and continued for more than a thousand after. The early Polynesians, so used to living with the sea, showed tremendous strength and courage to overcome such incredible hardships on their crowded giant double-hulled canoes. Loaded as they were with their families, supplies, root crops, and animals for any new lands they might be lucky enough to find, they could hardly have had enough comfort to enjoy the beauties of the night. The chilling wind-driven salt spray, the sweltering daytime heat, and the dazzling reflections from the often glassy surface of the water must have made them thoroughly defiant of nature's clashing maritime moods. But they fearlessly continued to discover and settle new islands after thousands of miles and many weeks at sea. Many of these expeditions must have ended in tragedy.

Where had they come from originally? Perhaps it will never be known for sure, but the best guess is that they originated in Southeast Asia. The foods they brought with them were pigs, chickens, taros, yams, possibly breadfruit, as well as many other useful fruits and vegetables to make life more comfortable, all were native to Southeast Asia or collected from intervening island stepping stones along the way.

The area they explored and settled is defined to the north by Hawaii; to the east by Easter Island, which lies 2200 miles west of the coast of Chile, in South America; and to the west by New Zealand. This vast area is known as The Polynesian Triangle, or more recently as the Maohinesian Triangle.

The early name for these adventurers was Maohi, pronounced MOW wee, rhyming with HOW wee. The Maohi navigators marked their domain in a most unusual manner. For example, an island in Hawaii is named Maui (MOW wee). The residents of Easter Island call each of the gigantic sculptured heads a mao'i (MOE eye), The original people of New Zealand are Maori (MOW ree).

My reverie was shattered by a sudden "Snap! Flap! Snap!" that cracked through the other noises on board at night. The jib! It was flapping wildly. I had been warned above all else to prevent that. We were off course. The sail could have ripped to shreds in seconds. In a flash, the captain was there to grab the wheel and set it straight. Keel-hauling was probably the only adequate punishment for such inattention, by which a heavier wind might have wracked severe damage.

The squall finally caught up with us before the midnight relief was due on deck. It was wet, cold, and grim. Life had hit a new low. The tropical ocean does not change its temperature much in the course of a year. But at night the rain and the spray, dashing from the bow or flipping from spar and shroud, felt like needles of ice. When driven by a storm, the combination of biting wind and slashing water is unbelievably miserable. It dribbled down the side of my face. It trickled down the back of my neck. It percolated into all of my clothing to chill my entire shivering body. Though we were almost on the Equator, it felt more like we were fighting our way through the Straights of Magellan. I can remember no sight as welcome as my relief when he came towards the bow dressed in his glistening wet foul-weather gear, reflecting patches of the red running light in the rivulets that oozed down his hooded jacket. I heard "eight bells." It was midnight, my watch was over.

The night air, when stirred only by the motion of the boat, is surprisingly cold for the forward watch. It is welcomed for its cooling freshness by those sitting in the shelter of the deck house. But it is not cool enough to satisfy the comfort needs of the crew below deck sleeping in their sacks.

Once relieved, I passed through the galley, where there was always hot coffee ready. Warming my hands around the steaming mug made me feel better. It was now only five more steps to my sack. The fo'c'sle was suffocatingly hot, and the collective moisture from the damp garments mingled with the odors of the day's cooking in the galley. The noises of the restlessly sleeping sailors hung heavy in the oppressive stagnant darkness. Sweating naked men tossed fitfully in their sodden berths, unconsciously trying to nose out an unspent breath of air. Such have been the conditions for centuries as seamen sought rest from their labors. Though the ventilator was overhead, it could not bring the relief that was so close above my head. It had been turned around to prevent spray from being forced below. There was nothing to do but hang up my wet gear, crawl into the sack, and try to forget it all had happened.

Sometime later I was startled by coughing and cursing. My shipmate had just been baptized by a sudden rush of water down the other vent. It had not only cooled his body but also soaked his sack. It would be a long time before it dried. It took restraint to do no more than curse.

In the few moments before I became fully awake, I grew aware that the motion of the boat was decidedly different than before. The jarring of the hull as we smashed against each wave was noisy and sickening. The humid closeness of the hold was flavored with the new smells of breakfast cooking on the stove nearby. The musty clothing swayed from hooks as if it might have been a group of attendants at some macabre ceremony. The pounding of the sea, the lack of air, the smells, the swinging gear, were the proper ingredients for a recipe that was about to unsettle my constitution. I hesitated to admit to my unseaworthyness.

A large part of the small open space in our cabin was occupied by a table and two benches, all securely bolted to the deck. While breakfasting, we were obliged to maintain our balance, six to a bench, while our foundations rose and fell with gyrating violence. The utensils and the condiment containers on the table slipped and slid on the slick oilcloth cover. The table tossed like a bronco and would have rid itself of these things had there not been a wooden restraining frame around the edge. The brown apple butter, in an ugly, bulgy jar, shot from end to end, banging itself into the frame. A catsup bottle and the salt shaker, on their sides, defined smooth arcs as they rolled with each pitch, often making complete circles. These offered chances for keen betting among the crew. Some spilled bacon grease helped the bread plate to career recklessly, wantonly scattering slices of cold toast. Because the sticky jelly can was heavier, it was a slower starter and did not make a good contestant in the Mess Table Sweepstakes. Its progress was further impeded by the crystal-coated sugar can. Spoons, forks, and the jelly knife were more obstacles than contestants with no competitive spirits in the free-for-all. They merely cluttered the field for the real contenders. Above all the others and with a dauntless spirit, the contents of the bulgy apple butter jar had to be recognized as the champion, as it crashed dizzily from one end to the other of the course.

This mad spinning of food before me sapped an already indifferent appetite. My stomach began to feel very much like the contents of the jar. It was time to go on deck. At the wheel, it was brisk, sunny, and beautiful. Every lungful of fresh air rapidly helped to remedy my queasiness.

In addition to the brass, I had the officer's and the crew's quarters to clean up. Below again, the violent motion of the heaving hull still hacking at the sea made walking in the companionway difficult. Walls, doors, and the decking all moved too fast to place a foot or hand on some thing solid, with confidence. One step was short because it was uphill. The next jerked the leg out to its fullest extent because the hoped-for decking had suddenly dropped out of range. Both hands were needed on the railing to creep along from one part of the boat to another and to stay upright. With a sudden lurch, I reached for a steadying doorjamb. Instead of support, I was trapped under a torrent of books. I'd grabbed and pulled down the first mate's bookshelf. Throughout the gale I was compounding my own work. Minute by minute I was creating more disorder than I had been sent below to correct.

Some jobs needed a bucket of hot water. The galley was the nearest supply spot. Carrying hot, sloshing, nervous water in a pail proved more hazardous than the task of filling it. It included several dousings, and frequent re-moppings. I thought it might make a considerable improvement while filling the bucket if I should hang it from a showerhead. On went the bucket. On went the hot water. Out came the spray. As the pail swayed and banged into the wall, the water flowed first to the right, and then to the left, only getting water into the pail in the middle of each swing. Before the pail was full, all of the walls were flowing with precious steaming hot water. The entire head was awash with a scalding miniature sea. The sorcerer's apprentice had nothing on me. There was too much water and no place to put it.

Blinded by eyeglasses that were so fogged with steam that I could not see; I groped for a thick towel to wrap around my hand so that I could turn off the shower. Down in the belly of the boat, ankle deep in a deluge I had created, and hearing the crashing beating we were taking from the ocean, I was suddenly overwhelmed. I knew that I was about to lose my self respect and everything else that was not securely attached. To fight the feeling any longer was futile. Though I sincerely wanted to believe that seasickness was only a state of mind, it offered me little help in steadying my own interior. Then quietly, neatly, and privately, I let it go. I felt better instantly.

And who were the others on board? What kind of men made up the crew of a luxury schooner as it cruised the South Seas?

The chef was contacted four hours before sailing. He had never been to sea before and thought that this would be a great opportunity. It was the hope of seeing Tahiti and leaving a nagging wife that had compelled him to sign on. For the seven weeks of the cruise, he hoped to fulfill both desires. On the day of departure, he had cooked two meals. The crew ate at five, the passengers about seven. Before the latter had begun their meal, the cook had already gone up on deck to see Diamond Head and settled down in a comfortable coil of rope. He remained there the whole evening. He had already lost all interest in sea life. Even the allurement of the islands had drained from his mind. Sickening thought though it was, he would have traded all this for a chair in his home near his wife. Later in the night, someone thoughtfully covered him with a piece of canvas, and there he stayed for the following three days and nights.

The Sous chef had been in the islands during the war and was a great deal more seaworthy. He'd collected a remarkable pelt of tattoos representing the best artists in the business from nearly every major port in the world. He had recently divorced his wife and had left the mainland to live in Hawaii. He quickly became the favorite of the seamen, as he believed that they were the most important people on board. Under his supervision, we all ate well and as often as we wished. He thoroughly enjoyed the entire trip, even when the rough water was making his preparation of the meals hazardous on his great stove.

Don, still in his early 20s, was the youngest member of the crew. He was one of the crewmen who were picked up in Los Angeles while the boat was being refitted for its cruising capacity. He had seniority, and with it, he had developed an undeserved sense of superiority. He was my immediate superior on watch. During the lonely hours when the two of us were on the deck together, I watched him closely. I sensed he had a mental instability. One of the other fellows had warned me to "Keep alert." He had a look about his eyes that convinced me he could be up to no good. I thought I might engage him in a friendly conversation. As I was innocent of what I would find at the end of this trip, I naively asked him why going to Tahiti was so big a deal with some people.

His snide response was, "If you don't know, you'll have to find out for yourself." It had passed through my mind, and I am sure through Don's also, that he would take advantage of any opportunity to push me overboard simply to create an act of malice. He had been to Tahiti on the two previous cruises and had fallen in love with Doris, one of the island's major attractions. He had studied the Tahitian language during his off hours.

Edward, the Tahitian member of the crew, had said to Don, "Doris, she plenny nice. She love every man." Doris was only 16, but she was a Polynesian girl. These *hina* do not by nature or training languish for an absent lover. Don couldn't believe that she would not remain loyal to him, and only him, while he was away. He planned to bring her back to Honolulu. Where he was going to stow her on board was still to be decided.

Later, when Don greeted her at the dock in Papeete they kissed, and he greeted her in her language. She shook her head. He asked again. She shook with laughter. He slapped her almost hard enough to knock her down. They then went off together. He had learned at least one of the island customs correctly.

One chap in his 30s was more Pan than man. He was capable of all tasks assigned to him, but in his own life he could not face up to responsibility. He had ended his marriage for the express purpose of pursuing his wanderlust. As a modern college-educated nomad, he'd tried all ways of life, from the hectic clatter of Manhattan to the trade wind-swept shores of Polynesia. This he found to be the most appealing, and he'd been practicing the fine art of beachcombing successfully ever since. He did not write or paint. He planned on doing nothing more productive than absorbing sunshine, only interrupted by frequent halcyon ventures into the lagoon in front of a palm leaf hut that he was employed to guard. Certainly barefooted, probably bearded, and undoubtedly covered with nothing more than a *pareu* (wraparound), he was still managing to live out this phase of his life to the complete envy of anyone who ever had a taste of "going native."

Rich, an ex-Marine, a tanned Greek god-type, had been a war hero on every beachhead upon which his company had landed. He boasted of fantastic feats of bravery that indeed may have been conceived in fact. A scar ran through his head of wavy blonde hair, under which he claimed had been installed a silver plate. That he had a wound was true enough. But the life he led seemed to be too much for a fellow with a roof repaired with such a delicate artifact. His exposure to possible serious accident was not lessened by life at sea. He had earned his keep in life at many jobs. Among them was gathering abalone on the coast of California for the local black market. The legal limit for taking these mollusks from their shallow water homes could never have supplied the commercial demands. This Marine hero had been a professional poacher.

Another sailor who was making only the one-way trip had been in the Merchant Marine. He'd been in a bad motorcycle accident and had lost a leg. He turned to painting and had been refurbishing the *Te Vega* while it was being refitted. This trip was to give him time to finish the job and also satisfy his genuine desire to get back on the salt water. He'd completed all of his watches and his painting, also. He was going to return home and continue his domesticated land bound life. Aside from the officers, he was the most experienced, and certainly the most tolerant, of the mistakes of a novice.

There were other sailors with varying talents and backgrounds. Most were looking for some form of escape. The sea seemed to be the outlet for those dodging irate spouses or the law.

We crossed "the line" (Equator) one beautiful day shortly before noon. A special ceremony was held, complete with a costumed and properly bearded Neptune who climbed up over the bowsprit onto the boat to perform the rites. He sat down on his throne. Among the crew, only Tahitian Edward was crossing north to south for the first time. It was his great good nature that produced the show. He accepted the messy lathering for the ritualistic shave, then scampered through the rigging like a wild one. Three passengers surrendered to the Oceanic Court to face their fate. A court assistant, draped in seaweed, steeped forward and ordered each initiate to "Kiss the fish!" he held in his outstretched hands, before they were doused with a bucket of water. Then the chief steward broke out a bottle of champagne.

The celebration marked the halfway point of the trip, but it was remarkably different from the crossing I'd made two years before in South America. I had naively thought it would be an interesting adventure to hitchhike the so-called Pan American Highway. In truth, the route was not by any means a highway. It was but a mere scratch along the precipitous shoulders of the frightening Andes Mountains. There, I was hitchhiking and riding in the back of a truck. At mid-day it was crispy cool. My companions were the descendants of the Incas, the Conquistadores, or both. All men and women wore ponchos of hand woven striped wool and dark-colored felt hats for warmth against the cold. We were all part of the cargo, along with a cow, a goat, half a dozen sheep, crates of chickens and pigeons, bundles wrapped in bits of blankets, boxes, burlap bags and several children, one nursing.

In Ecuador, we crossed the line between the northern and southern hemispheres where the land is very high, arid, and treeless. Not far away were snow-covered peaks. I was able to take a photo of the Equatorial Monument from the vehicle to prove it. It was one of the supreme travel moments up to that time of this adventurer's life.

Of these two sharply contrasting equatorial crossings, it was hard to decide which one I enjoyed more. This time we still had over a thousand miles to go before we were to see land again.

The second week was perfect sailing weather, though we were seldom without the boost that the motor gave. An improperly sewn seam parted, and the jib ripped. It was repaired by three of the crew who went out on the bowsprit and wrestled with the canvas until it was under control. As the *Te Vega* bounded along, this scene was a re-enactment of a sailor's task since time immemorial. Seamen at work made a real picture of a very old profession.

I was invited by Captain Darr to remain with the crew to make the cruise around the group of Society Islands after a brief stop at Papeete, the main city of Tahiti. This meant another two weeks on board. This bit of island hopping was the real reason the passengers had come. We were scheduled to visit the island of Moorea, which lies about a dozen miles northwest of Tahiti and is plainly visible with its fantastic steep sided volcanic mountains. Also on the itinerary was Bora Bora, a hundred miles to the west. True enough, the stops were only to be short ones, but it was quite an attractive offer that would double the length of time I could remain on the boat. By now, I'd gained my sea legs and felt really quite good about this sailing business. However, I did long for a stable night on shore where the footing would be sure and the air would be neither too hot nor too cold.

It was early on our 14th day at sea. At the first light of dawn, the hazy form of the volcanic mountain that is Tahiti was dead ahead. It was hardly more than a misty image on the horizon of the dark murky water. It seemed so small. It was so welcome. As the light increased and the glow from the still-hidden sun glazed the clouds with blotches of gold and crimson, the island's central peak grew darker and bolder. The oily-looking surface of the quiet sea took on reflections from above and shimmered in tints of rose and gray. The sky became streaked with color, and there was a bright spot where the sun would push out from the watery depths with a dazzling light. At first only a speck, then bit by bit the glowing fireball took shape, spreading its glorious radiance as it burned its way into the brightening sky. Once above the horizon, it consumed the purple cast of the mountain ahead. There were contrasting hues, highlighting brilliant greens and blues against the deepening shadows. Minute by minute the picture changed. The sea sucked in the solar rays and absorbed their power, became a luminous sapphire blue. Ahead of us, deep shadows formed on the rocky crags at the summit, which seemed to become jagged teeth savagely biting chunks out of a wreath of white clouds. The gentler slopes glowed in fertile emerald greens. The whole image was floating in a lagoon of iridescent aquamarine that shimmered as if sprinkled with golden sequins. Surrounding this and stretching for miles was a ring of sparkling spray where the ocean smashed itself against the encircling coral barrier of the reef. Only at this moment did I discover what I was to look for during my watch on the bow that very first night on board.

A small launch came outside the reef to greet us and pulled alongside. The harbor pilot climbed aboard and guided the vessel towards the pass, or opening, of the treacherous coral reef. A pass is generally located where there is an outflow of fresh water from an island river or stream, which probably stifles the growth of the coral. The nearer we approached, the more dreadful became the truth of the natural bulwark. The pass was narrow enough so that we could see the yellowish, stone-like walls on either side, but wide enough to permit large oceangoing ships to pass through. Like a fortification awash with a few inches of frothy torrents, the reef broke each ocean swell into countless billions of harmless particles of mist that formed into a magnificent rainbow for us as we entered the tranquil lagoon beyond. Once inside the barrier, the *Te Vega* steadied immediately. The water was many fathoms deep, but it was so clear and calm that formations on the bottom became visible with the penetrating light.

Along the shore at the base of the great central mountain, I saw a row of white specks, the buildings and the yachts that lined the waterfront. As we got closer, I could distinguish their red roofs. Standing in the midst of the town of Papeete (pah pay AYE tay) was the white steeple of a church, looking like a beacon of safety. The buildings became more distinctive as we got closer. I could pick out the coconut trees with their constantly moving waxy leaves waving at our approach. Under them were shorter trees splashed with screaming scarlet blossoms. Gracious clusters of purple, fuchsia, and orange bougainvillea climbed up the walls of many of the low structures. Some of the shops were painted yellow; others were green or blue. Papeete appeared to stretch along the edge of the harbor for a mile or more. It was a sleepy, weathered, waterside village.

Dozens of boats were moored along the quay in front of the main part of town. Some were fine sailing craft from other parts of the world, and others were dingy little coastal or inter-island water trucks. The bigger boats were dressed in holiday flags. It was Armistice Day, 11 November 1955, and they were honoring the end of World

War I. On the quay behind the boats was a constantly growing happy crowd of hundreds. They had come from all around the island on foot, on bicycles, on motor bikes, on scooters, and in tiny French cars to see the parade and join in the celebration. The timely arrival of the *Te Vega* was just another happy sight.

Most of our welcoming hosts and hostesses were walking barefoot while dressed in shirts and dresses of *pareu* with bold tropical designs and colors. They wore jaunty crowns of ferns and scented flowers and around their necks were strands of *heis* (leis). Ukulele music vied with the tooting of horns and whistles. The shouting increased as the pilot backed our boat stern first towards the seawall, where it was secured by tying our lines to a couple of ancient bronze cannons that had been jammed deep into the turf. The crew rolled out the gangplank. Two of the island's most respected citizens, proudly erect, walked aboard. The port doctor in his dress whites, and the customs officer in navy blue, had to check the crew and the boat before any of the enthusiastically waving and shouting visitors would be permitted aboard. When they gave the signal that all was clear, the mob streamed aboard shouting, laughing, and shoving across the narrow gangplank. Each of them looked for someone to welcome with *heis*, or crowns of flowers, and kisses. I deservedly got my *heis* and kisses, but could return only the latter.

Sailboat arrivals were always popular events, as the islanders appreciated the great distances and hardships suffered by everyone coming by sea. The sea was their life, and it had been a part of them since birth. The town was celebrating a holiday, and the mood was explosively joyous. They seemed to be drunk with the sheer delight of being with strangers who had come to visit their island home. Once their curiosity was satisfied, they cheerfully departed.

We resumed our duties to finish the many chores still to be taken care of before we were granted shore leave. I was helping the ex-Marine stow some gear that would not be needed again until the compass was pointing north on the return trip to Hawaii. He was below in the hold, while I was above passing him lines and tackle. Somehow a line tangled itself, and in pulling it free, I yanked the hatch cover from its leaning position and it crashed down on the head of my shipmate. I wasted little time finding out if his silver plate had been dented.

I spoke to Captain Darr, thanked him for the great trip, added that I didn't think I wanted to stay on board for another two weeks for the cruise, and left.

Tahitian Words Used in the Text and Their Meanings

Aroha: Love, good-bye, Aloha
Aue: Exclamation for many things
Fare: Tahitian bamboo and thatch hut.
Fei: Mountain Banana
Hei: Necklace of shells or flowers, lei
Hine: Girl or young woman
Ia Orana: Good Morning
Maeva: Welcome
Marae: Outdoor temple
Motu: Small island on the reef
Ni'au: Coconut palm
Noera: Christmas
Pae pae: House terrace
Popa'a: Foreign food
Tane: man
Tapu: Taboo, sacred
Taro: Starchy root vegetable
Tatau: Tattoo
Tiare: Tahitian gardenia
Ti'i: Carved image, Tiki
Va'a: Canoe
Vahine: Woman

Chapter 11
THE SOCIETY ISLANDS

This cluster of mountainous volcanic islands is about 100 miles west of Tahiti. Captain Cook, who arrived on the *Endeavor,* named the islands after the Geographical Society (London) that had sponsored his scientific trip to Tahiti to observe the transit of Venus in 1769, when our neighbor planet passed in front of the sun. The French call these islands *Les Isles Sous le Vent*, meaning The Islands Under the Wind.

Other boats made the trip to the Society Islands, but the *Benicia* (bay NEE she ah) was the most regular in its service. During the night it would cover the distance from Tahiti, arriving at the first port early in the morning. It would spend the daylight hours carefully negotiating the passes through the reefs that surround these high islands on its mission to deliver trade goods from the outside world for the local product of copra, dried coconut meat. This area, I was promised, would reveal to me the real way of Polynesian life, as it was supposedly untouched by the wave of westernization that had swamped the shores of Tahiti and its main town of Papeete.

The *Benicia* was leaving for the leeward group at five o'clock sharp. It was still necessary for me to get the police permit from the local government, and it was already after two. It was incredible the questions that had to be answered on their overlapping reports for a foreigner to take what I thought would be a simple trip. "Why do you want to go? Where are you going? For how long? When are you returning?"

Each of these questions had to be discussed with every minor official, until I was finally awarded an interview with Le Chef du Bureau. Although I could have done the interviews in French, I chose to make them use their English. It made me feel that at least they were forced to use a language they disliked as much as I disliked theirs. By this time my patience was wearing thin, which was their object, I assume. But instead of a full questionnaire, Le Chef simply wrote a permit in my passport, apologized for his subordinates, and wished me "Bon voyage."

The next important step was to buy some basic supplies that I'd need in a pinch. I had no idea what was facing me in the next phase of my adventure. I'd have to carry whatever I bought in my backpack, and it was already full of other necessities. I'd never learned to travel light. In addition, I'd been duly warned that though available, these items would be more costly in the outer islands. It was true that the prices were high enough in Papeete, without the additional 40 percent markups allowed the merchant copra traders on these islands. Living on an outer island was quite expensive for the Islanders, but they really didn't have to buy very much with their small incomes from making copra. They depended a great deal on what nature provided.

The cost for second class passage on the *Benicia* was one-half the price of first class. Thinking that I could stand anything for one night, I decided to save the extra

$10. The ticket entitled me to a round trip, but I could break my passage and stay at any stop. As the *Benicia* made a trip about every week, this made it easy to schedule my moves.

Down at the quay where this monstrously ugly trading motor vessel waited, a group of well-wishers and the curious had gathered. It didn't take much to attract a crowd. At one time this near-hulk had been white. Its dirty bloated sides bulged and sagged so much that it had earned the name "Old Roller." It was owned by a Chinese merchant in town who must have felt he would get all he could out of it before expending one more sou on repairs. I contemplated the safety factor momentarily. However, I considered the price of the ticket a bargain I couldn't afford to miss. This was a case of valor over discretion.

The second class passengers had already spread their sleeping mats on the salon floor, which was black with ground-in grime. Arrayed around each mat were the family possessions, including bundles wrapped in old, faded *pareu*, bunches of fruit, a few chickens, a potty, and an enameled basin. Scampering around the deck was a group of young unattended children. The amount of clothing most of them wore decreased with advancing age. Babies were heavily swaddled. The more mobile youngsters had divested themselves of what they could remove.

First class, or "Deluxe" as the ticket read, entitled the bearer to a place in one of the six mattress-less bunks that lined the walls of a large, dark, airless closet. Though marked "reserved," it did not necessarily mean "single." The little privacy that this condition afforded was far outweighed by the fact that the occupants were off of the floor, hence not in the paths of night walkers. These were people who would not be sleeping because there was no place to lie down, or they were not feeling well enough to trust being so far from the railings. Though tied to the sea for centuries, many Polynesians seemed to be an unseaworthy lot of travelers. Many preferred instead to remain inert and take it as it came, rough or calm, as there was nothing they could do.

After checking the sky, I unrolled my sleeping bag on the roof. Though not a sheltered spot, it certainly offered an opportunity for more comfort than being inside.

Goods imported from the outside world crammed the decks. Boxes or cans of everything from kerosene to toothpaste, cement to sugar were packed onboard. Four lifeboats were on the vessel, the ropes and pulleys of which had been painted so often that they had become solid. The lifeboats were not. The lifeboats were filled with the odds and ends of things that could not be stowed away anyplace else.

On the return trip, the *Benicia* would bring back only a load of copra and, with it, the heavy smell that is so much a part of the dried coconut trade. It is sickly sweet and permeates the clothing to such an extent that for days afterwards it seems impossible that there could not be a chunk or two concealed in a pocket.

From my rooftop perch I had a wonderful star-strewn sky over me as a blanket. It was comforting to lie there and know that here, as nowhere else, the stars were shining on a part of the world that was at peace and without fear. "Old Roller" puffed her way over the familiar route.

Chapter III
HUAHINE

At sunrise I saw the twin peaks of Huahine (hoo ah hee NAY), which I was told was the "Bali Hai" island of song and legend. Once around the point, it was only moments before the *Benicia* was tied up at the small village of Fare (FAH ray). The passengers got off at the little dock and swarmed into the two little dockside Chinese-owned cafés for breakfast. They were served coffee and tinned milk in a bowl and a slice of baguette with a dab of tinned butter. The tiny crude tables and chairs in these open air eating places were crowded only at ship time. The rest of the week, the casual customers of the island's residents drifted in and out and would not be enough to fill either of them.

Inside each café was a shop that had a cluttered array of packaged and canned items and almost anything an isolated population would need, from bush knives, lamp wicks, soap, and flour, to long out-dated aspirin. It was all in such a jumble only the owner could know where anything was to be found. The oven for the bread was an old oil drum in back of the shop, fueled with burning coconut husks.

The main "street" filled the tiny area between the dock and the two cafes. It was wider than it was long. It stretched lengthways only a few yards and then became a grass-bordered sandy track in both directions through the green shadows along the shore line. I had decided to stay on the *Benicia* until the next stop at the island of Raiatea (rye ah TAY ah) and make my visit to Huahine on the way back to Papeete later. So I had only a short while to explore until I'd hear the blowing of the conch shell that warned of our departure.

I made a quick decision to go to the right, down the sandy track along the shore. I passed a small empty school and an administration building. Lurking almost out of sight among the shadows of the coconut trees, I saw a scattering of small, brightly painted, boxy, wooden homes with thatched roofs. There was a slight rise in the path until I came to its crest. Below was a beautiful inlet glistening in the early morning light. In the water, a long line of men stretched across the opening. On the beach, there were dozens of other townsfolk, mostly children. This gathering explained why so few people were on the dock when the boat arrived.

Before me I saw a community fishing party. It had started when the tide was about to change to go out. The men had stretched a net across the opening of the inlet, trapping the fish that had entered with the flooding tide. Gradually, the men worked their way through the water, pulling their net along in a wide arc. They steadily decreased the area, never allowing an opening to develop back to the sea. Very quickly, the arc of the net was closed and became less than a hundred feet across. The men were struggling to keep the net together and keep the fish from jumping out. The women and children jumped into the water and began slashing at the fish with their big bush knives as the fish darted between their legs. Using their bare hands, others tossed the entrapped fish up onto the sand. The tempo was feverish, as here was food for many people, and it had to be collected quickly. The accumulation of beached fish grew rapidly as other women sorted them out, dividing the fish into piles for each of the participating families, for sale, or for barter.

Operation Foodstuff seemed very successful as the delighted, shrieking children pranced around with great excitement. The youngsters took a moment to stare at me but were soon satisfied, so they plunged back into the water to wash off. It was almost time for them to go to school where they would begin their French recitations. These quaint sessions of group repetitions of the lesson could be heard in every village. It's a pleasant sound as it floats through the air from the open-sided schools.

Back at the dock a crowd had gathered for the departure, cheering and shouting and in general having a happy time jostling each other. There was much double-cheek kissing and hugging.

Meanwhile, some cattle were being herded onto the deck of the *Benicia*. Cows get nervous when walking over water on a narrow gangplank. One of the luckless beasts slipped and fell into deep water between the dock and the boat. Apparently, cows can swim if forced to do so. She kept her head above water and did a paddling motion. She looked like a horned orca. There was some loud agitated screaming from the Chinese captain. A seagoing cowpoke jumped into the water beside the cow and secured a rope to one of her front legs. The ship's crane hoisted the wretched critter up high enough to clear the railing, swung her around, and then deposited her onto the deck. At best, cows are graceless critters at sea, but when she took to the air, this loudly protesting bovine became absurd. On deck at last, she quickly rejoined the herd, her dignity thoroughly ruffled. She tried to pass it off as if nothing had happened.

Chapter IV
RAIATEA

A short trip took us to the high mountainous island of Raiatea (rye ah TAY ah). Raiatea is considered by most anthropologists to have been the population and cultural center of the classical Polynesian world preceding BCE (Before Common Era) through 1400 AD, when the major dispersal of the Maohi people is thought to have taken place. Raiatea might have been the Polynesian Athens of its day. It is possible that the various exploring groups left from here, each carrying small parcels of sacred soil from the Marae (mah RYE, temple compound) of Opoa (oh PO ah). The mother of the sacred soil is Mount Tamehani (tah may HAH nee), which rises almost 3400 feet and is by far the largest volcanic mass in the area. The Polynesians, constantly growing in population on this fertile island, were forced to find new land, which was scarce in the middle of the vast Pacific Ocean. They navigated by charts made of sticks woven together in such a way as to indicate where known islands were located in combination with the stars, plus the wind and ocean currents. These charts led them to far away specks of land between which they fearlessly navigated their giant canoes.

The *Benicia* arrived at the dock at Uturoa (oo too ROE ah), the main town, on a Wednesday. It was Market Day, when the dock area was crowded with inter-island workboats, coastal craft, and *va'as* (VAH ahz, outrigger sailing canoes). The passengers got off "Old Roller" and went into the local cafes for another breakfast and social hour with their friends. Others, residents of nearby villages and the outer districts on the island, had come by other similar watercraft tied up at the dock, bringing with them whatever they had to sell or trade. Like market day everywhere, the exchange of goods is secondary to the exchange of gossip.

The Chinese café was doing a brisk business in local coffee and sweet brown bread. Most everyone was barefoot. Working men mostly wore faded blue shorts, while some added a loose singlet undershirt. In the cafés, it was rare to see a Chinese girl waiting on tables. Instead, Island girls were hired for the job. There were two reasons for this. Many Chinese had married Tahitian girls in order to remain as citizens and enjoy an unmolested life. The offspring of these mixed marriages frequently become very attractive adults. The other reason is that there is less resentment at the prosperity of the owners in running a successful enterprise.

One of the serving wenches was dressed in what was then considered the latest island interpretation of European high style by wearing a *pareu* wraparound and a lacey French bra. She looked exactly as if she had stepped out of one of the advertisements in a woman's magazine. Another lass showed off her dressmaking skill — or sense of humor. She'd made a blouse out of cloth printed with scenes of Paris pictured on it. A pair of appropriate pictures bulged across her ample breasts, each with the phrase "Arc de Triumph."

In the front part of the café was an old 44-gallon oil drum full of collected rainwater, into which the customers dipped their hands before using an ancient and grimy towel. The enameled metal coffee bowls were also rinsed in the barrel, as well as the spoons and other dining utensils, before they were dried dry with a deft swipe of the same towel. Some of the tables were covered in aged oilcloth with patterns of wild strawberries and their blossoms or a blue plaid with a pansy motif. The décor of the walls was equally striking. Patches of green, gray, and blue showed that the contents of three cans of paint had not been enough to cover the walls and that the proprietor was not willing to invest more to cover the planking, which had originally been parts of other structures still boasting faded remnants of their previous colors.

"Do you speak English?" I heard someone ask as I walked into the café. I turned to see an elderly, white-haired, slender, attractive, European woman, apparently in her 70s, sitting at a table behind me. Next to her was a Tahitian woman who must have weighed twice as much and whose face was heavily wrinkled. The one who had spoken English invited me to come and sit down and talk with her and her equally aged companion, whom she introduced as "the princess." We shook hands and exchanged a warm "*Ia orana*" *(ee ah oh RAH nah,* Good Morning.*)* We went through the stages of introductions in English, French, and Tahitian. The other woman apparently spoke only the two local languages. They asked several questions about where I had come from and why I had come to Raiatea. We chatted on about things in general when finally the thinner one introduced herself.

"I am Mrs. Fletcher Christian. I live here on Raiatea with my son on our plantation. I must go now and do some shopping, but I want you to come home with me. I think you will find it very interesting. I'll meet you at the dock at two, when the boats go." With that we parted, and I roamed around the small plaza, investigating the produce of the market place and the people milling around.

Most of the market goods were fruits of the land, bananas of many varieties, including the *fei* from the highlands, coconuts, breadfruit, taros, and less exotic things, to me anyway, such as carrots, potatoes, and tomatoes. When the haggling for the sale was completed, the goods were put in a palm leaf basket and eventually were hung on a branch of one of the trees planted for this purpose. Some branches were decorated with hunks of raw meat or strings of fish. The flies got to these choice items, but the packs of meandering scrawny dogs did not. Other trees were heavy with bunches of chickens, with their feet tied together and hung upside down. Long loaves of French bread wrapped in newspaper were tucked in anywhere. Half a dozen constantly squealing pigs were each tied to a separate tree with a strip of hibiscus bark.

Large jugs of wine also hung from branches. However, most of the wine sold on market day went directly into the purchaser. This made for a gayer and livelier crowd. Drunkenness was not only tolerated in French Oceania, it was considered something of an economic necessity by the controlling nation. They imported wine and wheat from North Africa, I was told, and traded it for copra from the islands, from which they extracted the vegetable oil and sold it in Europe. The oil was sent to other colonies for more of their products. This economic arrangement encouraged a state of semi-stupor that the islanders enjoyed, and it kept them quiet. It also forced more of the men to enter the workforce to produce more copra, so they could buy more wine. The time spent on producing copra reduced the time that might be spent following the traditional ways of living off of the land. Hence, their diet had become more bread and wine and less fish and taro. This had an obvious physical effect when a smiling mouth commonly displayed a set of rotting teeth.

While waiting for my appointment to catch the afternoon launch with Mrs. Christian, I did a small watercolor of the market, and then strolled around the little town. After a lunch in a Chinese café, I explored further along the beach. The heat of the afternoon sun beating down on the market was having its effect. The restlessness of the buyers and sellers, the pigs and the chickens, was very evident. The children were beginning to fight with each other. It had been a long day that started at "second cock's crow," and everyone was ready to call it quits.

Two little boys had caught two of the purplish land crabs. They had tied strings to one leg on each, and they held them in the air close enough so that the crabs could fight with each other. The crabs excavate holes all over the land that are dangers to both man and beast. By day the crabs are scarce, but they come out at night and skitter around. I found them obnoxious and very arrogant when I tried to camp on the ground. I was delighted to see the two boys giving them a hard time.

When I returned to the dock area, most of the people were milling around. I stayed with Elizabeth Christian in order to get onto the right coastal water taxi. Several of these picturesque craft were tied up to the quay, making ready to depart. I've tried to find a word to describe these water buses to prevent any misconception that they might be acceptable transportation for average tourists. They were mostly about 30 or so feet long. They may have had a couple of rows of benches for the passengers under an open-sided shelter. They generally permitted too many people to get on board with their bundles. The more agile youths climbed up and settled on the roof of the shelter, adding to the likely problem of the balance of the craft. Most of these water trucks were very aged looking. Maintenance was often thought of only when it was time to solve an emergency. The motor generally sounded as if it was choking as it belched out clouds of black smoke. In spite of all of the fresh air around, they smelled badly of filth and fuel. They may have been a "convenience," but one of a challenging quality. Most had no emergency equipment. Many seemed to have outlasted their life expectancy. They seemed to exist merely to attempt to make just one more scheduled trip along the coast inside the relative safety of the lagoon before they were ready to expire. But many others were taken outside the reef and became inter-island water buses without qualified equipment or crew.

Since I have been unable to find a properly descriptive term, I have chosen the word "chugger," mostly based on the sound of its power source, and hoping that it will do the job. A chugger therefore, was something to take only when one feels really lucky and can have a great deal of faith in prayer.

When Elizabeth and I got to the chugger that she knew went to her area, we saw that some passengers had already taken their places on the small launches. They seemed about ready to depart for various stops along the coast. A husky ancient Polynesian with a powerful set of lungs put a conch shell to her mouth and gave it a blast heard loud and clear all around the town. She did not need to sound it again, because from all quarters the people came with their goods to clamber aboard the one that would get them home. Their smaller packages were hung from hooks in the ceiling of the shelter under which most of the women and children had gathered. The larger things were put up on the roof of the shelter with the bicycles, bundles of produce, and some live barnyard critters. A trussed pig shared our shelter with the passengers. Most of the older men found places where they could and gathered in little groups swaying comfortably with the motion of the boat.

We pulled away from the dock and headed south down the east coast, the pilot dodging the coral heads in the shallow water. I could look back and see other people getting into their outriggers and pushing away to sail home on their own. It was a lovely sight.

Our route followed the coastline very closely, but I saw very few signs of settlement and no other towns along the way. We passed the mouth of a great bay named Fa'aroa (fah ah ROH ah), which cut deeply into the island. Beyond this point, there was no road or anything else that could bring development to the area.

Mrs. Christian began her story. Her father had left Denmark as a young man and had gone out to the islands to start a new life for himself. Once there, he changed his name so that he could never be found by friend or foe, and he married a "European" (white) girl and settled on the neighboring island of Taha'a (TAH hah ah). While his children were growing up, he made them work on his plantation all day, doing the work that the local people refused to do. It was hot, hard work hacking a place out of the virgin tropical forest land. Her memories of her father were not pleasant, as she felt that he had treated his children far worse than he treated his servants. He used to keep a supply of butter and cheese locked up in a closet for his own use, never sharing it with his family.

Gradually his little empire grew more prosperous, and he began to think perhaps he ought to have the protection of the strong man of the area. Many of the native Islanders resented seeing an outsider achieve any success in which they can't share. For this reason he sent Elizabeth, his oldest daughter, to the home of the king of the island to grow up in the court as a kind of hostage. She was brought up with all the customary etiquette of native royalty before the turn of the century (1900). She was happy there, and it was no longer necessary to work so hard. Her best friend was the daughter of the king, the princess, whom she still met on Market Days in Uturoa.

The father's plan to gain an ally of the king was successful. He was protected from the raids of the often marauding locals. It was about this time the French military landed on the island to force their sovereignty on the natives. In doing so, they destroyed much of the plantation. The king's men fought the battle diligently, but the invaders eventually won effective control. The new government granted land rights to the Danish pioneer and his family so that they could continue farming. The king lost his command, and the court was dissolved. Elizabeth had to return home.

For Elizabeth, going back to her family and the chores was not a happy prospect. Things had not changed. The repairs needed to set the plantation back on its feet again meant many dreadful months of hard hot labor. In the early 1900s she met Fletcher Christian, a descendant of the instigator of the 1789 mutiny on the *Bounty*. The original Fletcher Christian had a Tahitian wife as did the other mutineers and a few other Tahitians. They discovered and settled on Pitcairn Island. So this descendant was of mixed race. The dashing young man with the magical name captured her heart. Not only was this a way to get off of the plantation, but she imagined that a life filled with romance and adventure was at hand.

Her father protested the marriage to the Seventh Day Adventist, but she persisted. They went off together. They did not, however, go very far. They settled on Raiatea, the neighboring island, and for a third time she began to carve a plantation out of the dense brush. They were only married for ten years when he died, leaving her with three children, two girls and their older brother Chester. She brought them up as best she could, struggling to make enough copra to buy kerosene, matches, cloth, and a few other essentials that were available on their isolated island.

When he was about 25, Chester decided to go to America to make a living and change the pattern of life for his family. His plan was to get established and then send for them. It was a good time in America then, and he wanted to be a part of it. But within a few weeks of his arrival in 1929, and before he was settled, the stock market crashed. He went from place to place, but his work experience had not prepared him for work in a troubled industrialized world.

During his absence, his mother and younger sisters had done their utmost to carry on and keep themselves together until they should hear from him. He never wrote. When he returned, penniless, and bitterly disappointed with the outside world, all of their hopes for escaping the plantation were lost.

During the 1930s, a movie company filming *The Hurricane* was on location in Tahiti. Chester thought that this might be his big chance. He had the ideal body of a young islander, so he was photographed in costume to take a leading role. Then he was demoted to a lesser role. A second time he returned, dejected.

Within a few years, the two daughters married and both left the island. One settled in Hawaii, and the other went to California. World War II cut them off from each other for several years. When it was over, the daughters pleaded with their mother to leave the plantation and come to live with them. She hated to leave her son. He refused to go, but he insisted that she make the trip. She was to spend a very happy decade with her daughters and their families in the modern bustling world of post-war America. A whole new unimagined life had opened up to her. She drove herself to the supermarket and bought things to put in the freezer or to cook on an electric stove. The homes had air conditioning and hot running water. Everything about a modern bathroom was such a treat for her, contrasted with the crudeness of island life. She enjoyed her grand-children so much that her old life began to slip from her memory. It was simply too far away in time and distance.

But time and distance have a way of catching up, and she began to get letters from Chester that he was sick and needed her. He complained that there was too much work, and he could not manage to do it all alone. She was torn between the two choices, comfortable America, or returning to a primitive jungle life of constant labor. She pleaded with him to give up the place and join them. Again he refused, telling his mother that her life was in Raiatea and that she should come home.

Our small boat had stopped briefly a few times to let passengers off as we rode the several miles south from Uturoa. They seemed to be jumping-off places for paths that led straight into the overpowering green growth just beyond the shore. We stopped at a narrow shaky dock and got off as someone handed Mrs. Christian her bundles. We walked barefoot up a narrow path for about a quarter of a mile. I was carrying my backpack on the first of many tropical island treks. The recent heavy rains had turned the volcanic soil into a sticky mess. I had not walked barefoot through squishy mud for many years. In the beginning, it was a treat.

We had not walked very far when we stopped to meet Chester. He was sitting on a box amid the many coconuts he had split that day. His actual work in progress was scooping out the ripe white meat and spreading it on the rack to dry. He was well-built, deeply bronzed from the sun, and wearing only a shredding straw hat and blue work shorts. Instead of the dashing hero type I had imagined, he appeared tired and sad beyond his 50 or so years. He was cordial, but a lack of company over the decades had made him more interested in his work than conversation. He spoke correctly the few English words he uttered, thanks to his mother's constant use of the third language of the island. He gave me the impression that he felt he was going to be burdened with another person with whom he would probably have to chat later. I assumed that Eliza-beth brought home company when she could to have some diversion. Our greetings exchanged, Elizabeth and I pressed on towards their home.

We walked a little further and stopped to inspect Chester's latest project. He had begun to raise vanilla. The vine is very simple in appearance. It has a single, plain, smooth, oval leaf at each section of the vine. Each section is about two inches long, and alternates direction as it zigzags up the trunk of a coconut tree. The long thin beans are a profitable export crop for the colony.

The house was typical of all the island houses I had seen so far. It was raised up on stilts and built of boards that had once been painted a barn red many years before. It had a rusting, corrugated metal roof and a few framed windows. The structure was merely a box of two rooms with a covered verandah across the front. A classical old Seth Thomas octagonal-faced clock was on the outside front wall, but both hands hung forlornly straight down as if it had died at about 6:30, perhaps decades ago. On the porch were an old rocker and a straight chair with broken webbing. The flight of stairs up to the porch would have profited from some carpentry to make it a bit more secure.

All in all, it looked more like a tree house than a plantation manor house.

To the left was a smaller building made about the same way, but noticeably newer. It had a new corrugated metal roof. It was raised up to the level of the main house with a little bridge from the verandah to the entry. This was the eating hut.

A bit further off to the left was a still smaller hut made of roughly woven split bamboo. It offered protection only from the rains. It was covered with a thick palm leaf thatching blackened by years of smoke. This was the cookhouse, and it was here that Elizabeth Christian began to prepare the evening meal. Outside was a very narrow bench not made to be a comfortable seat. It was on two broad-board legs, one on each end. It had a slim piece of wood extending about a foot or so beyond one end of the seat. At the far end of the extension was a disk-shaped piece of metal about three inches in diameter with many tiny saw-like teeth in the circular edge.

To my offer to help, Elizabeth suggested, "Straddle that and grate the coconuts." She continued, "Take that basin and catch the meat. When you are done, put it all in a piece of cloth and squeeze the juice out into this bowl. I have to go to get the fire started."

So I had my first lesson in Polynesian cookery. Grating the opened nuts proved to be easy. Squeezing the meat of half a dozen nuts produced a couple of cups of thick, creamy, hearty liquid. This is what is used in cooking, not the water that comes from the interior of the nut. Coconut cream is used in several dishes, fresh, or cooked. It is put in coffee and is used also as one of the main ingredients, along with lime juice and a bit of salt, to marinate raw fish, or "poisson cru," which is so good. The coconut cream can also be baked into a delicious pudding or added to tender young taro leaves, wrapped in a fresh breadfruit leaf, and baked on the hot stones. It becomes like creamed spinach. Oh! What a treat.

Inside the cookhouse, barefoot Elizabeth had already started the fire with several dried coconut husks. These tough protective outer coverings for the center nut must be removed as the first step in using the unopened nut. A nut with a green husk is for drinking the water inside and eating the soft flesh. When the husk is brown, the nut inside is ripe. The husk is removed by ramming it onto a sharpened stake that has been set solidly into the ground. Once the husk is rammed and given a sharp twist, the first crack appears. A second or third ramming and twisting can generally separate the nut from the husk quite easily. Four rammings and twists ought to be enough to remove it even for a novice like myself.

The dried husks and empty nut shells are the most readily available fuel of the tropical islands. Chester always kept a pile of them under cover in the cookhouse to protect them from the frequent rains. He had an even larger pile outside under a shed roof, the result of his days work extracting the meat to dry in the sun.

For making copra, a bush knife, or machete, is used, and a single hefty whack ought to split the husk and shell in half from top to bottom. When they are opened, instead of the usual watery liquid, sometimes there is a foamy pulp inside, which is delicious and interesting to eat. This is a nut that has become fertile. The pulp is making the food for the seed to survive, like the yolk of an egg.

When a fertile nut from a tree near the beach falls and gets washed away by the surf, it can float at sea for a year or more until it becomes beached on another island. The nut (the seed) has three "eyes" on the top of its hard shell, one of which is relatively soft. A fertile nut will then poke a slender root out of the shell through the single soft eye. The rootlet will then pierce the tough outer shell of the husk and continue to grow as it explores down to the nearest sand into which it burrows. Once it feels established, another growth will come out that will be the start of the new green leaves, and they will grow upwards towards the light. Soon there is a new tree. Of course the fertile nut can fall onto dry land and sprout the same way without a lengthy cruise at sea.

Elizabeth's cooking fire was inside a ring of stones set on the earthen floor of the cookhouse. She placed a metal bar about six feet long that had been bent into a tight U-shape onto the stones. Then she placed on it the only thing she had brought back from America, her most prized possession, a fire-blackened pressure cooker. As she leaned over, poking the embers with a stick, I could see a face that showed both the sadness at the events that had forced her to return to this life and the resignation that she would never again stand up straight to cook. That modern life seemed to her so remote now, and yet it could be so readily available if she could ever make the decision to move on again. Chester never would decide.

We took our plate of poisson cru into the newer hut to eat. The single room was just big enough to hold a table with a chair and a bench. Somewhere they had found a box, and so we three sat down at our own places. They did not have guests often enough to need extra furniture or utensils. In one corner there was a screened food safe, or cabinet, with three shelves on which were kept all of the cooked and uncooked edibles. Ants were prevented from getting in, as all four legs were standing in tuna tins filled with kerosene.

While we chatted, the chunk of meat she had bought in the marketplace was stewing in the pot near the fire. We had talked a long time when suddenly she heard a noise in the cookhouse. She ran out and found the pot overturned near the dead fire. The meat was gone. "The dogs again!" she moaned. Her neighbors had many of the semi-wild beasts and seldom fed them. They had come raiding before, but never when there were people so close in the eating hut. I reached into the backpack and brought forth dinner, a can of corned beef. It didn't much help the feeling of hopelessness at the vagaries of island life.

Elizabeth led vespers that evening on the verandah but there was little joy in her voice. If it could help, prayer was all that was left to fill the longing she felt to return to the few years of happiness she had known so briefly in the other world beyond the reef.

The next morning I carried my copy of *War and Peace* with me to the outhouse. I had become used to tearing out a few pages each day, which forced me to read as quickly as I could to keep ahead. When I got back to the house, Elizabeth asked about the book. I showed it to her.

When she saw that several pages were missing, she stared at me and then said sadly, "That's a terrible thing to do to a book out here on the islands." I felt so guilty. I asked if she would like to have it, and she eagerly accepted the abridged edition. I wondered if she ever actually read any of it. As for myself, I had another paperback in the pack.

Upon departing, I bid the Christians a warm "*Ia orana*," and walked along the shore on the route leading back to Uturoa. It was interesting to stop off to see the ruins of Opoa, birthplace of the ancient gods, which had been the subject of an archaeological investigations a year or so before. In their present state of neglect and decay, they still stood as tragic memorials to the once proud and powerful Polynesian culture. Here was the religious heart of their entire race. Many of these large blocks were four feet or more in diameter. Many were chunks of coral lifted from the reef. Some were slabs of lava rock. All had been transported and erected into a meaningful structure without use of wheel or beast. One rectangular enclosure consisted of a base layer of stones about eight feet tall. Worked crudely with stone tools, these gigantic monoliths testify to the power and the ambition held in the hands of the mighty rulers. I had been told to look for a single stone, little worked, that stood in a clearing. Again, it was a stone about seven feet tall. My informant said that it measured the height of the kings. I do not doubt the possibility of the people being of great stature as I met Marquesans as tall as my own six feet plus, and much heavier. They were merely the remnants of a magnificent race. It was a good experience to view this acropolis of the seafaring islanders. It did not take long for missionaries to purge the minds of the populace of their old beliefs. Now few even recall the legends and the history of their own race.

I was following what was called "*La Grande Route*." "Grande" though it may be to the locals, and to some Parisian bureaucrat city planner, it was only a pleasant footpath following the shore through the cocos. Most of the time my eyes concentrated on the track in front of me, in order to prevent stumbling into the holes of the land crabs. I was completely taken by surprise to see, incredibly, a steel suspension bridge crossing a rather pleasant little stream. The floor boards were wide and strong enough to hold a truck of many tons, not withstanding the fact that no such truck existed in the whole archipelago. "Now," I thought, "I am coming to *La Grande Route*." To my utter amazement there was not a route, or even a pair of car tracks, on the other side. It was merely a continuation of the very same footpath. It was truly a bridge that went from nowhere to nowhere. The explanation was that someday there would be a road there and then the bridge would be ready. At the time it seemed to me to be terribly far-sighted wishful thinking.

La Grande Route rambled on towards Uturoa. Only a few scattered wooden huts indicated that I had twice walked through small settlements. In each I heard the ever present sound of squealing pigs. It was an inescapable noise, as nearly every pig was tied to a tree by one leg with a strand of hibiscus bark rope. For some reason, smart as pigs are, they hadn't learned to chew through the restraining bond. Perhaps it tastes badly. In any event, they spent the day complaining.

I watched two girls out in the lagoon. As they walked through the water, they dragged a long trailing thing made of green coco palm leaves tied together to made a kind of long rope with the long leaflets spiraling outwards. Every few steps they tossed stones into the water ahead of them, or beat it with sticks. They were fishing and driving their victims ahead of them as if they were sheep. The palm leaf thing was a kind of net, or trap, through which most of the fish would not swim. Up ahead in shallower water was a trap made of coral stones into which the girls would corral the small fish. They would then block the entrance with stones already piled there.

I came to the mouth of the Fa'aroa Bay and had to turn inland to follow the shore. The bay, which is narrow, goes westward deep into the island like a fjord. Much gaiety coming from one of the houses by the side of the trail aroused my curiosity. Ahead, there was no sign of any more path as it seemed to terminate at the little beach in front of the last house. Beyond, there was nothing but a deep stream bed and an extensive mangrove swamp that appeared to stretch far into the valley.

Before I could figure out my next move, I was surrounded by celebrants who wanted to know all about me. "No time for so many questions," shouted one of them in French as he pulled me towards the house. There were dozens of merry makers inside and out. It was a wedding, and there was much drinking. The rest of the ceremony and feast had been finished hours before. They apologized that there was no more wine, but I must have a drink with them. At this point, they were serving home-brewed beer made from bananas and papayas. Courtesy to such willing and open hospitality demanded that I swallow a glass or two, of which I can fortunately no longer remember the taste.

"Yes, it is very good. Now, would you please tell me where the trail goes?"

"*Il n'y a plus*," I was informed. They laughed and shrugged their shoulders. I could see that they were telling the truth, there was no more. If I had to make my way through the entanglements of the mangrove swamp with the sucking black mud, I knew at best it would be a terrible trip, in which I would more than likely get completely lost. Yet, there on the other side not a quarter of a mile away was another settlement of a few huts.

"*Il faut bateau*," one said as he urged me towards his *va'a* (a dugout outrigger canoe) that was pulled up on the bank of the estuary. A *va'a* was just that, a hollowed out log. Because the trees are not all that big, the logs aren't very thick. Since the dugout outrigger *va'as* often had to be handled by one man, or sometimes two, they did not want them too big and heavy. They take them out of the water and up onto the beach to dry out when they are not in use. The slender lines of the *va'a, or pirogue*, (pee ROUG, fr.) make it sleek and fast in the water. The "balance," or "outrigger," is an additional length of wood, a float, secured a meter or more out on one side of the *pirogue*, which helps keep it from capsizing.

I got in as instructed and walked the length of the hull, some eight feet, and then had to sit down on a narrow crossbeam. My difficulty was the pack on my back, which was not balancing properly. We managed to get it down so that it rested across the gunwales of the hollow log. To sit, I had to put one foot in front of the other, as there was no room for them side by side. He shoved off and we were soon gliding over the smooth water to the opposite shore. As my savior paddled with strong even strokes and we coasted along, I mulled over what fun it would be to have a *va'a* of this sort that seemed so easy to navigate. I then realized that it was all in the expertise. For me, it was too short a trip, but the ferryman was anxious to return to the party, so he was not wasting a moment.

As I got nearer to the next village, there were significant signs of a real dirt road that came from Uturoa. The mangrove swamp and the bay were the end of the road for any trucks. They would somehow have to bridge the mouth of this bay for *La Grande Route* ever to see any motor traffic passing over the suspension bridge. I continued northwards.

That evening, I did not find anyplace to stay. I did see a shed with a two-wheeled cart in it and thought about that as a shelter. I did not want to sleep on the ground because of the many land crabs that skitter around at night. They might decide that I was a delicate morsel on which to dine. I decided to try sleeping in the cart. This crude vehicle was used in the coconut plantations when the workers picked up the fallen nuts to bring them to the place where the meat was to be removed and dried. I took my sleeping gear and mosquito net out of the pack and got onto the cart. It was big enough to lie down in, but it kept getting unbalanced and wobbled up and down every time I moved. I had to get out and find something to secure it, and eventually settled down again. It was not long before I heard the crabs clicking their claws as they roamed around under my unsteady bed. At least I was under a roof, and not crab bait.

The mosquitoes sang their songs all night outside my netting. I had been told that these noxious insects had been introduced to the islands when they hitched a ride hiding in the water supplies of the earliest explorer's ships.

Another day as I walked through a village I was stopped by a young *tane* (TAH nay, man) and engaged him in conversation. Fortunately, I'd had years of French courses, starting in grade school. It was one of the scholastic exposures that I never liked, but which did come to me fairly easily when necessary for conversation, verb tenses be damned. I even pursued it a year in college, along with Spanish. I had no mastery of either of these, but, correct or not, I uttered them. Listeners seemed to make enough sense out of my babble so that the traveling life was far more pleasant for me.

Tarangi (tah RANG gee), the young *tane* I had just met, invited me to join him for a walk in the lagoon. It did not take long to get ready for that. I had only to put on my sneakers. I had heard some of the tales about the beauties and the dangers of the reef, and so would not go barefoot. Our small adventure was very interesting as I was shown various kinds of coral. He had been sent out to find something for the family dinner. He was looking for *pahoehoe* (pah HO ee HO ee). These mollusks are in a beautiful white shell, basically the same size and shape of a pair of clasping hands with interlocking fingers. The outer part is covered with what resembles ruffles. When enough had been collected, we returned to the shore. His home was the familiar wooden structure of old boards and tin roof raised on stilts. It was no different than the Christian's home or any other I had seen along the way. I was welcomed by the family and was advised that I was expected to stay for dinner and the night.

The following morning we spent snorkeling out on the reef. I carried my gear, and my young friend had his own primitive goggles. The pair he wore had been carved out of small pieces of wood and small lenses had been inserted. They did not keep out the salt water, but they were better than nothing. I exchanged with him frequently so that for once he could really see what wonders the reef displayed.

After a mid-day meal, Tarangi asked me if I would like to climb Mount Tamehani. I jumped eagerly at the idea. We both started up barefoot as by then the soles of my feet had become a bit used to the various terrains and the soles of my shoes were quite slippery on the damp surfaces of the stones. After we passed through the coco grove we began to climb from the coastal plain. On the slightly higher ground we started to walk in a forest of the larger hardwood trees. Among them was the chestnut. It was not really a chestnut tree, but it produced large lima bean-shaped nuts that tasted like the European variety. The roots are marvelous. They looked more like medieval buttresses supporting the huge trunk for many feet up the sides. We climbed through gullies and in the stream bed. We passed through a fantastic tree-fern forest where the ferns were a dozen feet tall and the spread of the leaves from tip to tip appeared to be even more. We had to fight through vines with clothes-gripping tentacles and through barriers of grass so tall that we could not see over them, and through saw-toothed edged leaves that scratched the bare skin. We had to climb over ledges of coal-black volcanic stone, up through a bridal veil waterfall, and around two more. Then we walked up the stream itself and it was somewhat easier.

The next stretch was one of the most beautiful scenic gems I have ever seen. We were sloshing our way up the stream as it splashed its silvery spray over the slick jet black boulders when we entered a bamboo thicket as dense as it could possibly be. There was not another kind of plant in sight. All I could see were the dark green stalks and their leafy plumes as they soared skywards, more then 20 feet tall. The trunks of many of them seemed to be almost a foot in diameter contrasting in size and color with the delicate shades of the tender new shoots. Short stumps here and there indicated that many of these had been harvested for lowland use. There was a harmony of the living greens, and the tans of the dead leaves on the ground. There was a look about the place as if we were the first explorers to stumble in on nature's first experiment with tan snow. The thick silent covering muffled our footfalls so that the tinkle of the stream was all that could be heard. It was a happy spot, this silent little chamber in the woods, and I hated to have to leave and fight even further up the mountainside.

The rain began to fall as soon as we left the last cover of overhead growth. We had climbed quite high but there was little view, just the thick grey, wet, low-hanging cloud that looked like churning masses of fog. Underfoot the path was almost impossible. Even the toes found it hard to grip in the buttery red mud. The rain was cold, very cold, on the hot body of this sweating climber. Progress had become too slow. There was still a very considerable distance to go to reach the summit. It was already late afternoon and Tarangi said that if we went on to see the crater that we would have to spend the night on top of the mountain in the cold rain, as the path back down would be too difficult to follow in the dark. The choice was a difficult one. To turn around meant that our effort would be almost wasted. To continue meant facing a very uncomfortable and very long night, shivering in this unprotected area. The only wise decision was to retreat.

I was upset that Tarangi had not gotten this expedition started early in the morning, but did not make any comment. I was getting too cold. We had to make time in our descent before it got too dark in the dense forest. We trod our way through the fading light. It changed the bamboo grove into a veil of shadowy forms. We scrambled down the waterfalls and the slippery cascades.

We had passed over the worst part of the trail and literally felt our way along with our toes in the complete darkness. We could then pick our way slowly with no more real danger than comes from stumbling. Once in the great forest of big trees it became easy. By the time we got our still-shivering bodies down into the coco trees, the moon had turned the beach sand into silver, striped with shadows from the trunks of the palms. Was the moon also shining into the awesome crater? Or, was it still raining? Frankly, I was glad that we had arrived at the shelter of the house for this night.

Tarangi and his family had been most pleasant hosts. I left them with a large can of meat and a package of cheese that I hoped I could replace if I passed a shop along the route to my next stopping point. We bid each other good-bye with firm single-pump handshakes, said "*Ia orana*," and I was on my way.

The trail changed little along the way and I made some good time. I did stop at a small Chinese store and replaced my essential supplies so I could be ready for an emergency. Part of the afternoon was spent on the beach and in the lagoon.

Towards late afternoon I spotted a small empty thatched roof hut, or *fare* (FAH ray). *Fares* are often abandoned if a family moves away, or if someone dies in it. I put my gear down in it and took an exploratory stroll to acquaint myself with the area. It was too late in the day to attempt to walk further, and I had found a shelter for the night. These huts of woven split bamboo walls and coconut palm leaf thatched roofs represent only an investment of time for the owner, and it was often better to rebuild than to bother to repair it. When a new *fare* was needed, it was a matter of getting the word out. The new home owner collected the materials needed. Everyone around contributed a day of labor. The beneficiary supplied the food. There was a great deal of happy interaction in the women's work of weaving the thatches and the men's construction crew. There were pleasant food breaks, and everyone had a great day together.

It took me no time at all to settle in my *fare* for the night. I had no more than gotten out my emergency rations, when a *vahine* appeared from the nearby store and suggested that I move into the better *fare* next door. It appeared that this was probably her own home and I accepted her offer, made the move and again set about to prepare my meal of canned meat, cheese, and half of a French bread baguette. In a very few minutes the *vahine* reappeared with several drinking cocos. Seeing that I had nothing to open them with, she came back with a machete, or bush knife. A few minutes later she was back with hot coffee and sweet bread. While we were talking, her sister arrived with meat, tomatoes, water, and an ancient kerosene lamp, all on a tray. Before we had finished, another couple appeared.

By their gestures and expressions, I was certain that they were the owners. Their sense of hospitality was not as keenly developed as that of the two girls of the store. I was asked to depart. I was to find that some native hospitality puts the direct burden on the shoulders of an unsuspecting neighbor. I returned to the abandoned *fare* for a quiet, if not insect- and crab-free sleep. The next morning I arrived in Uturoa and awaited the *Benicia* for the short voyage northwestwards to Bora Bora.

Chapter V
BORA BORA

By New Year's Day 1942, America was at war on opposite sides of the globe. The Germans had occupied Europe and North Africa, while the Japanese were occupying or advancing on Southeast Asia and many of the strategic islands on the western side of the International Dateline from Alaska to New Zealand. Our one-sided declaration of neutrality was not an option. We were surrounded by enemies.

Within a month after the attack on Pearl Harbor, Rear Admiral Ben Moreell of the U.S. Navy had devised a plan to enlist skilled and experienced civilian construction workers into self-sufficient units to set up emergency fuel and supply depots across the Pacific. This was to create a series of positions from which further anti-enemy activity could be carried out, to halt the Japanese advance towards Australia and the rest of the Western Pacific islands.

Admiral Moreell structured these quasi-naval units so that they would be under the Civilian Engineer Corps officers with naval command. The men would have basic military training for self defense and bring their work experience with them. Many had helped build Hoover Dam, national highways, and New York skyscrapers. They'd worked in dockyards, quarries, mines, and subway tunnels. Sixty skilled trades were represented. The volunteer enlistees ranged in age from 18 to 50 or more, with the average age being 37. The construction battalions were designated as CBs, which became known as Seabees. Their motto was, "We Build, We Fight." This unit was called "The Bobcats."

The first fuel tank farm and supply depot was constructed on Bora Bora, a small mountainous island. The island had a safe, reef-protected, deep harbor, and it was far from the enemy. Located some 1500 miles directly south of Hawaii, Bora Bora is about halfway to Australia from America's west coast.

They made a road around the island. In March 1943, an airstrip on Motu Mute on the outer reef of Bora Bora was inaugurated. It was the first airstrip in French Polynesia. In April 1943, the fuel and supply depot was completed and was ready to service naval and supply vessels. Other depots were established on Tonga and in the New Hebrides.

James Michner was the author of *Tales of the South Pacific*. These tales were the basis for the play and movie *South Pacific* featuring a unit of Seabees. Michner did his writing in the New Hebrides, later called Vanuatu, in Melanesia. This was far to the west of the Society Islands, between Fiji and northern Australia. The movie was filmed on Kauai, in Hawaii.

During the afternoon I heard the conch horn warning that the *Benicia* was ready to depart from Raiatea for the next stop on its weekly circuit of the Society Islands. .I headed for the wharf in Uturoa.

Once settled on the deck of the *Benicia*, I could relax and enjoy the overnight voyage to my next adventure on Bora Bora. From a certain viewpoint across the water, the island's profile is like an inverted "W," with two huge and impressive peaks bursting out of the vast blue lagoon, ripping at the horizon like a pair if gigantic shark's teeth. But as the ship's course curved towards the harbor, only one captured my imagination. Shaped like a huge book on end, 2,385 feet high. Otemanu (oh tay MAH noo) surpassed all the other landscape around it. Tropical vegetation had managed to smother the rest of the fabulous scene. Otemanu, thrust naked and erect into the sky, was shorn of anything that would soften its lines. Yet it is not rude. Its rounded crest is capped with the green of daring plants that hang by their roots to be whipped by the wind and seared by the sun. Sometimes a passing cloud is caught and anchored to the peak as if it had been speared like a willing vahine. Otemanu is such a mountain. Bora Bora is such an island.

The Polynesians, or Moahi People, believed that Ta'aroa, God of the Sea, fished all of the islands up from the ocean floor, and that Bora Bora was the first of all of them. Bora Bora is a magical name that rightly brings excitement to the minds of men. If they have not heard the fantastic stories told by servicemen who passed through there during the war years, they may have read in novels about gorgeous, luscious island beauties who rescued shipwrecked heroes from the surf. These were mostly wild imagination.

There is a good basis for the imaginings of dreamers of fiction and non-fiction about the South Seas. The physical aspects of Bora Bora are perfect for any exaggeration. It is awesome! Those lucky enough to have seen it could not soon forget the sheer majesty of the great peaks soaring out of the sea. They must long remember the fabulous lagoon and the spectacular beaches. They could not forget the interesting people who live there. They dare not forget to embellish their stories when they repeat them endlessly to others. The very name Bora Bora is enough to set the adventurer's travel juices flowing. However, there were no young girls and few females of any age there when the Americans arrived in 1943.

The French administration well knew what to expect if the base was to be set up in Tahiti. After all, they had brought their own troops out in the 19th century. So they offered the Allies the harbor of Bora Bora. The natives also knew what to expect. They had already coped with a lot since their own power was crushed by the French colonizers who promised "protection" from other nations during the 19th and 20th centuries. So when the Islanders learned that their harbor was to become a port for American ships, they sent the females in their families, mothers, sisters, and daughters, to a safer place, off to the romanticized island of "Bali Hai." This safe island was actually just out of sight over the horizon. Its real name was Huahine.

And so the invasion of the Americans began. The first to come were the Seabees. Their landing, the unloading of their ships, and the beginning of their construction work, was something the likes of which the islanders had never seen before. This invasion was good, the natives found. There was plenty of money to be had for practically nothing. These guys would buy anything. They would trade anything. But the Americans were disappointed. What they had heard most about, and wanted most to encounter, were the fabled young girls of the South Pacific.

One man expressed it to me this way "Plenny cigaretti, plenny chocolati, plenny choon gum. An for wat? For nutting. The *Mariti* (American servicemen) were plenny rich, plenny good spenner. But, "*Mariti* wan wun ting not nuff of, *vahine.*"

It was said that one of the more erudite of the Seabees vocalized his unit's disappointment in one of these paradise assignments. It was universally acknowledged that what they lacked was the equivalent of an incomparable, incomprehensible, complex, yet essential, totally unique creature of the opposite gender, "DAMES!" Eventually the thought was put into more simple terms and became a show-stopper tune in a Broadway show about the war in the Pacific.

So the call went out to all the islands around to send back the *vahine.* When the word was spread about how easy it was to earn plenny cigaretti, plenny chocolati, plenny choon gum, there were suddenly plenny *vahine.* Mothers, sisters, and daughters all returned, eager to meet the new young *Mariti* who were "plenny rich and plenny good spenners."

Almost every traditional activity in any Polynesian village was gender defined. Males did some things, females did others, and they rarely shared. The *tane* hollowed out their *va'as* and went out fishing in deep water. They constructed *fares*, they tended the gardens in which they raised food crops, and they cooked in the underground ovens. These activities were taboo for the women. The *vahine* gathered food from the sea, they made tapa cloth and wove mats, they did the family laundry, and they cared for the children. No males would consider doing female things. These were *tapu.*

When the *vahines* returned to Bora Bora, they immediately responded to the needs of the *Mariti.* Most frequently, the *vahines* were rewarded with chocolate bars and bubble gum, which had suddenly become the coin of the realm. Obviously native *tane* were excluded from this trade. Some of the *vahine* must have earned a lifetime supply, and banked it. A decade later, the bubble gum still seemed to be available, perhaps in the Chinese stores.

One evening one young *tane* chatting with me was extolling the virtues of his sister. He boasted with manifest jealousy, "Oh, she one very cleva girl. She make big bubble."

When the sea routes to Australia were safe again, the base was pulled out of Bora Bora, and with it, the Seabees and any other servicemen. They lined the decks of their departing ship and waved good-bye to the *vahines* they were leaving behind. There were very few who did not say: "Boy, when the war is over I'm going back to Bora Bora." The war had been over for a decade. The flood of returnees was long overdue. On Bora Bora some were still waiting. Some *vahines* had little young reminders of the time when the *Mariti* came with plenny cigaretti, plenny chocolati, and plenny choon gum.

The *Benicia* pulled up to the cement pier that was big enough to hold the Navy's ships. Off to one side was the small settlement of Vaitapi (vie TA pi, rhymes with "my pappy"). The remains of a weathered thatched hut were empty of anything but a couple of broken chairs and a table, with a sign outside announcing the "Bora Bora Yacht Club." On the other side was a large pile of rusting scrap iron, much of it earth moving and construction machinery. When the American base had been abandoned, much of their equipment was left behind for whatever benefit it might be to the Islanders. Because they returned quickly to their coconut culture, the villagers had little use for it. It was up to an enterprising Chinese merchant to enrich himself by removing the heavy equipment bit by bit, and selling it, with none of his profits going back into any form of beneficial development for the locals.

Beyond its natural beauty, Bora Bora was noted for its dancers. During July all the islanders joined in with their French co-inhabitants for a week of celebration of Bastille Day on the island of Tahiti. The festival, "La Fête," (lah FET) in Papeete, presents the competitions to which the various islands send their best dance teams, athletes, and boatmen. It was rare that a dance team from Bora Bora was beaten. Their skill, their teamwork, and their exquisite costumes far surpassed the others. They worked hard in practicing the traditional dances. Their finely shredded bark skirts and other adornments had become their second major source of income. These outfits were sold to tourists in Papeete, or to the more adventurous ones who came to visit the village of Vaitapi.

The costumes, the "grass skirts," are made from the shredded soft inner bark of a certain tree, and then trimmed with perfect shells collected from the reef. Shells washed up on the beach were never used, as they were never perfect. The shells must be gathered during the nights when the tide is low as the animals within are nocturnal. It is time-consuming and dangerous work searching with flaming torches for the dark shells. The collector had to be cautious, as there was a constant threat of getting stung by the rightful owner of the shell. Another hazard was being scratched by the sharp corals. Once lodged in the flesh, these bits of coral tend to fester and can abscess, causing great discomfort and dangerous infections.

When the fabric parts of the dance outfits are completed, the men sewed the handsome dark brown shells, along with tiny yellow ones, on to the waistline of the soft bark skirts. Headdresses and chest bands for the males are also created, with designs that add richness and luster to the costume. When finished, these dance outfits were willingly traded for used clothing or a few dollars. No longer did they sell their talents for choon gum. But in spite of the fanciful travel posters promoting the island put out by the Papeete Visitors Bureau, and these Islanders concentration on this one product, I never saw anyone wearing anything but shorts or *pareu*. The blue or khaki shorts were made by almost every Chinese trader on every island. It was another monopoly.

I had not gone far from the dock near Vaitapi when I heard tap, tap, tap, tap, coming from under one of the huts raised on stilts. Investigating, or rather nosing around, I saw a family group sitting in the shade working. They beckoned me to sit down, which in itself was not surprising, as it was common Polynesian hospitality and curiosity. The interesting thing was that the language they favored was *Mariti*. Though halting at first from a decade of little use, there was no doubt that the fellow and his wife took every opportunity to communicate with visitors to their isolated island. I came closer, and put the backpack down. The noise that had roused my curiosity was coming from the striking of a wooden mallet that the woman was using, to mash the inner bark of a tree, on a log. She was making the off-white tapa cloth used for trim on the dance costumes. When beaten many times, soaked, folded over, and beaten again, and soaked and beaten, the bark eventually takes on the appearance of paper. Tapa was the only form of cloth made and worn by the ancient Polynesians. The roots of this special mulberry tree were carried with them as a necessary plant on their trips of exploration and settlement on new islands.

I accepted with pleasure their invitation to stay and visit them. When it came time to prepare dinner, I asked if I could help by grating the coconuts. They were surprised that I knew how and seemed happy that I helped. When the cream was squeezed out, my host threw the white meat on the ground for the chickens and a pet cormorant. Within seconds the cat arrived, scaring the fowl away and began to eat its fill. A scraggly dog gingerly joined the cat. Their tenuous peace did not long last because some grunting pigs moved in to finish off the small nutritious offering. That is about all that any domesticated animal is likely to get, and to get that, they have to be quick. On their own, all of the animals scavenge what they can from the shells of partly cleaned nuts. What they have left by nightfall, the insidious land crabs finish.

When the meal was over, my host's *vahine* prepared some coffee. Some days before she had collected the beans from a hillside grove, husked them, and dried them on mats in the sun, And now, with the strong black brew mixed with coco cream, we relaxed and chatted in a patois of French, *Mariti*, and Tahitian. My footstool under the table grunted and moved periodically, but who can deny that a warm black hairy hog is more comfortable than a box, especially when barefoot?

Between the two cots on the verandah, there was a door that went into the only room in the house. I was to sleep on one of the cots and the grandfather on the other. Inside in a double bed slept my host and his oldest son. On another cot in a corner slept the two younger sons. The grandmother, the wife, the five daughters, and a baby all slept on mats on the floor. Those on the cots had well-worn Army blankets. Those on the floor had each other.

The following day I walked to another part of the island and found an isolated part of the lagoon in which I could spend the afternoon contemplating its beauties. Up to this time, I had been so occupied that I thought it was fair to take some time off from my talking, watercolor painting, and general investigating. Wearing nothing but my sneakers, I brought my diving mask and snorkel to the edge of the crystalline water of the lagoon. I was prepared to spend a delightful part of the day just lazing in the water enjoying the offerings of this magnificent spot. I swam the hundred yards or so out to the reef. I was new at this game and had no idea the dangers that could be faced. I am from New York. What would I know about a reef?

The actual reef is a rocklike wall that that grows on the outer shoreline of tropical isles. It is formed by the never ceasing production of tiny polyps that, when they die, leave a diminutive deposit of lime to add to the total growing structure. These organisms build in many strange, but pre-determined ways. The variations in color stagger the imagination. It can briefly be said that they range from hair-thin flower-like elements to solid barriers that can tear the heart out of the stoutest ship. To swim amongst these sights is like gliding weightlessly in the most beautiful of gardens. There are trees as solid as stone, flowers as rigid as steel, branches as brittle as glass, and giant brains as sturdy as concrete. The beauty is in the constant and unending diversity of color and form.

The outer rim of the reef is a formidable rampart that shatters the forces of the ocean. Beyond the outer edge, the blue depths plunge down directly several hundred feet where there is another world, full of the great fishes. They seldom enter the shallow brilliant kaleidoscopic precincts of the lagoon. The corals at the outer lip screen out the roughness of the open sea and its wildlife. Each new wave rushes over the myriads of forms harboring themselves within the limits of the whole. Little terraces confine tiny pools, and when these are awash they form miniature cascades and rapids.

As I stood on the solid reef watching the swells build up I could look into them as if they were made of glass, and down below could be seen the shadowy forms of the titans of the deep. Though I was sorely tempted to plunge into the outer ocean, I realized the risks of a rip tide that could wash me out to sea. Or instead, being tossed wantonly onto the sharp corals and ripped to shreds. No, that was one risk I was not going to take while I was not in sight of another human … but I was tempted.

Swimming in the quiet water behind the safety of the reef I found to be most exhilarating. In the waters of my native Long Island Sound between New York and Connecticut, there was little charm, there was little visibility, and the colors ranged from maroons to dark greens and browns. For anyone used to that, a lagoon was a revelation. As I swam underwater, I rolled over and looked up at the ceiling of the sea. I could see that the glassy surface reflected the images of the forms on the bottom. Every wave washing through the coral set the surface alive with millions of tiny bubbles, each reflecting a tiny rainbow.

The many kinds and colors of the fishes were fascinating. There were those that lived exclusively within the confines of the formation of a chosen coral host. Others darted in and out. Some came within six inches of my hand to investigate the creature invading their world. Some fish were invisible to the eye unless I could see their shadows on the sand at the bottom under them, and was aware of where to look. But I think the most wondrous were schools of tiny pale blue and silver sardines that darted back and forth doing military maneuvers, while they traveled in a great crowd of a ball-shaped formation. I tossed pieces of coral into their midst to watch them explode with fear in every direction, and then re-group instantly into their sphere, and move on as if nothing had occurred. They are firm believers that there is safety in numbers.

I saw many creatures that have to crawl or slither over bottom sand, and they were just as diversified. I saw many varieties of starfish. Some were big and slow, others were small and fast. Some were red. One kind I saw was a bright blue. One was so brittle it came apart with no effort. Another was more than a foot and a half across and wore a coat of terrible spines on its 16 arms. It is called the Crown of Thorns. Then there was the sea slug or sea cucumber, so called because it looked like one. It was a brownish, leathery looking, unattractive resident that seemed to be inoffensive and just stayed on the sand. It was considered by the Chinese to be a delicacy when dried. I poked it with a stick I carried. When bothered, it ejected a white latex-looking substance. When this got on the stick or on my sneakers, it was very difficult to take off. I supposed that this is how it traps its prey. I could not see any way that it could devour anything it caught as it did not seem to have a mouth. But I was not going to worry about it.

The reef has some very dangerous residents. Sitting motionless in the broken chips of coral, its skin camouflaged with pink and gray blotches, exactly matching that of the lichens on the dead coral, is the very poisonous stone fish. It is the ugliest creature to be seen. It is the most dangerous when not seen and stepped on by accident. Along its back is a row of spines that stand erect in moments of stress. Many an unwary reef walker has stepped on one of these villains. Its poison causes unbearable pain and terrible swelling, and it is often fatal. It is the cobra of the lagoon. Any explorer must wear shoes.

Another nasty critter is the sea urchin, which comes in a variety of forms. But they are more obvious and can more easily be avoided. Some have brittle spines, maybe eight inches long, which easily break off in human flesh. The instant first aid is human urine, but if there isn't a nearby donor, the victim is in for a painful time. Years earlier I went for my first reef-peeking excursion in the Florida Keys. I stepped out of the rowboat onto a coral head but also right onto a sea urchin. I got spines in my left foot, which felt like lightening had struck me. I got back in the boat and my companion was handy with first aid. It offered little comfort. For almost a year I suffered with 14 bits of spines in my foot. I swore I would never try that activity again. How quickly we forget. This obsidian-black crawler seems always to be where there is a good place to sit down.

As an act of revenge to make me feel better about my first experience, I carried a diving knife and a stick with me, and when reasonable, I stabbed a number of these spiked creatures. As their innards floated out of their brittle, round crust of a shell into the water, tiny fish in great numbers and varieties darted towards this offering, to dine on the fresh food source. I learned that fish do have memories. I stayed at the same beach for a few days and crushed urchins in the same locale repeatedly. After the second time, small fish sensed my presence and gathered for the feast before I began poking at the urchins.

In spite of the known hazards, and not being aware of others, I did not stop venturing out on the reef alone. It was a whole new life, and I wanted to live it to the fullest. Through sheer dumb luck, I never had a more serious accident than a few coral scratches. Some of those eventually needed medical attention, but I was in a land where the cause of the problem was well-known, and treatment was readily available in the larger villages.

Towards late afternoon I began to think of dinner. The possibility of foraging on the wealth of food in the surrounding water intrigued me. Here and there, nestled in small crevices in the coral were many *pahoehoe*. With the aid of my dive knife, I was able to pry several of these mollusks out of their homes. The *pahoehoe* is quite interesting. It is first spotted by seeing the bit of flesh that protrudes beyond the edges of the two halves of its open shell, which acts as a bait to attract its prey. This bait comes in several velvety colors. It is embellished with contrasting black spots. When anything comes along to investigate and touches the bait flesh, it is drawn slowly inside the shell. When the creature feels the prey is involved, it snaps its two shells shut so quickly that it traps a meal. It then waits patiently until the struggling prey is quiet. Meanwhile, other fishes in the neighborhood arrive and attack any exposed part of the victim. All that is left for the host is what it successfully trapped inside the shell. Its muscles inside the flesh contract in such a way so that they work anything available into the middle of the mollusk, where it is digested.

Since I was now the hunter and the *pahoehoe* was now my prey, I had to work hard to pry it loose from its lair in the crevices of the coral. But once it was mine, it was no trick to jam the knife in the opening in the back of the shell and pry the two halves apart and cut the flesh loose. It can be served raw after being marinated in lime juice and coconut cream. It is mouthwatering. The *pahoehoe* is related to the infamous giant clams that, in fiction anyway, can trap unwary humans who venture too close and too carelessly.

By the time I reached the shore after several hours in the water, I realized that I had not escaped without injury after all. It became painfully clear that I had fallen victim of the most common enemy of northern land people. I had become terribly sunburned, not on my shoulders, which were already browned, but on my bottom, which I had left bare while luxuriating in skinny dipping. I nicknamed myself Rosebutt.

It was a Saturday evening, and I had been invited to join the guys in a pub to help them drink beer. Well, it was hardly a "pub," just a dilapidated hut of palm thatches. Five of us were seated on a built-in bunk in one corner. It was a crude affair made of saplings with an old mat thrown over it. Two more celebrants were seated on a rickety chair in another corner, while another sat on a broken rocker. Among us we had several bottles of beer and three glasses, all different. Seated on the sandy floor, around the walls, were a dozen or more women and children, including one attractive girl braiding and unbraiding her hair continually. Crowded at the low doorway and the single window were even more friendly smiling faces, all having come to meet the *Mariti*. Long remembered phrases like, "Any gum chum?" brought peels of excited laughter. I was asked repeatedly if I had "cigaretti" or "canny pars."

In the group was one man who had suffered terribly from the tropical scourge of elephantiasis, or filariasis. I had heard ugly tales of this mosquito-spread disease, which at one time had been prevalent in French Oceania. This fellow, short and 40, had been attacked so repeatedly that he had an advanced case. His body was badly swollen. He was wearing a *pareu* because he could never get into a pair of pants. His legs were shaped like nail kegs, and in his lap he carried a pair of grapefruit. As the disease advanced over the years, he must have endured terrible sieges of wracking fever, but tonight he was playing the role of village jester with clumsy and heartbreaking enthusiasm. Not being able to participate in the production of food or cash crops for the communal good, he had become a figure of ridicule for the entertainment of others. To me, the entertainment proved to be a failure. This disappointed him and the others. Unfortunately, I could not laugh at his antics as I was so overcome with pity.

A great deal of the medical research for treatment of elephantiasis had been carried on by the University of California, Institute of Tropical Diseases, I was told. The local French administration had cooperated with the program, which began during the American occupation of Bora Bora. It was this, and the memories of the Seabees, which prompted many of them to ask me, "When *Mariti*, he come back?"

When I asked why they thought they wanted the Americans to return, they smiled and longingly said, "Ah way! When *Mariti* here, plenny money, plenny choon gum, plenny big road round Bora Bora, plenny good time."

Then I suggested that perhaps it was only because of the times, and that if the Americans were to return as administrators, then the islanders would have to work to earn their "plenny good time." They answered that they wanted to stop working for the profiteering Chinaman and basically have a life of "plenny good time," which means, "plenny fish, plenny pig, plenny poi, and plenny breadfruit. Plenny beer would be nice too."

The music for the party was made by Tomi, a strapping Mr. Polynesia, who played a guitar with great skill. His singing suffered from the fact that at 20 years old he was nearly toothless. This was the most obvious and appalling apparent development to come out of the gradually increasing Europeanization of the islanders. Working for the low wages offered by the profiteering foreigners, both native-born Chinese, and immigrant Europeans left them little time to pursue the traditional skills of growing and catching the food to which their bodies had become accustomed over the centuries. They desired to become modern, so they succommed to commercially produced white flour, biscuits, jam, and sugar for their now-standard "Continental breakfast." From there it was just a short but expensive step to acquire tastes for more imported goods. Almost all looked down on their traditional diet that offered them all the nutritional elements that they needed. A pretty *vahine* with her natural teeth was an unforgettable sight. But alas, she was quite rare.

The following morning I attended a funeral service of a little boy. The church was full with everyone wearing their best, which was white. They sang with great fervor, trying to lift the departing soul to Heaven on the very waves of sound. We then went to the family home, where a grave had been dug beside another, a dozen feet from the porch steps. The little coffin was lowered into the ground, and as the local minister was speaking each person present filed past the grave and tossed in a handful of dirt. The mother tried to control her feelings until her turn to toss in the earth. Overcome with grief, she threw herself screaming into the little pit, and it was with some difficulty that the others were able to pull her out. The group then crossed the road and had a feast for all the family and friends who had gathered together. Some time later, the family would place a ring of coral lumps or sea shells around the grave. Heads of the family rated a cement block that, as time passed, became a convenient place to scrub the newest baby, deposit fishing equipment, or dry coffee beans. In any event, the family was kept together.

That afternoon, I decided I wanted a change of scenery. Instead of continuing to walk around the shore road made by the Seabees when they were there a decade earlier, I turned towards the central mountain to take a trail over the pass between two of the peaks. The trail offered several places where I had wonderful views of the surrounding lagoon and even some of the other islands. I could easily see Raiatea and Taha'a and possibly the ethereal form of Huahine on the far horizon.

All of a sudden, I was attacked by a big black wasp-like thing that landed on my arm and gave me a terrible sting. Frantically I searched for something to ease the pain before the possible swelling developed. All I could see was a bunch of green *fei*. I was desperate enough to try anything. I broke one off, cut it in half, and rubbed the cooling banana on the reddening welt on my arm. It was a miracle. By the time I had walked down the other side of the pass, the swelling had gone down, and all the pain had vanished. It must be by sheer luck like this that many natural medications and treatments have been discovered.

Chapter VI
TAHA'A

After a week on Bora Bora, I returned on the *Benicia* to Uturoa. I wanted to go to the island of Taha'a (tah HAH ah) easily seen to the north, and I had to change here. I hung around the dock until the blast on the conch shell announced the afternoon departures. There was nothing different about the inter-island chugger in which I was sitting from all the others at the dock, except that it was going to the town of Patio, on the northern end of Taha'a. We were ready to go, and we were overloaded as usual, with the usual animals and produce, all up on the roof. There were maybe two dozen people aboard, sitting and standing wherever there was space.

The men, still celebrating the pleasures of a nice day in town, had gone to sleep everywhere. They had left their island at third cockcrow, around daybreak, and now it was afternoon and hot. It had been a long day for people who don't particularly like long days. My neighbors were friendly, but they could not understand why I was going to their island. Why did I, in truth, want to go to Taha'a? Nobody else does. I had no answer, except that it was there and plainly in sight of Raiatea, and that was enough reason.

There were three overburdened inter-island chuggers squatting low in the water. They were all going across the lagoon and the ocean to the neighboring island. Fortunately, both islands are enclosed in an enormous reef so that the miles of ocean between Raiatea and Taha'a are fairly calm. With luck, they might make it. We left the dock, one after the other, and followed like a line of ducks, until we cleared the tight little pass out of the reef guarding Uturoa. Out here in the middle of really nowhere stood a cement post with a small metal cage on top with a bit of old newspaper in it. If, at night, a skipper wanted to bring his boat into the harbor, all he had to do was light the paper and the town pilot would come out to guide him into the town dock; that was if anyone happened to be watching. The water below was so clear that it looked like we were suspended in the air. I could see with devastating clarity the treacherous coral heads that made navigating in the area so hazardous. Poor piloting could be disastrous.

The distance between the two islands was perhaps four or five miles. Once out in the open water between the islands, we were fortunate to have gentle surf running with a light breeze. Our little waif of a craft chugged along following the other two through the glorious afternoon. Basking in the delight of being in the midst of another unfolding adventure, I took out my sewing kit to make some repairs. The *vahines*, aged women, nursing mothers, and sweet tender young things, all offered encouragement, or help to do the task, being sure that no man had the ability to sew. I had already threaded the needle, and that, I thought, was the hardest part.

The boat ahead of us was suddenly going nowhere. It was no longer making its coughing sound. It no longer spewed puffs of black smoke into the trade winds. It had completely died. The lead boat waddled on towards Taha'a. Our captain approached the wallowing craft in what I thought was going to be a friendly gesture of assistance. My guess was that we would toss them a line and tow them back to Uturoa. However, nothing of the kind was to take place. We pulled alongside and more than half of the passengers with their possessions, jumped onto our already over-taxed puffer. Our captain was going to try to make the trip across a few miles of open sea with a double load. It took little imagination on my part to visualize our tub simply giving a sigh and rolling over. I grabbed my pack and leapt over the already widening space between the two launches. Far better to founder on one that could at least still float than take such an obvious risk. If the Tahitians have a word for "chicken" in their language, I'm sure that they shouted it at me as they pulled away, very low in the water, leaving us to our fate.

I soon discovered that the only activity among our crew was a scary bailing operation undertaken by two men below using soup cans with which they filled a bucket. This they handed to a small boy up on deck to throw overboard. The Chinese skipper said something to the effect that it was the mate's fault, and he would have to fix it. Then the captain joined the passengers in a sound sleep. Typical of Polynesia, if there was trouble, they went to sleep. When they woke up, they hoped it would be all straightened out. If it was not, they went back to sleep.

The bailing activity increased in tempo, but aside from that, little else appeared to be happening. There were the usual tapping noises that a man makes while fooling with a motor, but nothing more concrete. Meanwhile, the bailers had discarded the soup cans in favor of simply scooping the bilge out with the bucket. I was concerned with the increasing amount of water coming into the hull. Something had to be done. At the top of my pack was my diving face mask, which I thought the mate might possibly use to discover something on the outside of the hull that concerned our condition. I called the mate and showed him the mask and explained how to use it. Over the side he went, and we did not see him for an agonizingly long time. At the start of this new project, the bailers had lost all interest in their jobs in order to watch any new development. I began to feel that I should not have interfered.

When the mate finally did break the surface for a breath, he screamed something excitedly and plunged below again. Then I felt reassured. He'd found what was wrong and would soon be set to right, or so I thought. The second time he surfaced he climbed aboard and gave the glass to one of the other men in the boat. He also jumped overboard, and stayed down a long time, and came up with a burst of words and wild hand motions. By now, nearly everyone on the boat was leaning over the rail, the same rail! We were sinking and listing very much to starboard. I was shocked to see yet another guy go down with the mask on, and then another. They all were taking turns, but nothing was being done. I protested, to the mate who was reveling in the excitement. He spoke plenny good *Mariti,* and told me, "Plenny good dat glass for see fish. Plenny good. All men must make look see."

In all the excitement, our welfare had been forgotten. The pleasure of the new toy had been too much of an attraction. When all of them were satisfied, the bailers returned to the job, which now looked hopeless. They had to make up for lost ground. The mate dove below again, attended to something, and returned to the deck, saying all was well. There was more tinkering with the motor A few chocking coughs, and smelly black smoke from the engine proved it still had life. On our way again, the boy ran to the stern and pulled up the sea anchor, an aged tire on a four foot line.

Once inside the reef at Taha'a, we chugged along the beautiful coast, passing the mouth of Hamene Bay (HAH may nay) poking deep into the center of the island. To port, the late afternoon shadows accented the clefts and ridges of the central mountain mass. To starboard, maybe a half mile away, we saw huge jets of white water shooting many feet into the air, as great waves became shattered on the reef and turned into harmless spray. The roar of the water on the rock sounded like a freight train passing by.

Patio, a small village on the north coast of Taha'a, was to be my home for the night. I had met the mayor of the town on the boat, and he had invited me to stay with his family. Of course I gratefully accepted. As soon as we got on the dock, we had to take off our shoes. The town was on a water-logged mud flat, and there were only pairs of logs of coconut trees bridging the many drainage canals. They would have been difficult to cross with muddy shoes and not much easier with my still untrained bare feet.

We eventually came to his home, a typical wooden box of a structure with a red corrugated metal roof. It was newly painted a bright red, possibly his reward for becoming a government official. At his front steps was an oil drum of water with which to wash our feet before we went into the house.

Once inside, he made himself comfortable, bidding me to do the same. Off came his town coat, his tie, his shirt, and his town pants, each of which he hung on a separate nail in the wall. It was my first official reception with a mayor, and the dress code was undershorts.

The crowd that gathered that night was interested in the picture postcards that I carried. They accepted the pictures of our natural wonders of the western National Parks without question, but when it came to the pictures of New York City, they balked. To them, the buildings were individual houses. "Why so many little windows when a few big ones would be better?" "Why were the buildings built upright? Couldn't you sleep better in them if they were lying down?"

I had to take a second look at the pictures before I understood what they were asking. It was not long before I realized it would be far easier for me to say I was from Honolulu. Such words as Honolulu and Waikiki are already in their vocabulary. To them, Hawaii was something of a heaven, a place they all want to go sometime. It was thusly that I made myself an honorary Hawaiian.

The next day I followed the footpath southwards along the windward (east) shore, through a village like all the rest except it had a new social center in the middle of the town. It was the *robinet* (roe bee NAY), the French word for faucet. Piped water was not all that new. The ancient Polynesians had pipes made of lengths of bamboo. The robinet with the system of metal piping controlled the flow of cleaner water from further up the hill. This had saved the women many miles of walking everyday to keep the domestic needs fulfilled. Women did their washing at the robinet. Young girls went to get water, tarried there with the hope of meeting boys there who come for a drink. Young children played in the splashing water. Most children got at least one good scrubbing a day at the robinet, and then they were given an affectionate slap on the back and sent to play in as much mud as they wanted. They would be washed again before the day was over. It was a happy spot.

Towards evening I was invited to visit in a *fare* (FAH ray). A *fare* was a native-style hut. It was generally a square box raised on stilts about four feet above the ground. The few domesticated animals make their own headquarters under the house. Its walls are made of strips of split bamboo woven together. The walls in this house were high enough to keep children from falling out, while the upper part remained mostly open. It had a hip-style thatched roof. This was my favorite *fare* of all in which I had stayed so far. A wall on one end of the building was missing. An extension served as a covered porch area where visitors sprawled on mats and pillows. It was big enough so that a dozen people could eat and enjoy a pleasant evening watching the rest of the activity in town. Behind the porch area there was a single room about twice as big. The walls went up about two-thirds of the way to the eaves. The remainder was open for the night's cooling breezes It was well protected against the rain by the wide overhang of the roof.

This *fare* had a system of bamboo pipes that brought running water in a constant stream to the front porch. Merely switching the last section of pipe from one direction to another, the flow could be directed to the wash house for private bathing, to the laundry stone, or to the big oil drum to hold water for domestic needs. The rear of the single room was piled high with thick mattresses, plain sacks filled with lumpy kapok.

There was something genuinely satisfying about the feeling of the *fare*. It belonged to the land. Across the footpath, over the tidal water, was the outhouse. Perched on stilts like cranes, a line of these structures stretched along the beach for the length of the village. They too were of split bamboo, offering privacy on every side but the front. They had no doors. Doors were harder to make and install. If a door was closed, the occupant would miss seeing anything interesting that might happen in the vicinity.

The next day had been great just to walk around the delightful shoreline of Taha'a, and I had not paid attention to the time. Suddenly it was late afternoon. I had always been fortunate to arrive at a village early enough to get myself settled for the night before it got dark. For whatever reason, there had been no signs of settlement for several miles. I turned the corner of the trail I was following along the shore and saw the wide opening of the very large Hamene Bay that went deep into the center of the island. There was not a village in sight on either shore.

I met an elderly man, bent over with age and labor. He seemed intensely sincere when he invited me to stay with him and his family for the night. "You do not know when you will get to town," he insisted, "It is very far away." He appeared to be correct.

We walked a short distance, and on a rocky point of land I saw a nasty pair of small thatch shacks. The word *motu* means a small island. A *tiare* is a delightfully fragrant, small, star-shaped, white flower. Motu Tiare was neither. It was a small rocky bit of land, useless to anyone else but the three people who lived there. It was to be the site of the single most unpleasant night I'd had on the whole trip. Both shacks were storage sheds for bags of copra. One was full, and the other was also quite full of bags, but the front part was still open, much like the home I had so enjoyed the night before. It had been a long time since any repairs had been made on these hovels. But it was a place to stop for the night.

As we talked, his old wife, the only dirty islander I had seen, peeled coffee beans and dropped them one at a time into a well-worn, wretchedly filthy sneaker. My stomach heaved when I saw the diseased leg from which the shoe had been taken. I knew then that we were in for a cup of brew in the morning. I hoped that the old woman's sight was good enough to tell which were the beans, and which were her scabs.

In exchange for his help, a young orphan lived here with the elderly couple. His only possession was a dirty shrunken red and white striped tee shirt. He made an effort to tidy up the place and re-arranged a few copra bags so that the four of us could sleep under the shelter. I had arrived in time to be offered a plate of cold rice and a cracked glass of water. The man had only a saucer to eat from. I added my usual contribution of a can of meat, but the woman put it aside for a time when they would be hungry, I guess. The woman and child ate from a shared piece of banana leaf. We ate with our fingers. They had no lantern, so when it got dark we were all settled down on top of the sharply lumpy copra bags. It was not comfortable, but I wanted to be a gracious guest, and I tried to make the most of it. Once they were horizontal, the three of them started to cough and continued through the night, all night, first one, and then another. It was wretched.

Before the first real light of day, the woman was up roasting the coffee beans in an old herring tin can by a most modest fire on the ground. The boy was washing the few dinner utensils from the small rickety bridge that led to the outhouse. Here, dishes were washed before they were needed, not after they had been used. When the boy was through with the dishes, he ground the beans in an old fashioned hand grinder. He then put the powder into a blackened piece of old *pareu* rag and poured hot water through it again and again until there was a steaming bowl of jet black liquid in it. The man had grated a couple of coconuts to make the cream, and we sat down for breakfast. I seldom looked a gift horse in the mouth, but I was glad when they had only three cups, and I had the excuse to use the one from my backpack. The coffee may not have been good, but it was hot, and it was strong. I hoped that it was hot enough and strong enough to kill anything that might contribute to a health problem. I departed soon after, saying something about getting to town to meet a friend, and headed off into the unknown.

I decided to go up and over a hill as a shortcut rather than around the long point of land ahead. The sun was so bright. The air was hot. The hill was steep. My pack seemed to be getting heavier in the heat, and my clothes became unbearably sticky. If only it were possible to find a nice refreshing stream at the crest of the hill. The cool morning breeze that swept across the ridge I was climbing was most welcome. If I had looked back, I could have seen the acres of tall reeds that blanketed the hillside. They were useless to the islanders, and it was most discouraging to try to break a trail through them. The sharp edged leaves scratched the bare flesh. Small chips got into my eyes. The fuzz from the dried blossoms got up my nose. But it was over, and down below at the end of the red clay path I saw Hamene Bay.

That was not all that could be seen. Storm clouds were racing over from the opposite shore of the bay and would hit momentarily. With no shelter in sight, there was nothing to do but to walk down the track. Within seconds I was in the midst of a deluge that was crashing down on all sides. The path instantly turned to syrup between my toes. The rain was cold when I had been so hot only a moment before. My glasses became useless from the drippings from my forehead. I couldn't see with them, and I was almost blind without them. I wondered about the damage being done inside the pack, especially to my sleeping bag. It would take a long time to dry out.

Thoroughly miserable and uncomfortable, I reached the shelter of the big trees just as the downpour stopped. The sun broke through the clouds. A second shower began as the drops fell from the leaves overhead. I seized a big leaf from some huge plant and, by holding it by the stalk, I managed to make a reasonable umbrella. Why I bothered, I can't remember.

I must certainly have been the most dejected-looking traveler ever to pass through the clearing on the shore. A voice called out from a flower-surrounded cottage asking me to come in. This was a real house with freshly painted planking and a shiny new metal roof. Screens covered the windows, and there was a cement patio at the front door. Surely it was a mirage. The voice belonged to a young man, perhaps in his early 20s, who spoke rapid French as he urged me to come inside the house. He startled me by looking at the wet pack and saying that everything inside must be soaked and to take everything out and hang it up to dry. How different his reaction was from others who merely had curiosity as to what it was.

The young man was named Tamu. He was obviously disappointed when I emptied my pack. He asked me why there were no knives or guns inside. I soon found out that he was pack-wise because of a treasure he had keenly guarded. He showed me an issue of *Life* magazine from the early 1940s that displayed the contents of an Army pack and the personal gear of an American soldier. Apparently in the years he had kept the magazine, he had studied the material and knew the contents by heart. I imagined that never in his wildest dreams had he ever expected to see one come down his back path.

Tamu wished me to remain with him for a long time so that he could teach me his ways. I had to tell him that as much as I would like to stay and learn from him, I was only to be on his island a very short time. However, I had much to teach him in return. I said that if I could learn some of his ways, then I could teach my people.

His face shined with delight. "But to learn our ways, you have to act like us. You are not dressed properly. Take that off and put this on," he chided, handing me a length of red and white *pareu* cloth. It is a simple matter to put on a *pareu* securely, just like a towel after a shower. For wear around the house, as a sleeping garment, or as a quick cover-up, they are unbeatable. At the end of this chapter there is a description of several ways to wear a *pareu*.

My first lesson in the Tahitian way of life was out of the way. The second and more important was to be spear fishing. We went out to the rear of his house. We each had a three-foot long metal reinforcing rod with one end sharpened to a point and the other end flattened with a notch cut into it. The rest of the equipment was a short length of bamboo, about a foot long, to be held in the left hand to use as a guiding hand grip. Each of us also had a two inch wide strip of rubber from an inner tube that was about a foot long. One end had been folded over and secured so as to make a small loop big enough to slip in a thumb. The other end had been similarly fashioned, except that there was a kind of small wire stirrup in it.

The metal rod passed through the section of bamboo. The right hand held the stirrup in the notch of the metal rod. The left hand held the bamboo, with the left thumb in the rubber loop. The right arm then pulled back, stretching the rubber band as much as possible. With proper aim and some good luck, this would drive the spear through any fish.

After repeated efforts, I still missed any target by a wide margin. We stuck at this task until I had made some slight progress, but no fish would have any real worries if we should ever meet eye to eye.

For those who didn't choose to get wet or have no goggles, there was another traditional way to spear fish. The water must be clear. It should be quiet. A dozen pieces of stiff wire, each about six inches long, were secured to the end of a light bamboo pole about four feet long. The fisherman stood quietly on a rock and waited. Patience would reward the fisherman with the sight of a fish within range. He must judge sudden movement and light refractions. If the fisherman could hit the passing fish he was lucky. Boys were sent out when they were very young and told not to come home until they had something.

Sunday after church Tamu, his brother Eta, and I set out to go on a "piquenique." From their porch we could see a *motu* out on the reef with enough green to make it look like any desert island in a movie. They said that it was a popular place for Sunday picnics and family outings and that the fishing would be very good. The mother of the two brothers packed a nice lunch of baked fish, breadfruit, poi, and fresh fruit wrapped in fresh green leaves, which was put in the bottom of the *va'a*, outrigger canoe. We lifted the small craft up from the rack that kept it high and dry between tides set it in the water. There were three spars: two masts and one boom, all three stepped in one spot in the *va'a*. Each spar supported a different corner of the sail.

Once we were out in the water and under sail, we had a fine trip. The breeze was strong enough that the outrigger fairly scooted along the surface towards the *motu*. We heeled over so far that Eta had to go out and lay on a bar that was strapped across the beam and extended several feet on each side. His weight helped balance the craft. The steering was done with a wide-blade paddle, used on either side of the craft, and at either end.

The *motu*, the high spot on the reef where we were going, was covered with palms and other plants that like their roots near salty water. The sand was the brilliant white of powdered coral. No one could live there, as there was no fresh water. But many fishermen come here for a day or so, and we found many of their little thatched shelters. No one else was to be seen on the *motu* this beautiful Sunday afternoon. On the outer side of the *motu,* we checked out an old fish trap made of a small rectangular stone wall of three sides. The fourth side had a narrow opening with two wings of low stone walls that gradually widened to about 30 feet apart. It was much like a cattle or sheep corral. The procedure was to go around the outer side and locate a browsing school of small fish and herd them into the open jaws of the trap. Then they could be caught individually for bait to catch bigger fish.

Eta was the first to spot a blackish cloud in the choppy water. It was a school of fish, no doubt about it. Here was a chance to use the trap. "Quick! Get a stick," Eta yelled, and I rushed onto the beach to find one.

Back in the water Tamu pointed for me to go over to the other side. When we had gotten into position, we began to close in, beating the water, shouting, and splashing as we ran in the knee deep water of the lagoon. Like sheep, most of the fish struck together, and it was easy to herd them in towards the wide mouth of the trap. The nearer we got, the more often I saw some peel off from the school and dart off on their own. As fast as we could, we ran to drive them into the mouth of the narrowing walls of the corridor. Faster and faster we ran as we had to close the trap quickly with some of the loose stones piled at the entrance. Luck smiled down on us. We had trapped a small portion of the school, but more than enough for bait. The hunt was over, but the screaming was not.

In his haste, barefooted Eta had cut his foot on something. The pain was agonizing, but there were only two drops of blood on his big toe. With a heart-rending wail, he shouted that he had stepped on an odious stone fish and had been pierced by two of its poisonous spines. He limped to the beach.

Tamu ran back into the water with his stick and looked for the terrible creature in the trap. There it was, less than a foot long, the ugliest, and deadliest of the fishes. It was perfectly camouflaged with blotches of the rusty pink and gray colors of the dead chunks of coral lying about. Tamu stabbed it and stabbed it again and again. It was dead, but Tamu could not control his anger. He stuck his stick into the shredded body and walked up on the beach to the fire and burned it. But this was too late to be of any help to his older brother.

Eta's foot and ankle began to swell, and the pain was excruciating. Eta lay down, not knowing what else to do. Quite some time passed while he rested. He must have been braver than many, as he said nothing more. He just lay there dumbly.

We had no use for the fire now, so we put it out. Tamu and I went to the trap. We had trapped a couple of dozen oval shaped flat fish about six inches long, maybe one percent of the original school. We caught them and put them in a basket, packed up, and sailed for home. Once back in the village, they would have to take Eta to the town where he could get medical attention. I had my own medical problem, as a boil had developed on my shin, the result of a coral scratch, and I wanted to get to the hospital in Papeete.

The next morning it was with real sorrow that I saw the little *motu* getting smaller as the chugger taking me back to Raiatea passed the scene of the fishing expedition of the day before. My return to Uturoa meant that my stay in the "Isles Sous le Vent" was over. Though it had been quite short, I'd had a most fascinating time.

In Uturoa, I awaited the *Benicia* to take me back to Papeete. It was nearly Christmas, and I wanted to be with friends. But even this great holiday would be an anti climax to the happiness I felt, and wonderful things I had found in "The Society Islands."

***

Instructions to Men for Wearing the Tahitian *Pareu,* or *Pareau (fr.)*

The material preferred for these examples of men's *pareu* is soft, well-washed, cotton with boldly printed patterns, generally florals, in two colors, red and white, blue and white, or any such. The measurements given are general for men of average height with waists of around 32-34 inches. Make your own allowances for your own body type.

Style A. Take a piece of material a meter wide (a yard and three inches) and a length of two meters or more, up to about seven feet long. This is easier to do than to explain. Follow the same action as in putting on a large towel after a shower. Place the center of the cloth waist-high in the middle of the back, with each hand holding a top edge in front, as in drying the back. Bring the right hand across the stomach and pull the material ("R") snugly just above and past the navel to about the lowest rib on the left side. Hold it there. Bring the left hand part ("L") across the front, overlapping the "R" part so that a small section of several inches of "R" (the part you held) remains above the waistband of "L." Pull "L" snugly across to the navel and tuck a few inches of the top edge into the waistband of "R" at the navel. Let the remaining material hang in front in a bunch. Adjust to feel snug. This is the most common way to wear a *pareu* around town, in the home, or to bed. In public, it is commonly worn over boxer shorts.

Style B. Proceed exactly as above. Reach under the bunch hanging loosely in front and grab the lower corner of "R." Give it a little twist to make a kind of loose rope, and pull it between the legs, out and over the material in back. Tuck the end of the rope "R" into the waistband at the center of the back. Adjust. This forms a long piece that hangs down over the left leg, and a sort of "short," over the right hip and upper leg, with a visible twist of material between the buttocks. Adjust. This offers comfort and security. This is how many Tahitian fishermen wear their *pareu.*

Style C. For the next time you have to climb a coconut tree, here is a simple and quick way to make a bikini. Bunch, or twist slightly, the whole piece of the material lengthwise into a loose rope. Reserve and hold a flap in front of about nine to twelve inches at the navel. Pass the rest between the legs; bring it through, up, and over the right buttock. Pull the rope snugly around to the right and to the front. Pass it under the loose material of the flap, and continue around the left side and to the back. Push it under the material already there, give it a pull towards the left hip, and tuck it in the left part of the waist band. Adjust the loose rope and flap in the front as needed. This could have been the original pattern for a "thong."

Style D. The sport style is the neatest Tahitian style. You may prefer a shorter length of material, about six feet or so. Take only one short edge, the width. Holding one corner in each hand, center the material in the middle of the back, and bring the two top corners to the front and tie them in a square knot. If the waist measure is nearly as much as the width of the cloth, forget this one, or get wider cloth. With the knot tied in front, the rest is hanging down in back like a bridal train. Gather the train and pull it between the legs to the front. Tuck all of the material behind the knot and bring it all through. Now the "train," or "apron," is hanging in front. The apron should be about 30-36 inches long. Straighten out the bunched material in front and spread it around the waist line a bit, so that it is neat, and snug. Bring the bottom two corners of the apron up to the waist. Get each corner around to the back and tie another square knot in back. The result should be a kind of two-layer kilt or mini-skirt about 15-18 inches long. It is secure, neat, and very comfortable. This is the regulation way to wear the *pareu* for competitions during the July Fête for spear throwing, dancing, and the *va'a* races when the regulations call for "corps nus" (bare body). It is also comfortable and convenient for just strolling around or relaxing.

There are many other ways to wear a *pareu.* Try experimenting on your own.

There are various styles for *vahine* also, but I can offer no instructions. Sorry.

Chapter VII

PAPEETE,

AND CHRISTMAS IN PUNAAUIA, TAHITI

Returning to Papeete after an overnight trip from Raiatea, I was very happy to see a real town again. As I leaned on the railing of the *Benicia* for the last time, I felt an excitement I did not have the first time when I entered the harbor on the schooner *Te Vega* from Honolulu. I knew more what to expect this time. I had a few friends here among the sailors who had navigated their boats from different ports around the globe. I was anxious to meet and greet them again. The waterfront was the perfect setting for any tropical tale to begin …or to end. To the east, the commercial area of the docks was busy with the inter-island traders, and occasionally a great steamer carrying freight, or immigrants from Europe to New Zealand or Australia docked there. To the west was the quay where the private sailing yachts were moored. These sleek beauties represented the fortunes made by their owners. People of every section of society passed through here, all with the same dream of a tropical adventure. For some it may have come true. For others it may have been a disaster ready to happen.

Papeete was a town of some 12,000 souls in 1955. There were tawny skinned Polynesians. There were also the descendents of the Indo-Chinese brought in from Southeast Asia to do agricultural work. Many now owned most of the small businesses. There were also French colonists. Some were government employees or entrepreneurs. Others were enjoying the good life. There were also a few international wanderers who had been to the four corners of the earth and sailors who had navigated the Seven Seas. They were here to satisfy some primal urge for escapism. But, could they have escaped in a place that did not welcome the escapee? The authorities wished no one would come who had a dream to stay. Visiting yachtsmen were greeted cordially because they had their own transportation onwards. Anyone else who did not have this proof of departure was required to leave a deposit of a considerable sum of French francs or U.S. dollars in the Banque de France to guarantee their prompt departure within the time limit allowed, or sooner, if their funds ran too low.

I limped along the quay. My shin was very painful with an obvious infection. There was only one way to get to the hospital, walk. I passed the row of small private businesses that line most of the waterfront, the face that Papeete turned to the world. I glanced at a souvenir shop, a travel agency, and the Air France office that, although open for business, offered no flight schedule. Next was the office of TEAL, the New Zealand airline that boasted the only air connection with the rest of the world, and this was via Fiji, over a thousand miles to the west. I nodded at occasional acquaintances, the same faces that seemed to haunt the waterfront week after week while they sat in open air cafes or bars.

Next I passed the green and white four-story skyscraper, the tallest building for thousands of miles around. Each floor was surrounded by an open veranda with nice views. I guessed that it was after this structure was erected that the ordinance went through limiting the height of any further buildings to be no more than "two thirds of a coconut tree." It was regarded as a "professional building." The top floor was hostess to seaman in search of female companionship. Le Circle Français met on the ground floor. It was a sort of open-membership club, where visiting yachtsmen found some hospitality and friendship. Actually it was nothing more than a big room with a bar and a shady sidewalk terrace. But there the local elite met and contemplated the beauties of the lagoon and the sidewalk, while sipping refreshing beverages and trading spicy town gossip, or nautical tales, mostly of misadventures.

Next was the house where Nordoff and Hall collaborated in the writing of the Bounty Trilogy: *Mutiny on the Bounty*, *Men Against the Sea*, and *Pitcairn's Island*. These three books offer a wonderful read to any would-be adventurer.

There was a very picturesque building a few paces further on, the "Postes et Télégraphes." This apple-green, three-storied structure with the phony round dormer windows on the red Mansard roof looked like it had been designed to face the square of some small provincial town in France. I often thought that the plans must have been switched by accident, and I wondered what had been built in that little town in the motherland instead, which would have been designed more appropriately for the tropics. Properly enough there were three flights of steps leading up to three doors, but only the center one opened. A pair of handsome metal lamps stood guard at the center steps. Under the red, white, and blue tricolor flag, was the red and white sign proclaiming the business that was conducted inside. A little blue and white enameled sign had been placed stating the days and hours of business. Not much business was done here except on every alternating second or third weekend when a TEAL plane landed to bring in and take out the international mail. It was, I think, the most interesting building on the island.

Across the street, the yachts were tied up to a row of huge weighty anchors that had been the salvage from several big sailing vessels that had met their fate on the nearby reefs. The row continued with several antique cannons, their formerly threatening muzzles stuck indignantly into the soil. To these rusting relics of days gone by, several visiting yachts had been secured, stern first. They boasted flags from Australia, New Zealand, America, Britain, and a few European nations. I had to take a second look when I spotted a Swiss ensign one day. Switzerland? These shimmering examples of the luxurious life of the real world rocked gently in the quiet swells of the harbor.

Intruding in this display of courageous adventurism was a dirty gray, boxy, fishing boat with a flag swaying in the slight breeze proclaiming that it had made the trip from Chile. The *Tres Damas* had brought five would-be settlers from Chile with whom I had become friends before going out to the Society Isles. Valparaiso, Chile is half again as far away from Tahiti as is Brisbane, Australia, and across the very lonely open ocean.

Two more recent arrivals were also moored to the old cannons. One, the *Yasmine*, was a sloppy 40-foot sloop, its begrimed Union Jack dangling spiritlessly from its pole. The other, named *Happy Return* was a neat sloop sporting the ensign of New Zealand. I took note that I would have to investigate the owners of these boats later.

Continuing in the direction of the hospital, I passed the public wash house. It was an open building, little more than a rectangle of cement posts with a large red roof. Inside were a few large, cement tanks where clothes could be washed. The tanks were waist high, and they were generally well-used by locals and foreign visitors alike. It was a tropical laundromat. All of the running water is from a stream so it is cool and plentiful. On two sides were showers and restrooms for men and women. Any passerby was welcome to use the facility. On my visits to town, I often took a cooling shower before the evening activity. I still wonder if the little fish-like lizzardy things are slithering up and down the wet walls in the men's room today.

As an aside, giving or receiving directions in these islands was not generally done with words like east and west, or north and south, or left and right. Rather, they reflected more obvious physical conditions, such as: "into the wind," "with the wind," "towards the mountain," "inland," or "towards the sea." In every case of which I was aware, the mountain, if there was one, was in the center of the island, or certainly obvious. For example, "Go with the wind until you cross the second stream, then turn towards the mountain."

To get to the hospital, I turned inland at the next corner on one of the many tree-lined streets. On this, the widest and straightest avenue in town, I had to pass the Police Station, which also had the same look as those in the provincial towns in France. On each side of the main metal gate was a small yellow cement "guard house" building with the cornerstones painted red for trim. They were roofed with Mediterranean arched tiles. There were two shuttered windows in each side facing the street. Overhead the tricolor flapped in the constant trade wind.

Next I passed the government administration building with its cobbled courtyard. It was from here that the foreign control flowed that ruled the lives of the 150,000 people living on the collective land mass of French Polynesia. Squished together, the many islands would be "equal in size to half the area of Rhode Island spread over a part of the ocean four times the size of Texas" (source unknown).

Finally I arrived at the hospital. The building was bigger than most of the other edifices in town and had a cobbled courtyard. Once inside I asked a nun for directions. After sitting on a gray wooden bench in an unclean office for a while, I was ushered into a dark room by a Polynesian girl dressed in white. I showed her the boil that was bothering my shin. She poked inquisitively at it with her finger. We decided that it was due to a bit of coral poisoning that I had picked up when I was scratched on the reef. It was red and yellow and very angry looking. Suddenly she stabbed the bubble with a bare fingernail and pulled the covering off of the boil to drain it. She cleaned out the spot with a purple fluid, "gentian violet," akin to iodine, the islands' cure-all. After wrapping my calf with a big gauze pad and yards of bandaging, she said I could go home.

I had to retrace my steps to the waterfront, walking quite stiff-legged with my new cotton cast. I stopped to chat with the two recent arrivals moored to the cannons. The first one was Tom Akland, a New Zealander who had been a prisoner of war in Germany and had been very badly treated. During the decade after the war he lived in England but wanted to return home. Finally he began to realize his dream. He bought a boat some 40 feet overall and was sailing her home. He called her *Happy Return*. Tom and his crew of three had sailed across the Atlantic, through the Panama Canal, and on across the Pacific. After all these years he could see that with a little bit of luck, his homeland might be reachable within another month's travel. He was looking for a new crew, as those with whom he had come preferred to remain in the island for a while longer. I was indeed interested in going to New Zealand, but I wanted even more to stop in Samoa and Fiji on the way, stops that Tom was not willing to make. That was why I declined his repeated offers to join his crew.

Sometime later in the week he got his crew together to depart with the blessings of the townsfolk with whom he had become acquainted. He hoisted his sails, and with a blast of his horn, bid farewell to the town he had been so anxious to quit. As the *Happy Return* caught the trades and began to sail, and the sun was setting in the western sky, the folks on the quay turned and wandered off. Another day was ending.

Most of the people who had gathered to wave good-bye had gone home by the time it was dark. Sailors come and sailors go. Most of them just use the harbor as a rest stop along their course to encircle the globe. Each one leaves behind a story that the residents repeatedly tell each other. They are similar tales with different details. Along with fresh supplies, each one takes away a little memory.

In the bright light of early morning, the town awoke to see something it had not expected. It had not seen the last of Tom. Stranded helplessly on the teeth of the reef at the passage to the sea, like a skewered sea gull, hung the ghost of the man's dream. The *Happy Return* had not made good its escape from the harbor and would never sail again. The news got around the island by "Radio Coco" (gossip) before Tom had been brought back to shore. In fact, some said that the salvagers had boarded the wounded hulk before it had even been abandoned. This prize played the central role between the eager salvagers who wanted to gain profits at a low cost and the man who had only lived for the day he could sail into his home port. Time was running out, and it was costing the castaway more than money. Completely discouraged, and on the verge of despair, he sold his hulk at their price and bought a ticket on the next plane. His was to be far from a *Happy Return*.

I next visited with the Englishman, Danny Weil, owner of the smaller and untidy boat. He told me that he had purchased a coastal life saving boat from the British equivalent of our American Coast Guard and converted it into a sloop. One of his purposes was to be the first Englishman to make the round-the-world trip single handedly. The second purpose was to make ham radio broadcasts from many out-of-the-way islands that had never been heard from before. When he went on the air, transmitting his signals, hams around the world picked them up. Then they would send him a card that they had received his signal, and in return they wanted his card with a stamped confirmation of the broadcast. For this he required of each listener a dollar bill to help defray his own expenses. Danny had a world wide audience who followed his every move. He made his contact every night at six o'clock sharp.

Within a few weeks he began to receive the mail from his backers. Then, much more secure financially, and physically well rested, he started out again with the favorable wind. The worst was behind him, having conquered the Atlantic and the vast open wastes of the Pacific. From here on, islands would be popping up every few days. He would make calls from the Cooks, Tokelau, Samoa, Canton, the Fijis, the New Hebrides, and New Guinea. New Guinea was not to be the end of the line. He was within a short run for Port Moresby when a storm broke upon him and smashed his rigging. He drifted for hours in heavy seas sending out S.O.S. signals, which were picked up in Port Moresby. Eventually help came to save him. The *Yasmine* was towed to port. When the repairs were completed, he sailed bravely out of the harbor again. Again a storm. Again a wreck. Again a call for help. But this time, it was too much. His grubby little boat was destroyed. Danny jumped onto the reef to save his very life with only his shorts and hunting knife. Danny would not finish his single-handed trip around the world.

The post-Tahiti part of his voyage was published in monthly installments in a periodical named *P.I.M. Pacific Islands Monthly*. For residents of many of the areas bordering the Pacific Ocean, this was a most fascinating collection of "local news."

Located at the east end of Papeete, the market was a huge roofed shed with strange sights, sounds, and smells. It always held a fascination. It opened around four o'clock in the morning and was pretty well finished by eight. But Sunday mornings before church it was at its busiest best. Everything could be found, and the casual tourist could have fun wondering for what some of the things for sale might be used. Surrounding the market area was the business center of town with almost all of the two-story wooden shops owned and operated exclusively by the Chinese merchants. They never seemed to close. One or another would have anything anybody wanted, from pink plastic toothbrushes, to parts for outboard motors, from gooseberry jam to powdered dragon's teeth, stacks of blue work shorts and lacey French bras. All the storekeeper needed was time to find it. These shops were fascinating jumbles. Less pretentious entrepreneurs had little pushcarts out in the tangle of narrow streets blocking the Sunday traffic, vending sweet breads, cold drinks, fried squid, and ball point pens. Some served complete meals, generally on a banana leaf. They had prepared meals of Chinese, Tahitian, or "popa'a," food for foreigners.

Papeete after dark wasn't much. Three movie houses seemed to be just emerging from the silent movie era. Since most of the films were from America, and most of the residents preferred to speak Tahitian, Chinese, or French, the sound was often turned off. A few night spots, called "Boites du Nuit," (boxes of the night) existed in the town, but most activity was in the few small hotels on the out-of-town beaches.

Head and shoulders above the rest of the places in town for ambiance was Quinn's Tahitian Hut. It had the best band, "Eddie Lund and His Tahitians." It had the largest dance floor. It served the biggest crowd and the roughest characters. It had the best fights. It was often a riot set to music. It held the odors of sweat, smoke, and stale beer. It had what it took to make this place the best place to be. It had no neon lights, no blue mirrored walls, no chrome furniture, and no waitresses in uniform. The place was not brightly lit. It had only raw wood walls, tables, chairs, and tiny booths around the room, which tended to keep some kind of order. The music was loud, and the chatter was louder. When the music started, there was no order. No order except the rhythmic upheaval of partners thoroughly savoring every moment of the world's earthly pleasures together. Those on the dance floor got more out of each other than mere dancing.

"Showtime" was announced by a spotlight piercing the dimness and shining on a rear door. The band played a fanfare. The floor cleared. Suddenly out came Marie, the island favorite of the moment. She shook her way to the center of the room. She wore a magnificent Bora Bora dance skirt of shredded bark, trimmed with glistening shells. The rest of her was covered only with a couple of flower *heis* hanging around her neck. With a roll of the hollowed wooden drum, she started her performance of the *papeo*, the Tahitian Hula, something not to be missed. If any place could be considered "authentic ethnic," Quinn's had to be it. It was the most written about single spot in the entire South Pacific Island chains. One of my prize possessions is an Eddie Lund record that I have played when I wanted my dreams to soar back to the islands.

Outside the Hut there was always a gathering of town folk and visitors taking a breather. Amongst us strolled several of the aging barefoot "flower girls." These were ladies of past fame who had been entertainers at whatever occupation they could perform to earn a living. They were presently dealing in flower *heis*, also fern crowns with flowers, waiting for a big-time spender to show up.

One night when I was out on the street in front of Quinn's cooling off, I noted two women marching out of the Hut together. It seems that one of the women had been dancing with a visiting sailor, and the other had cut in. That started a ruckus inside, and the bouncer threw them both out of the hall. Once out on the street they had a face-off. One growled, "*Ça va?*" (sah VAH? OK?)?

The other snarled a negative response, "*Ça va pas!*" (sah vah PAH! No! It's not OK!).

With that the fists began to fly, and hair began to be pulled. The crowd of jubilant onlookers, mostly men, gathered around the fighting pair, egging them on while laughing their inebriated heads off until one girl wrestled the other to the ground. Once settled, the two *vahines* stood up, shook off the debris from the street, straightened their dresses, got each other in a double cheek kiss, and marched back into Quinn's as if nothing had happened. I assumed they re-entered the arena and began dancing while musically arousing some other lucky sailors on the dance floor. This must have been what Don meant that night during our watch on the *Te Vega*, when he answered my question, "Why is going to Tahiti such a big deal?" by saying, "If you don't know, then you'll have to find out for yourself."

At this time (1955), the only air service was TEAL, a seaplane service that connected Tahiti with Fiji, which was called the "Crossroads of the Pacific." The "flying boat" arrived twice every five weeks when it brought the mail and occasional adventurous tourists. On any scheduled Friday afternoon at about one o'clock, the leeward (western) sky would be watched by most of the residents along the shore. The pilot would fly over several miles of the coast to give notice that the plane had arrived and would soon land in the lagoon. By the time the plane was empty, the town was filling up. People were pouring in from the outer districts on foot, on bikes, on "mobelettes" (motorized bicycles), scooters, camionnettes, and bug-shaped French cars. Far more exciting than market day, mail day was celebrated by almost everyone on the island. Everyone showed up in their very best while trying to look casual. The shade of the huge mango tree at the corner of the Postes et Télégraphes was nowhere near big enough to shelter the crowd gathering there. Children who couldn't read were there just to see the crowd, and they brought their dogs. Old people who were not going to get anything came to see who the new couples were. The Consuls of Austria, Norway, Belgium, Chile, and the United Kingdom all showed up, the latter in a safari suit and a pith helmet.

By four o'clock the mail was sorted and being placed in the boxes. People would break away from their conversations to see if there was anything in their box. They would return, talk restively and soon check again. As I was present at several mail days, and I took pleasure in people-watching while I was waiting for Poste Restante to collect mail for me, I took note of many in the crowd.

One really lovely island *hine* named Doris showed up regularly. Doris was on the quay to greet the *Te Vega* upon our arrival. She was so attractive she had even appeared on a magazine cover and in a few tourist ads for Tahiti. The first time I noticed her at Postes she apparently had on a new dress. I watched as she approached clusters of people and sort of modeled for them. They all knew her and all seemed to admire her. The next time she had a new dog, a white fluffy creature that she carried in her arms. She went from group to group greeting friends and allowing admirers to pet the pooch. This particular Friday, the crowd was surprised to hear the sputtering of a new Vespa motor scooter. Here came Doris and her dog on a glistening new red Vespa. When she stopped and got off, the dog got off. When she got on to start the motor with some false tries, the dog got on. Around the block she would go, and then stop near another section of the crowd. She stopped and get off the scooter and so did the dog. This time of course, she was showing off her new machine. She was apparently having some economic success at her modeling career and making sure everyone knew about it. But I noted that she never went into the Postes et Télégraphes. Her connections were all in Papeete.

As the hours passed and the ripe mangoes fell from the branches overhead, the crowd came and went. When the children saw the fruit fall they scrambled to be the first to get there and grab it. There was lots of excited shouting and fun pushing each other. There was plenty of fruit on the island, so this seemed to be more of a game with them. At 7:30, a voice from behind the window shouted "Ç'ést tout" (say TOO, that's all), and the gathering dissolved into the darkness. Those who had received mail, however, burned lights late into the night. More than a hundred people were writing letters to get on the departing flight. It would not leave until Sunday afternoon. By then all the mail had to be written, sealed, stamped, and in the Postes.

Bureaucracy was at work here to the most astonishing degree. No matter how many letters one would have written, even if they were all exactly alike, as for example identical postal cards of the same scene, Postes insisted on weighing each and every one of them to make sure the postage was correct. Sometimes they even counted the number of words on the card to see if they could charge more postage. On Saturday the lines were long and desperately slow. With little accommodation to the people, Postes stayed open Saturday afternoon no later than one o'clock sharp. The clerk called out to those still on line already angry at the slow operation, "You can put it on the next plane!" and slammed the windows closed. The next scheduled plane did not leave for two, or even three weeks. Vive "Liberté, Fraternité, Egalité!"

Mme Jacquimen ran the Government Visitors Bureau, and there was nowhere a finer or more helpful agent. She had the finest collection of sea shells to be seen in any of the islands. Admission to see the shells was only granted upon presentation of a perfect shell from anyplace. These she either entered into her collection or traded with other conchologists all over the world.

Mme Jacquimen was most kind to me one afternoon. Leading me by the hand, we hurried to the small inter-island boat that was going to the neighboring island of Moorea where there was to be a big native luau. I went and had a terrific evening. The luau had been set out on a beach with an incredible view of the spectacular volcanic peaks unique to Moorea. The silhouette of Tahiti across the water on the horizon was the perfect backdrop.

Several woven mats were lined up on the beach. The guests sat on the sand along both sides of the mats. In front of each guest was a placemat of banana leaf to be used as a plate. Each had a sea shell of *poisson crue* as an appetizer and a drinking coconut. Down the center of the mats was a row of fresh banana leaves holding a continuous line of a wide selection of tasty, finger-lickin' delights. There were shreds of roast pork, sections of chicken, pieces of fish, and several kinds of vegetables, like breadfruit, yams, taros, and leaf-wrapped packets of steamed spinach leaves. It was Polynesian food at its best, all within easy reach of every guest. It was an all-you-can eat affair, and the food disappeared with gusto. The feast was followed by a music and dance demonstration illuminated by beach fires and torches. It was a spectacular evening.

I was lucky to find a beach shelter for the night. Then I spent the next wonderful day by hitching a ride around Moorea with the visiting Administration Doctor. He was checking out all of his patients, so we made frequent stops. Many of them suffered with elephantiasis. The doctor explained that once the mosquito-spread disease was noticed, it could be 98% stopped if the patient would continue with the treatment and sleep under a net. Unfortunately, many felt better, discontinued the treatment, got re-infected, and suffered further enlargement of various part of their bodies. This allowed the disease to continue.

Together we made a tour around the island, the most spectacularly beautiful place I had ever seen. It was my first taste of the real Polynesia. This island could have been my Paradise.

Every new traveler to Papeete stopped in the Visitors Bureau to find out what to see while they were there. They could rent a car and drive the 60-mile long road around the island and see everything in a day. Heading into the wind (eastwards), there was Matavai Bay where Captain Bligh moored the *Bounty* in 1789 before the infamous mutiny. Next there was Point Venus where Captain Cook landed from the *Endeavor* (1769) to make his observation of the Transit of Venus. Close by was the tomb of Tahiti's last King Pomerare, with a carved stone copy of a brandy bottle on top, memorializing his favorite pastime. Further on there are a couple of natural blowholes where the surf forces water up through holes in overhanging black lava rocks. At the southern end of the island the road crosses a small isthmus. To the south another smaller mountain grew up from the bottom of the sea, and it was close enough to join with the bigger mass to give Tahiti the appearance of a "figure 8" from the air.

The Chinese owner of the local ice cream truck made the trip around the island every day. One day he went one way, the next day he went the other. His young customers stood patiently by the edge of the road awaiting his regular arrivals. He had a most pleasant business.

Around the leeward side on the west coast was the site of the house where Paul Gauguin lived. (He was buried in Atuoana, on Hiva Oa, out in the Marquesas in1903.) The surroundings were lushly tropical. It was a part of the island that the visitor would like to absorb slowly because it was so different from home. This area had to be a sample of Paradise.

Further up the road was a restored marae, or temple compound, that made an interesting stop. Basically it was a rectangular few acres with a recently constructed too-neat stone wall enclosing it. At the upper narrow end there was another rectangular block of similar stones serving as a foundation for a smaller block on top. A few recently made wooden panels represented something unexplained.

Between a few scattered settlements, the well-maintained land of the several coconut plantations along the way offered miles of superb vistas of pristine beaches and the lagoon all along this leeward coast. But that was about it for the sights for the average tourist more interested in the sun and living a life of luxury for a few days.

The more observant travelers would see the fishing nets hanging like bridal veils in the trees to dry. Some would notice the homes of the well-to-do residents that have adapted many of the ideas of the original native *fares* with their thatch roofs and woven bamboo sides. A few visitors might have seen a fisherman out on the reef tossing a circular net, or someone in a *va'a*. They might even spot a taro patch and wonder what it was. A taro is a large plant with great arrowhead-shaped leaves and a rutabaga-sized bulb. The bulb is a basic starch food in the tropics, and it is the primary ingredient of poi, an island favorite.

All those passing around the island would be impressed that this paved road appeared to be guiding the visitor through a tropical botanical garden. Trees often arched over the road dripping with bright red blossoms in their season, while other colored vegetation offered vibrant contrasts on either side. There were frequent views of the beautiful profile of Moorea Island only a dozen miles away to the northwest. It was one of the most satisfying tours a visitor could make anyplace.

* * *

About mid-day on the 24th of December I was waiting for all of the others to get ahead of me boarding the camionnette (cah mee oh NET.) I wanted to take the local version of a bus, also known as *le truck,* to Punaauia (poo nah AH wee yah) part way down the west coast from Papeete. A camionnette was made from the chassis of a truck that had been converted into public transport. It had a sturdy shelter built over the load bed and had roll-down side curtains for the rain. In the rear were three long benches going lengthwise from front to back. One bench on each side was bolted down, but the one in the middle was loose. On market days, when there was more freight than passengers, the middle area was a tangle of legs, livestock, and baggage. But today was the beginning of a holiday, so more people wanted to ride. They filled the middle bench. Holiday makers going to the outer districts had been loading up the camionnettes all day for the happy, bouncy trips.

I was waiting to be the last onboard, but not because I wanted to be the first off, as I was going to the end of the line. Rather, I was giving serious thought to my injured shin in its bulky cotton cast. The other passengers imagining that my wound was worse than it was, urged me to take the last seat, as they squeezed in to secure their own. There may have been only a dozen and a half people sitting on the benches with their bundles on their laps, but I know that there was not room for one more of anything. The men had all climbed up on top to sit on the roof. It was a staggering load for the camionnette.

Across from me, a young *vahine* had a small pig in a palm basket and a child on her lap. The elderly lady next to her had a chicken in a basket. The hen kept pecking the defenseless backside of the piglet, who squealed almost continually. Next was a huge woman with three small children on her lap; one was nursing. A very large woman sat on the middle bench in front of me. She was dressed in black. Most of her upper body had settled into her lap. She apparently knew most of the other people on *le truck* and actively carried on three conversations at the same time without a break during most of the trip. It was interesting to see her facial expressions change from hearty humor to tragic, according to what she heard. The young woman next to me was in her party dress, and she had a bird in a cage on top of a huge bundle wrapped in bright red and white *pareu* cloth. Her dog had been stuffed under the bench but did not complain. From here on into the depth of the bus it was impossible to see more. The bigger bundles were put up on the roof with the young men, who were already making music to entertain the merry mob.

With happy squeals of "*Aue!*" (AH WAY), we bounced along, and the driver took curves quickly so that we were constantly falling merrily onto each other. When one of the passengers screamed "Içi" (eee SEE), the driver would stop on a "*sou*," and the whole tangled shrieking crowd would smash gaily forward. When he jerked forward, they all rolled to the rear regaling in laughter, except for me. I thought I would be regaled right off the end of the seat. The back end was open, with no form of safety barrier in place. The driver had started his celebrating earlier in the afternoon, and this was his last trip to Punaauia. He was making the most of it. The only serious complaint was heard from the great trussed-up hog that was hanging, feet up, from a hook on the ladder above my shoulder.

We joggled along, stopping and starting. We stopped to let people off. We stopped to let some on. We stopped so that someone near the front could squeeze out over everybody, get off, run to the house, kiss everyone on both cheeks, deliver a present, have another round of kisses, then get back on the bus and push herself back towards her seat, where she disappeared from my view. They delivered presents of flowers, both real and artificial, live scrawny chickens, and loaves of French bread wrapped in old newspaper. One had a fresh salad made of chunks of the giant clam, packaged in a section of green bamboo big enough to hold a quart bottle. She kindly offered me a sample, which I enjoyed. One delivered a cake of ice that had been considerably larger when we left town. The driver made stops for some little children who stood by the roadway. These tiny watchmen then ran to the house and called someone who ran to the bus, kissed the driver, and give him a present of breadfruit, bananas, or some small little remembrance, which he stuffed into a palm leaf basket hanging on the side of the door-less camionnette. The eight miles to Punaauia took two and a half hours. I could have walked as fast.

The camionnette arrived near the end of the line, and the driver let me off. He had taken my friends out before and knew in which thatched roof *fare* they lived. Someone helped me get my gear from the roof, and the bus departed. I was making a surprise visit, mostly because I didn't want to be alone at Christmas. I arrived expecting busy preparations for a big feast, but when I knocked on the door I realized it was really "Gloomsville." After a round of greetings they told me their story of how the last month had gone for them. I would tell them about my trip to the Society Islands later.

My friends in Punaauia had come to Tahiti in the ugly gray fishing boat moored on the quay in Papeete. It was named *Tres Damas* for the three women aboard. They had arrived in mid-November about the same time I did. They were a young couple from Chile, Bea and Arturo and an American named Dan, his 12-year-old daughter Susan, and Dan's recent French wife, Odette. There were also two Peruvian crewmen who were living in town. During the voyage, which had lasted several weeks, they had survived on rice, beans, spaghetti, and other dried foods. They had come to Tahiti with a cargo of sheets of copper for boat building and repair, with the idea of selling them and starting a business with Chile. The venture so far had been successful only in that they had reached the island. On their arrival they had leased a *fare* right on the beach.

Since then their problems had been compounded. They were not allowed to open the business, sell the copper, sell the boat, or find jobs. Christmas *(Noera,* no AY ra, *Noël)* for them was going to be far from merry. None of us had ever been away from home before during the holiday season.

We still had to have *Noera*, so I gave them my contribution of assorted things I thought would go with the holiday week. I had brought canned corned beef, avocados, wine, cheese, sweetbread, and fruitcake. Little did I know when I picked them up in town that they would be the bulk of a meal. The groceries had been planned for a New Year's celebration.

The Tahitian neighbors next door had given my friends some raw fish and a pair of live chickens. No one knew what to do with the two birds or the fish. The two women, Bea and Odette, stared at them in fright. Fortunately I had raised chickens and knew how to kill, pluck, and clean them, so that was a great relief to the women. The fish I turned into "poison cru," by marinating them in lime juice and coco cream. Things began to look up. Dan went out and got a large branch of an ironwood tree, which has very long flexible needles and set it up so his daughter Susan would have a Christmas tree. She, in turn, went around collecting shells and some fallen baby coconuts that she painted red and made decorations. She found some purple water hyacinths and three long shell necklaces. She topped the tree off with a spindly dried-in-the-sun blue starfish. Discarded wine bottles held sprays of red, yellow, and orange hibiscus, and scarlet and purple bougainvillea. At the base of the tree she placed a picture of The Virgin. She was busy and contented.

Another stroke of good fortune for Susan was that Dan had met one of the TEAL Airline pilots in Papeete and somehow the pilot had agreed to bring Susan a jar of peanut butter when he brought in a plane. Where he got it was a mystery. It would certainly not be available in French Tahiti, and most unlikely in English Fiji, New Zealand, or the other island groups. The pilot may have had a connection with Hawaii. Susan probably had the only jar of America's Gourmet Gift to the World's Epicurean Arts for thousands of miles around. This lucky American girl could feel a little less homesick, but Dan and I were obviously extremely jealous.

Inside the *fare,* Odette and Bea busied themselves with enthusiastic efforts to get a meal ready. They were trying to combine their own and local customs. Later we sat around with our after-dinner guests from next door, in a room that was dark except for candles. We talked and laughed in four languages. We had balanced our various cultures so well that Christmas for this small band of beachcombers on this far away island had become a meaningful and memorable celebration.

Tropic boils need attention, and by the following morning, Christmas Day, I felt that I was about to lose a leg. The pain had increased measurably along with the swelling. The boil was now about the size of a quarter. Dan had a complete medical kit and started me on pills and wet compresses. For three days it was most aggressive looking, and then it began to ease up.

Later on Christmas morning, our Tahitian neighbors came to the water's edge to have a beach party. They invited us to join them, and it turned out to be one of the happiest experiences of my stay on the island. Two of the young men went fishing with their spears. The smaller boys went about collecting old dry coconut husks and black volcanic stones for the underground oven. Someone dug a hole in the sand and lined it with the stones and then tossed in the husks. A raging fire began to add its heat to the mid-day air. By the time the stones were hot, the fishermen had returned with fair luck, and what they brought was wrapped in fresh green breadfruit leaves and placed on the stones along with ripe bananas, the long ugly kind, and peeled halves of breadfruit. In the center of it all was an aluminum pot with poi to be baked. The oven was then covered with several round doormat-sized pads of fresh green leaves that the women had just made by twisting the stems together in a continual spiral.

Everyone enjoyed the next couple of hours talking or fishing. The islanders are marvelous at both, due to centuries of practice. By mid afternoon it was time to eat. The pads were taken off of the fire, and the food was served on tin plates, the only concession to modern times other than the match to start the fire, and the baking pot. The boys played their musical instruments. It was a wonderful Christmas.

Later that evening, three of the boys from the same family next door passed our *fare* on their way to the beach. They paused to say they were going to catch bait and would we like to go along. For equipment, they had only a half a dozen poles with dried palm fronds tied to the tips, which would be lighted and used for torches. The small boy carried a bucket with no bottom, and an older brother carried a small, tubular, split- bamboo cage that was pointed at both ends. On the top, it had a small trapdoor under the handle. As we walked quietly into the gently flowing current of the black lagoon in water almost up to our knees, the lighted torch cast long shadows of the small group. We stopped and waited. The light was beginning to attract small fish. Moe (MO ee), the young boy with the pail, was poised for instant action. Suddenly he pushed it directly into the water. He put his hand in the bucket and felt around without any apparent luck. He lifted the pail to try again. Down went the bucket with a splash. All was quiet as he felt again. This time he had trapped a fish, not six inches long, which he put into the floating cage. This kept up for quite a while until they thought they had enough bait fish. Next, we headed for the beach. The cage was tied to a stake in the lagoon and would stay there imprisoning the live fish until they were needed. The men were now ready at a moment's notice to dress a hook and go deep water fishing.

Dan and I returned to our own *fare*. We were in the midst of telling the others of the evening adventure when we heard a cry from the neighbor's place. It was not a cry of anger, but a plaintive wail of pain. We listened attentively, but there was no further noise. A moment or two later we could make out the shadowy forms of three figures leaving the thatch *fare*. In the limited moonlight we saw that the smaller boy was being dragged towards the shore. As they passed nearer our porch, we heard whimpering and the gruffer voices of the bigger two. Once at the water's edge they marched determinedly right on in, splashing noisily. They were not going fishing. We could see that they were not going very far when they stopped and made the smaller one sit down in the water. While the bigger figure stayed with the child, the other walked back to their *fare*. This did not seem to be any kind of emergency. Dan called over to find out what had happened.

Chati told us that his youngest brother had recently turned 12 and that it was time to become a man. The uncle had taken the large bush knife from the corner of the hut, and with a deft slice, he had quickly and painfully super incised (a semi-circle cut across the upper ridge) the youngster. Now the boy would have to sit in the sea until the bleeding had stopped. Only then could he return to the house, a man. In olden times there would have been a greater ceremony for this important event. There would have been priests, and a pig would have been killed for a feast to mark the occasion. Times have changed. Now the only ceremony was to have Moe prove his manhood by catching bait fish in a bucket without a bottom.

The catching of fish is important to the Tahitians, as it is the most reliable readily available food supply. They raised pigs, chickens and even dogs, but these animals could be eaten much more quickly than they could multiply. On the other hand, with the relatively small population sprinkled along the shore, there always seemed to be food in the lagoon, if it could be caught. A man had to be able to fish to feed his family.

Only a very short walk along the beach from the *fare* was a lovely beach hotel called Chez Rivnac (shay RIV nak). Monsieur Rivnac had built a series of bungalows in more or less a native style with a few nods of modernity. There were inside showers, but the water was not heated. There was electricity, occasionally. The central building was not much different from the cottages, but it was bigger. It had all developed bit by bit along the grassy rise just above the sparkling white sand. A wide open terrace was the most favored spot for the guests to sit at tables. By day the view from there was a constant symphony of changing colors of the water and the sky. When the sun set everything in sight was tinted with rusts and gold. When it became dark and the sky was sprinkled with the southern stars, the only thing that could be seen out in the sea was the spray of the waves against the reef a half of a mile away. As soon as the moon rose it cast a silver glow on everything. The flecks of light danced on the surface of the sea as the soft breeze rustled the palm leaves overhead into a constant whisper. Life was good.

Inside, in an excusably casually maintained taproom, there was a small bar. Unlike beachcomber bars in cities all over the world, there were no nets, glass balls, sea shells, or stuffed fish to decorate the room for atmosphere. Bare-chested, barefoot fishermen dressed in red or blue *pareu* standing at the bar with their spears leaning in the corner were enough. When a drink was served in a coconut shell, it was not to be picturesque, it was to save washing unnecessary glasses. The music to which we did a kind of shuffle step came from a band that seemed to be made up of guests who would play on anything that made noise.

Here in Chez Rivnac we celebrated the arrival of the New Year 1956. No one sang "Auld Lang Syne". No one cared that the old year was at last finished. Everybody looked forward to the New Year starting, and bringing with it 365 more nights of fun.

Chapter VIII

A CRUISE ON THE VAITERE
JANUARY 1956

The New Year was less than a week old. It was time to start adventuring again. I had just boarded the copra schooner *Vaitere* (vai TERR ee) at the dock in Papeete. She was being readied to depart for the Tuamotu Atolls and the Marquesa Islands. The brilliant afternoon sun was turning the little puddles on the dock into steam. The puddles were all that remained of a tropical downpour that had been just one more thing to delay the scheduled noon departure. The *Vaitere*, a 110-foot long, motor-driven, two-masted trading schooner, would eventually start on its monthly voyage among the low atolls and the high, coarse, Marquesas further to the northeast. The voyage was intended to bring necessary goods to the islanders and collect copra, for which the industrialized world had found many uses, mostly for the vegetable oil the copra contains. Eastward, beyond these islands, there is nothing but lonely Pitcairn and Easter Islands until the shores of the Americas are reached.

In spite of her few years, the *Vaitere* looked like she had been plying the trade routes for decades. The rough handling of the heavy goods being put aboard attested to the crew's attitude of indifference. The cargo was still being loaded onto every available space on deck. There were cases of canned meat and fish, powdered milk labeled "KLIM," and fruit preserves. Sacks of flour and sugar, onions, potatoes, taros, and lemons were all stacked in any corner. Demijohns of red wine in wicker baskets from Algeria, another French colony, in North Africa, and odd bits of cheap furniture, a bicycle, and an American outboard motor, were put temporarily in a more protected place, the lifeboat. Much of this would be rearranged later. Bolts of *pareu* cloth, bottles of patent medicine, heady pomades, and perfumes from Hong Kong, tools, and miscellaneous items of ready-to-wear were stowed in the main cabin.

The stevedores began loading 44-gallon drums of kerosene and gasoline upended on the deck, paving the area with red metal disks. These would become very hot to the bare feet when the sun was on them. On top of the drums, Canadian lumber and sheets of corrugated metal were stacked.

A large canvas awning was stretched taut over the boom covering the deck (roof) covering the main cabin. This provided shade and a sleeping area for the deck passengers. Crates of oranges had been placed in the front part of this area to break the headwinds. Claiming a sheltered spot to sleep, I spread my sleeping bag close to the orange crates and sat around to watch the action on the wharf.

During the next hour the other passengers came aboard and took a place by spreading out their sleeping mats. Before long the area under the awning was crowded with two dozen adults and several children. Each family group had piled their gear in such a way as to create a bit of privacy. They had colorful bundles that looked much like laundry. All of them had gaudily painted enameled pans, cardboard suitcases, cartons, bunches of bananas, breadfruit, coconuts, pineapples, and mangoes. For most of them there would be very little difference in their shipboard housekeeping than if they were at home. We would all share the same companionship and the weather, for the next month.

Back on the dock, the black-haired crowd swarmed like ants. The jumble of bicycles and trucks, screaming children and complaining animals, wandering fast-food and flower *hei* sellers, gave the wharf a sort of carnival look. The sadness of departure began to tell on the faces of those on the dock and on board as the hours dragged on. At first there had been gaiety with music and songs of friendship and even love. But it had begun to quiet down as farewell songs were sung instead.

Cargo was still being loaded, but no more deck space was available, so the crew began filling empty spaces in the lifeboat, also known here as whaleboat, or longboat. Crates of live chickens were stacked one upon another near the cookhouse next to the pile of firewood. Four unhappy mongrel dogs were tied to the mast. In separate crates, two huge pigs and a dozen free-running piglets had a place in the sun. Several palm fronds had been secured at the bow to create some shelter and food for other animals being hauled on board. These included a dozen shaggy goats, two sheep, a horse that had seen better days, and a mal-humored complaining cow. With luck they might survive the trip with little more to protect them from the elements and the spray than their fur. They had all brought their own flies. The captain had a puppy, and the steward had a kitten. The ship had a cat that may or may not have had some effect upon the domestic rat population. At night, I noted that roaches and the copra bugs came out and scurried around scavenging for tidbits. I soon realized how much the captain resembled the Biblical Noah.

A sudden blast from the *Vaitere's* whistle made the stevedores scramble down the gangplank. Blocking their passage was an aged hulking woman in a huge black Mother Hubbard garment, shaded by a wide-brimmed, flat-crowned, white straw hat. She was heaving her bulk step by labored step up the narrow quivering gangplank. Tucked under one arm she had a roll of sleeping mats and a pillow. In her hand she carried a small wriggling naked child and his puppy. In the other arm she had a tin basin, a cardboard suitcase, and a crate of three pigeon-sized nervous chickens. Bucking the traffic of the sweating workmen, she finally gained the top of the gangplank, deposited her load, and returned to the pier to kiss a friend good-bye.

Within seconds of the big woman's return to the deck, lines were cast off, the motor chugged three or four times while belching huge odorous black clouds, and then it died. The fact we were drifting along the wharf with no apparent control bothered no one. The crowd ashore followed us down the wharf, waving, crying, and tossing flowers into the widening span of water between us. Another series of agonized grunts and puffs from below, and the motor finally took hold. We pointed out to sea. We were on our way at last.

It took half a dozen lurches of the *Vaitere* bucking the inrushing ocean swells to clear the pass of the protective reef to gain the open sea. It was considerably rougher outside the lagoon, and this sent most of the passengers rushing to find a place at the rail. Though their ancestors had been marvelous sailors and navigators, scattering themselves over the vast Pacific Ocean, these descendants were proving themselves unseaworthy. Those who at first had not seemed noticeably ill soon looked as though they envied those who had. This group suddenly had lost their entire carefree attitude so characteristic of Tahitians on land.

Below deck in the salon were four pairs of double-decked, curtained, cubbyhole bunks for the Cabin Class passengers. Built to be large enough for the average Polynesian traveler, anyone with more ample proportions would have difficulty fitting their body into one of these bunks. They were like Pullman Car uppers, and each was designed to be shared by two persons. Their luggage had to be stored in that space with them.

Two of the pigeonholes were occupied by the Lie family. Henry Lie was an expatriate Norwegian, who decades earlier had settled in the islands. He and his Marquesan wife and teenaged son were returning to their place after a visit to town.

Next to them were two European nuns who immediately became sick and remained tucked tightly in their curtained slot for the entire trip. They were going out to do God's will, but were suffering miserably at his hands in the meantime.

In the bunk above the nuns were a young couple and their three small children, whose scamperings in and out of the bunk added materially to the discomfort of the constantly praying Sisters.

Across the cabin, three other bunks were occupied by the captain, the mate, and the representative of the Donald's Company, the owner-operator of the schooner and a chain of shops in Papeete and on the outer islands. The Cargo Supervisor had the fourth bunk. He was also the ship's "doctor," and he claimed also to have been the island "dentist" whenever there were problems. His basic supplies were the French iodine, gentian violet, and pliers. He told me that there would probably be a man waiting on the pier with a toothache. I could see no way he would know that. We were too isolated from Radio Coco for him to have received the news that way. He added that every time the *Vaitere* arrived, the man begged to have a painful tooth pulled. As a painkiller, the dentist gave the patient a stiff drink of cognac. Once that had taken effect, the man became violent and would not let the tooth be pulled. About the time the ship was out of sight, the effect of the cognac had worn off, and the toothache returned. The patient had to wait for the next visit. It was a painful way to get a high once in a while.

The middle part of the salon was filled with red leather-covered benches and a table. This is where the Cabin Class passengers had their meals. This was also the social and recreational center for evening games and chatter.

The "head," or toilet, was jammed into a miniscule space. The tiny sink was hung on the back of the door. To wash the hands, it was necessary to sit on the head. No more ambitious washing project could have been possible. I found it more practical to use the non-enclosed perch at the stern for the Deck Class passengers. There was no privacy, but no one seemed to care. It was a wonder no one fell overboard.

When I went to inquire about taking the cruise, I found that I had neither the money needed to travel Cabin Class, nor the desire to travel "cargo," or deck class. The Donald's Company representative suggested I compromise and sleep deck class and eat first class, and during the off hours, fend for myself. On the Passenger List I was recorded as "Monsieur Tourist." I soon found out that this solution was the very best arrangement possible. There was enough space in my deck claim to stretch out my six-foot, three inch frame in the cool fresh air under the awning. I was also able to enjoy decent meals served at the table. For about $75 (1956), I had the opportunity to enjoy a cruise of some four weeks. It would be a real travel bargain if I could survive it.

Every time I went to sea in the South Pacific, I had memories of a movie I saw around the late 1930s called *The Hurricane*. The main action of the plot was a storm that drove huge waves over an atoll and wiped it out. I was on my way to the atolls. Thus, I was aware of the dangers that could suddenly happen in this area. In 1938 I had lived through the first hurricane on record to strike Long Island, New York. That storm should have taught me a serious lesson. But I had always been more curious than cautious.

Life soon settled down to its casual tempo. Aside from the crew, who all wore only work shorts, everyone else was dressed in *pareu*, except probably the hidden nuns. My Levi's, my own native attire, impressed everyone as they all thought immediately that I must be a "kau poi," the six-gun wielding daredevils they had seen in so many American western films. Because of my height and narrow build, I fitted their image perfectly, though I had never lived west of the Hudson River.

On shipboard most of the passengers looked forward to meal times, as there was little else to break up the day. Though the life aboard this ship was more interesting than most, we generally awaited the dinner bell with conditioned salivating. For breakfast we had tea, or Tahitian coffee, fresh fruit, jam, butter, and a choice of pate or cheese to go on the freshly baked French bread. Lunch was the big meal of the day, when we had a fish course, salad, meat and potatoes, melon and wine. At evening meal we had soup, meat, spaghetti or rice, bread, cheese, fruit, and wine. The fish, which I guess was mostly barracuda, and very good, was caught on a line constantly being towed from the stern. The meat was mostly goat chops, which was supplied by one of the crew whose job it was each morning to catch, kill, clean, and butcher one of the bleating beasts in the bow. The menus of continental Europe have strongly influenced life in the South Seas, even on a trading schooner.

The deck passengers did not fare as well. They were served coffee in their own cups, bread, plus a bit of butter and jam for breakfast. For lunch and dinner it was cold bully beef (corned beef) straight out of the can, and rice, along with boiled green bananas or breadfruit. To be fair, the Polynesian generally preferred bully beef to all other treats, so they were eating the diet to which they had all become accustomed. I do not know if they ever were given any fresh fish. Each deck class passenger had brought their own utensils. They lined up, and each had a turn at the food pots placed on the deck and served themselves. Then they found some spot to hunker down and eat at their own pace.

The seamen were busy all the time they were on deck. There was always wood that had to be chopped for the chef's oven. Another seaman tended to the needs of the animals with water and a little feed, enough so that they would survive until they arrived at their destiny. One crewman, bare-chested and bare-footed like all the rest, also had steward duty in the cabin class dining room, where he added only a white jacket over his clean work shorts.

Besides the normal work on board, they were also the stevedores at each port we visited. They rowed the whaleboat, our lifeboat, back and forth between the *Vaitere* and the shore when there was no pier where we could tie up. They unloaded passengers and freight. Most times when we had to land on a beach, they carried the passengers up to dry land. They lifted the sacks of copra from the beach storehouse to the scales to be weighed, each one generally 60 pounds or so, then to the beached whaleboat. They had to row out to the *Vaitere* through the surf, which frequently was quite strong. They unloaded the copra into the hold so as to return the empty sacks to be refilled. They reloaded the longboat with trade goods and rowed back to the beach. This went on until all the copra had been collected and all the ordered goods for the trading shop had been off loaded. Then they brought the passengers back who were going onwards. They worked very hard. They were huge and muscular, most around six feet tall with the builds of major athletes. They could carry a load of three sacks of copra or flour on their shoulders, as if it were only one. This was all done at the quickest pace, as time in port was time lost as far as the captain was concerned. Upon the return to Papeete, the crew had to shovel the entire cargo of loose copra back into bags and off load them.

The crew fared pretty well. I did not envy the crowded fo'c'sle where they spent their downtime. They did have the unique privilege of being able to draw two buckets of fresh water a day from the large square tank on the deck, next to the galley, or cook-house. The water was for a shower on the open deck. On a small clear space reserved for this use, they could wet down with a coconut shell dipper, soap up, and rinse off. The daily bath was a most important part of the islander's lives. Even Cabin Class was denied this refreshing necessity. For them, it was cruel testimony as to who was the most important on board.

Chapter IX
THE TUAMOTUS (THE ATOLLS)

After three full days and some three hundred miles of motor-driven sailing north-east from Tahiti, we had our first sight of land. Sticking just barely above the surface of the mild surf was the atoll of Tokoroa (to ko RO ah). I was told that no part of this island atoll was more than a dozen feet above the average level of the surrounding ocean. In the dim past of geologic time, a chain of volcanic eruptions occurred on the ocean floor, which spewed out a large number of mountains that grew high enough to break the surface of the sea. But they were not long-lived. They were eroded back to sea level. Gradually their nearness to the surface was found by sea-borne coral polyps to be a good place to stop and colonize. Thus a reef was begun on top of each irregular ring-shaped pile of volcanic debris. Dead coral eventually broke off in storms, filled in, and sand was then formed. Thus, the atoll appeared above the level of the sea. This was land hospitable enough in which the floating coconuts from other islands could take root and thrive. These trees like their roots near salt water. As they grew, their roots collected more and more sand.

A chain of about 75 of these atolls now formed a treacherous area of random, unchartered reefs that cover an area roughly the size and shape of California. The atolls are known as the Tuamotus, or Low Islands, and also as "The Graveyard of Ships." When the Polynesians, or Maohis, were making their voyages of discovery, possibly a millennium and a half ago, they found these semi-habitable islands, which could sustain small populations. Their ability to collect and store rainwater was the essential skill they had to master, or perish. In the meager soil they could raise a few basic crops. With the natural riches of fish in the central lagoon, and coconuts without limit, they could survive without fear of meddlesome neighbors. They navigated their sailing craft between atolls by observing shafts of light in the sky caused by sunlight being reflected from the white sand at the bottom of the central lagoons.

From afar, the dark green of the leaves on the coco trees gives a far more substantial image to an atoll than it deserves. Many times great waves have washed over these islands, wiping out the tiny settlements.

The *Vaitere* slowed down as it approached the outer edge of the surrounding reef of Tokoroa. There was no pass to get through to bring us nearer the shore. The ship's motor kept us in a relative position outside in the open sea. The water was so clear that as I looked over the railing I could see the wall of the reef, which plunged down hundreds of feet. The light surf continued wave after wave into the shallow water of the reef, constantly flooding it with fresh nutrients the coral needed to stay alive.

The whaleboat was put over the side, and the six crewmen held it as steady as they could as several passengers climbed down and settled into it. As they pushed off, the coxswain kept his eyes on the incoming surf waiting for the "one in seven" that would contain enough water and power to lift the longboat up and over the lip of the reef and carry it into the quiet water on the other side. Any miscalculation could be disastrous. A happy crowd had gathered on the beach and welcomed the new arrivals, an event that only happened about once a month. At the edge of the beach the crewmen hopped out and carried the passengers up to dry land.

For the return trip, sacks of copra were put in the whaleboat, and a few visitors climbed onto the sacks to come out to see friends on board. The boat was pushed off by the islanders. The trip back to the *Vaitere* was far more hazardous, as the crew had to row against the current. The load of copra weighed about the same with the several visitors. To get back over the reef, the coxswain faced the sea and waited for the wave he hoped would bring enough water onto the reef so the men could put their oars in, and with powerful strokes, ride atop the inrushing water out to the open sea beyond. If they failed, the heavy load and the boat could be stranded or overturned on the coral and the cargo lost. Both boat and people could be savagely hurt on the sharp coral. "NOW!" shouted the coxswain and with mighty strokes, the loaded boat cleared the dangerous barrier. This same operation was repeated several times during the hours we were there.

Unaware that I too could have ridden in the lifeboat to shore, I stayed on the boat. The first to come aboard was the Chinese storekeeper. He had come to make the sale of the copra, select items to sell in his shop, and place orders for the next delivery date. He also brought a few pieces of mail. He selected lengths of material, as he was also the island tailor. He decided on the luxuries they could have and the tools they might need. He set the economy for the island. Left to themselves, the Polynesian islanders would select a few things that took their fancy, regardless of their usefulness. It has happened that a month's work making copra was traded for wine. After the big party that followed, and the massive island hangover, there were no supplies to be had until the ship came again. The Chinese merchant was permitted a heavy markup, but he did keep a balance of necessities.

Before we left Papeete, several dozen stalks of green bananas had been tied to the railings along the deck. During the four days of the voyage the sun and spray had turned them black. No matter. All the fruit was precious to the locals, as they could not grow them in the sandy soil of the atoll. Along with half of the oranges, half of the weathered bananas had been taken off of the railing and put in the whaleboat, beside the drums of kerosene for the lamps, and gasoline for their outboard motors, and delivered to the beach. Some of the sheets of corrugated iron and all kinds of packaged goods were also taken ashore. Some of the lumber was tossed overboard to drift ashore on its own.

The merchant and other visitors went ashore, and the longboat returned with the ongoing passengers. The crew made ready to go to the next atoll, only a short trip away. The next morning the captain navigated through a marked channel in the reef at the atoll of Tokopoto (to ko PO to). We tied up at a small, crude wharf crowded with welcoming adults and school children.

I was anxious to get on solid land regardless of how insecure the atoll appeared. As I stepped onto the tiny wharf, someone touched me on the shoulder and asked in English, "Do you want to take a bath?" "What a marvelous bit of hospitality," I thought, and I followed the young woman along the sandy pathway through the center of the settlement to her house. She was an attractive island woman probably in her mid-twenties. She introduced herself as Maeva (mah AY vah). She was dressed in a neat yellow print dress. Her skin was lighter than the others on the island. She told me that she had come from "the Mainland," meaning Tahiti. Maeva said that she was the teacher in town, and she always came down to the dock to welcome tourists on board and bring them to her home.

The bright sun reflecting on the white sandy path was blinding. The only shade at mid-day was in the star-shaped shadows of the leaves of the coco trees directly overhead. My guide pointed to a small church and said that most of the water used on the island had come from the rain that fell on the roof and was collected in the big cisterns at the corners. Owners of some of the other houses had collected their own water into empty gasoline drums. Sweet water was so valuable that it was mostly used for cooking, washing, and irrigating the small garden patches. When water was scarce, the residents survived by drinking the liquid inside the coconuts.

We turned off of the path in front of a small yellow wooden house with red trim. The house was raised up on stilts some three or four feet above the sand. On each side was a pair of windows with no glass in them. Each opening had wooden shutters hinged at the top and propped out at the bottom with a stick. On the front porch, I noted a round table and a group of chairs. Inside one of the two rooms, I saw a double bed in each corner, and a single bureau topped with a vase of artificial flowers. Around the base of the house was a small garden outlined with a ring of large sun-bleached white *pahoehoe* shells. Maeva led me around the back of the house to a little corrugated shed, which had a bucket of water, a bar of soap, a coconut shell for a dipper, and a bunch of coconut fibers from a fresh coconut, for scrubbing. I had learned how to bucket-bathe by watching the crewmen on the *Vaitere*.

When I came around the corner, refreshed, a crowd of young people had gathered on the porch. "These are my best pupils. I have told them that you will tell us something about your island." In halting French I tried to describe the things that I thought might interest them. My utterings were translated and greatly amplified by Maeva. She was widely read and, of course, had learned much of the outside world from films. They were amused at the need for such things as traffic lights, the changing of the colors of the foliage in the autumn, and the sensations of ice skating and skiing. They did not believe the stories of the tall buildings, although I had brought along picture postal cards for just such an occasion. I knew that if I wanted to describe the size of my island (America) to these young people, I would have to put it into some terms they might understand. I said that America was a land that was bigger than the distance from their atoll back to Tahiti. This was a distance of only some 300 miles, but one that many of them had experienced by boat. They giggled. They couldn't believe that most American children had never seen a *ni'au* (nee ow, coconut tree) or never even tasted salt water. I was sure that they hear the same stories every time an American comes to their atoll. There were other visitors from many different lands who arrived occasionally on the trading boats. The outside world must have been very confusing to them. Or else, maybe it was the act of bathing in the shed that creates the fantasies about which visitors raved. In any event, they were a wonderful and responsive audience.

A small girl in a spotless white dress handed me a green coco, the top of which had been chopped off. "All you visitors like these," Maeva smiled. They all stared as I drank the refreshingly cool liquid. It pleased them that I appreciated the offering. With a large bush knife, the teacher whacked the empty nut in half. I knew enough to use a sharp chip of the husk as a scoop to clean out all of the soft tender flesh. I devoured it with relish. Was I becoming a Tahitian?

"Let me show you the town," Maeva urged, as the children all rose to accompany us through their all-too-familiar village, all noisily chatting in a holiday mood. On the opposite side of the sandy path she pointed out her school. Framed in green and yellow painted timber, most of it was wide open to the constant trade winds. Inside there was a blackboard, a large map of France, and a shelf of various readers. The whitewashed church with its stained glass windows was next, and behind it was the bakery. The island bread maker was standing by his oven, a 44-gallon oil drum. He had affixed a section of corrugated metal in the middle. In the lower part he had a fire of coconut husks. The long strips of rolled bread dough were placed carefully in the grooves of the shelf. A similar bit of metal was placed over the bread to complete the oven. On top of the latter he courteously allowed anyone who wished to roast their fresh-caught fish.

We walked across the width of the ring-shaped atoll to the shore of the inner lagoon. Out in the middle we saw the outriggers of many fishermen. The varying depths of the water created many shades of blue. In some of these depths, the mollusks that make the black pearls thrive. But the host gives up its life when it is opened. Rarely, there may be a pearl inside.

We visited with the local boat builder who was working alone in his thatched shed. He was making a boat about the same size as the whaler from the *Vaitere*, suitable to use for neighboring inter-atoll traffic to bring back the copra for storage near the wharf.

Maeva pointed to one of several *ni'au* that we passed. Each had a coco leaf tied tightly around its trunk. The tip was secured up the trunk, and the butt end was near the ground. Each pair of leaflets was tied tightly around the back. She asked me if I knew why that was. I had no idea, but I guessed that they might have been left over from some kind of celebration decoration. She giggled. Then she said, "None of you visitors can guess the real purpose. When we have our brief heavy rains, the water flows down the trunks and the leaflets guide the water onto the main stalk so that it dribbles into a container where it is caught for our supply."

Most of the men of the village were out in the groves making copra. When the fallen nuts on one island are harvested, the men go to a neighboring uninhabited island to work. An atoll is uninhabited because of its size, or lack of water. However, the Islanders can thrive on the water inside the coconut if necessary. Often whole families go and live in thatch huts created on the spot. The family life is disrupted very little by this activity. Some men will still go fishing for the food for the group, while others work on the nuts. There is no season. Normally, nuts fall regularly all year long. To grow well, there should be no more than ten trees per acre. If there are ripe nuts still up in the trees, some men will climb up and harvest them.

To climb a branchless *ni'au* perhaps some 20-30 or more feet tall, a *tane* makes a loop of old *pareau* about a foot in diameter. He slips this loop over his feet to his ankles. Then with his hands and bare feet, he shinnies up the trunk without a safety belt and twists the ripe nuts off of the cluster. The nuts fall to the ground. The nuts are gathered and taken to the drying place. The outer husk with the nut inside must first be chopped in half. To scoop out the white meat, the men use a special blade that is curved into a half circle to fit the inside of the shell. The scoop is somewhat similar in design to an ice cream scoop, but it is not a half ball. It is only about an inch wide. They can extract the white meat with one or two deft movements. It is tedious work. The meats are then spread on metal sheets to dry in the sun. In case of rain, a thatched roof, on rollers, can be pulled over the copra to keep it dry.

It takes about six nuts to make a kilo (about two pounds) of dried copra. Each filled sack weighs about 30 kilos, or about 65 pounds. Between five and six thousand fresh nuts will make a ton of dried copra, which in 1956 sold for about $200. The amount of nuts available, divided among the number of men who work on them, does not make for a big income. Roughly, the meat of 50 nuts might earn about $2. I don't know how many nuts a man can process in a day, but I would guess between one and two hundred, all considered. A can of New Zealand bully beef, enough for two people, cost the islander about 80 cents. A kilo of flour was 17 cents, and sugar was 22 cents. A quarter of a pound of the most ordinary chocolate was 35 cents, a luxury. Thus, their basic diet is still fish, but fishing takes time and is never certain. The copra shipped to the Western World generally winds up as "partially hydrogenated vegetable oil." The so-called "palm oil" generally comes from another kind of inland palm tree. They are different. I did not see any in the South Pacific.

As we approached the wharf for our return to the ship, we met a lovely young friend of Maeva. She was sporting her most recent purchase from the trader. Above her *pareu* she wore nothing but a shell necklace and a very lacey white French bra. She was so proud of the latest fashion.

As the crew of the *Vaitere* made ready to depart, I noticed that the rest of the weather-blackened bananas had been taken off of the railing and apparently moved to the village shop by the local merchant. I also saw that the two praying Sisters had come to the dock to wave good-bye Though still travel worn from their ordeal, they seemed of good cheer to be on solid ground again, no matter how isolated it would prove to become. Their bunk space was now occupied by one of the more comely women I had noted during my stroll through the village.

I left Tokopoto with mixed feelings, thinking how exotically beautiful these atolls were. I was impressed that centuries ago humans had decided to settle on these isolated specks of land when they had other choices. They adapted to the precarious conditions to make a life for themselves which seemed to be satisfying.

I was told that the Polynesian language has 28 words to describe the colors of blue to indicate to the listener the condition of the water and the sky, the two things most important to the lives of the people of the atolls. These seem to be the only variables, as the temperature changes little. The breeze is constant. The rain is adequate, but no more than that. When a ship stops by, a movie film may be left for their entertainment, which is shown with the power from a generator. There were no cars, as there was no place to go. There were flies without number. Periodicals were rare, and alcohol was forbidden. However, the administration makes an exception for red wine. The Low Islands were not the ideal paradise I had thought they might be.

Chapter X

THE MARQUESAS
(LES ISLES TRISTES)

At about noon on the sixth day out of Papeete, the peak of Hiva Oa was quite clear on the horizon. We had arrived at the Marquesas. At just about 4000 feet high, it is one of several volcanic mountains in this group of high islands. I was surprised when I saw that the nearest part of the land we could see was bare rock and rust red. As we got nearer to Traitor's Bay, our anchorage at Atuoana (ah too WAH nah), the largest town, the landscape changed considerably to lush greens and abundant vegetation. Lei told me that while sailing west from Peru and searching for King Solomon's mines, the Spanish explorer Alvaro Mendana discovered the archipelago in 1595 and named it after the Viceroy of Peru. At that time, the islands were populated with thousands of people. Cultural misunderstandings between the natives and the explorers led to problems. After killing some 200 of the natives, the Spaniards departed. "Might makes right" even if you are only curious visitors, I guess.

Traitor's Bay is not a harbor. Rather, it is a long curving sweep of a beach of black sand and black polished stones. It would offer little protection from a storm. Trees come right down to the beach. From the bay, the only indication of the town was the tall radio tower. The valley looked like a half of a broken teacup, walled in by a long curved ridge of peaks eroded as if sculptured into the buttresses of some natural gothic cathedral.

While some of the crew was loading passengers into the whaleboat to go ashore, others on the opposite side of the *Vaitere* were tossing cargo into the water. In went a large number of planks of wood, a pair of chairs, and the horse. All but the horse would drift ashore in the gentle surf. The lifeboat towed the horse with a noose around its neck. When two huge wicker-covered demijohns of Algerian wine were tossed in, they hit each other and broke. Instantly that patch of sea went blood red. Just as quickly two of the crewmen jumped into the water and began scooping up the brine-wine mixture, frantically swallowing all they could.

A crowd had gathered on the shore, and when we got near they rushed into the water to help push the longboat up onto the beach. They offered to carry the passengers through the few inches of water to dry land. This was our welcome to the island that had been described by early explorers as being inhabited by a race of cannibals. I wondered if they were planning a big feast that day. Marquesans actually seemed to be much larger than mainland Tahitians. They certainly appeared to be more sturdily built. When they carried the heavy cargo on their shoulders, they proved their proverbial strength beyond doubt.

When he was in the South Pacific, the French painter Gauguin spent most of his time in Tahiti, but he is said to have loved Hiva Oa. When he died he was buried here on a small ridge overlooking Atuoana with a marvelous view of the mountains and other islands. He was not alone up there. I stopped to visit with him. I brought a cluster of yellow frangipani blossoms to place on his grave. An artist-to-artist thing, I guess. Several others were buried there also, as there were many crosses with Tahitian inscriptions on them. But the living residents seemed to avoid the spot, as it was sadly overgrown.

Atuoana was a town of only some three hundred people. There was a Catholic church, a convent, and a Protestant church. Donald's, the owner of the *Vaitere*, also operated the store. There was a radio station and a post office. The Gendarme, I was told, never investigated a crime. To do so would admit that crime existed. A male nurse completed the professional French administrative staff on the island.

Visitors unfamiliar with these islands ought to know that it would be most unfortunate if they planned to relax on one of the beaches. First, there are no reefs or lagoons. Second, most of the beaches I saw were black sand and rocky, but there were some white sand beaches. Third, there were small sand flies called "no-nos," and the unnoticeable bites of these tiny insects raised terribly painful blisters. The only protection is long clothing. With the rugged terrain, the inhospitable beaches, and the remnants of a once large population reduced to so few souls, it is no wonder that the French refer to the Marquesas as "Les Isles Tristes," The Sad Islands.

There were several towns, the only remains of which were the *paepaes* (pie pies), or stone platforms that raised the wooden and thatched huts above ground level. Very skillful labor was needed to fit the stones together by using only stone tools. The bigger the *paepae*, the more stones it had. The better fitted together they were, the more they represented the greater wealth and power that the owner held in the community. The fact that the roots of trees and vines had not split these ruins apart over the past two centuries indicated the quality of the work involved. The biggest set of these ruins that I saw was on a slope west of Atuoana, just off of the only road. The huge size of the layout is startling. Long since gone were the wooden structures that the ruins supported, leaving nothing upon which to reconstruct mentally what might have been there. If there were any sculptural elements to enhance the community, they have long ago been removed and were now collecting dust in foreign museums. What remained useful were the terraces built to form the level land where the basic food crops were still being raised.

More interesting to me was a small phenomenon at the base of a giant tree. I saw a small rock that had two holes in it with a jet of water coming out of each. It must surely have been a spring. When I placed my finger on one of the holes, the jet from the other hole increased in volume.

Since I had taken my meals with the first class passengers, they became good friends while on the cruise. Henry Lei told me many tales about his life. He had worked as a cabin boy on a ship. When they got to Tahiti he skipped ship and chose to settle in the islands. He had been there long enough to know much about most of these spots of land. As we passed the barren red part of Hiva Oa he explained that it was not a part of the natural history of the island. When the explorers on the first ships to pass through the Pacific discovered an island, they dropped off a few goats. Their plan was to let the goats multiply and the next time they came back there would be a fresh meat supply ready for the taking. The plan worked too well, and to the detriment of the islands themselves. The goats ate the young trees faster than they could grow so that much of the soil washed off. The land became barren and exposed the bare rock. The goats had since become a favorite source of food for the residents as well, and they were hunted as wild game. It was hoped that this would bring the herds under control and help restore the islands natural cover.

The sharp plunge of the cliffs into the sea prevented the formation of reefs around these high islands. There was a nice beach on the north side of Hiva Oa at Paumau Bay (POW MOW, rhymes with "how now,") where the early mission was founded. Many of the stones that made up the wall that surrounded the church yard had been carved into the figures of the traditional tikis. They stood there silent, as if to help the priests to convert the heathens. Behind the church was a path that led to a group of remarkable sculptures about a quarter of a mile inland. One was a gigantic figure of a *ti'i,* or tiki standing about eight feet tall with his hands clasped at his belly. His huge eyes were still staring blindly out to the bay. He had an expression of cruel power. Not far away was a fallen figure of a woman in the act of childbirth. The delivery was being made more difficult as her face was in the mud and her feet were aimed at the sky. This petrified Adam and Eve were among the few the remaining artistic achievements of the ancient Marquesan culture still to be seen in their probable original location.

Another master artist practiced his skills in the same area. There was a huge flat stone with curious shallow cups hollowed out of the surface. I was told that the local tattooer mixed his inks in these cavities into which he dipped his skin piercing instruments, anything from shark's teeth to sharpened edges of broken shell. Punctured or carved, the skin retained the coloring. In the stone was also a larger rectangular depression that, when filled with water, became a mirror for the proud owner to admire his new facial adornment.

Applying a tattoo was serious business, and the master's reputation was always at stake. He was highly paid for his professional skill. Since it was a most painful procedure, the client was often strapped to large sections of the trunks (logs) of banana trees to keep the body from moving, which would spoil the accuracy of the final design. The final result in the Marquesas was that the upper class members of society had tattoos covering their entire body.

In 1722 the Dutch explorer Roggewein arrived. Roggewein and his men observed what they imagined were the natives wearing some kind of garments woven of dark silk net. Later, many European artists accompanying the early explorers sketched the natives while the ship was in the harbor. The existing illustrations show that adult males had their faces tattooed, probably indicating their tribal association. Apparently each island of the group had a particular tribal pattern of bands with stylized designs, or solid monochromes, from one side of the face across to the other. One band across the area of the eyes and nose, and another across the mouth area, may have indicated a member of a Hiva Oa tribe. A single band across the central portion of the face probably indicated a male was from Fatu Hiva. A diagonal band from one side of the forehead to the opposite jaw was the feature of another tribe. There was great variety.

Joseph Banks, the artist who went along with the English explorer Captain Cook, was the recorder of anything discovered on the voyage to Tahiti in 1769. His sketches of South America were mainly flora and fauna. Then they reached the South Pacific. He suddenly became an 18th century *paparazzi* with a paintbrush. The first sketch he made of a tattoo was done by copying what he saw on the body of a dead Marquesan. His work began to preserve the extent and sophistication of this cultural specialty.

Captain Cook also picked up a young adult Marquesan named Omai who had an entire body tattoo. Somehow, Cook convinced Omai to volunteer to leave his island and spend the next months at sea for the long voyage back to England. Cook rarely sailed in a straight line, as he was always looking for new things. He went southwesterly to visit some islands thought to be in that area. After exploring some of the coastal area of New Zealand, he claimed it for England. He then sailed westwards and encountered the Great Barrier Reef off of the coast of Australia. Exploring the reef, Cook got into a jam and had to make lengthy repairs to the *Endeavor* before continuing. Cook and the others all eventually arrived back in London, where Omai's tattooed body became the star attraction of High Society. He was invited everywhere.

Other foreign recorders have left clues as to the extent of the appeal to the natives for the art. I did not learn if there was social pressure to be tattooed, or if it was purely voluntary, depending on the status of the individual. A few individuals were adorned from head to foot. Other bodies had various individual parts decorated separately, such as shoulders, arms, hands, or legs. Women had their own special patterns and locations, but generally they did not have as much work done on them as the men.

Some of the individual motifs were stylized designs representing *tikis*, or various land and sea animal life forms they knew, including lizards, fish, turtles, crabs, or even whales. Floral designs were also popular. The display of the cluster of leaves of a ni'au tree fit nicely on the sides of male buttocks, with the trunk extending down the leg. Their bodies were their cultural canvases. In that tropical climate the only other body covering that appears in the earliest sketches was a minimum *hami* (or *cache sexe,* as the French so discretely put it) covering the genital area

How did this Marquesan body art get started? The legend was told to me that a man of the village was sad because his wife had left him. He was advised by the god Tu to have his body decorated in such a way that his wife would think him so handsome that she could not resist him. He went to the local tattooer and had him start to work. After many months the job was completed, from face to foot. He became so handsome that he regained his wife. In a culture where there is little else to do but the work to survive, this might have been entertainment. An untattooed man was called a *kikino* (kee KEE no).

In the later part of the 18th century, Jean Baptiste Cabri jumped ship and fled into the interior of one of the Marquesan islands. He was allowed to remain with them and, either by choice or force, was facially tattooed. Apparently he went for more of the body art as time passed. Later he was rescued and brought back to Europe. He then traveled with a circus as one of the exhibits. When he died his skin was preserved and exhibited. Europeans marveled at this novelty. By this time, sailors of every nation had a new port-of-call pastime.

Henry Lei and his family got off at Iaone Bay (ee ah OH nay) where his plantation is located. He welcomed all visitors, if they had time to stay a while. Otherwise he treated them to a quick tour of his Swiss Family Robinson-style house. It is a fine example of modern European ingenuity with a tropical accent. He had planted a wide variety of fruits and vegetables in his well-tended garden.

He told me that the Governor of the archipelago wanted to promote the consumption of more fruits and had ordered hundreds of little pomplemouse tree seedlings. This green, oversized, sweet grapefruit is delicious. Once the tree is established, it thrives wonderfully in the rich volcanic soil and does not need any amount of care. He envisioned that the expected excess produce could be sold to the peoples of the atolls, which would increase the planter's income. The Governor knew that if he gave the trees to the islanders, they would think that they were not worth anything and they would not tend them. He knew that if he charged them the price that it cost to raise and deliver them, they would not buy them. Consequently, he decided to charge them half the cost, stressing the value of the fruit and the profits they could make. The men lined up and took their allotment. When they had all been passed out, one of the men said that they all wanted to be paid for planting them. The Governor sent them on their way with a gesture of annoyance. A few days later one of them returned and said that they had decided not to water the young trees if they did not get paid. There the matter died, as did the little pomplemouse seedlings. It went back to ancient times when in the original Polynesian culture, no one could have anything more than his neighbor.

There was a similar story relating to the running water that had been piped by the government from the higher slopes down to the houses. The island men demanded free parts if there were any repairs to be made, in spite of the fact that the pipes had saved vast amounts of time and effort carrying water from the spring. It was only the women's time that had been saved. Attitudes of initiative and self-improvement had not developed along with the demands for modern material advances.

I heard of only two other Caucasians who had taken up living in the Marquesas. I met an American named Fred Johnson, who told me of the months of difficulty it took to get permission to stay there. He had married an island princess who had title to a large amount of land on the island of Tahuata (tah hoo WAH tah). They wanted to live there, but the authorities threw every possible obstacle in their way. Finally, after a year and a half, he was granted the temporary right to farm the land. On the beach he built a small ways to haul his little boat out. He then began seriously to develop the sloping hillside that held out the most promise to be the best area. There was much work involved, piling stones up to hold the earth for terraces, and the raising of stone walls to keep his neighbors' marauding animals out of his garden.

One of the easiest things to grow is papaya. All that has to be done is to throw the mature seeds of the melon-like fruit out onto the soil. Within a few months there will be ripening fruit on the tree. This fruit was rare in the islands, as the seeds were generally not given the chance to ripen. Large bats called flying foxes loved the fruit, and at night they attacked anything that was on the verge of maturity. In order for the islanders to enjoy any of these gifts of nature, they had to pick the fruit before the bats get to it first. When they did pick the green fruit, they ate it immediately instead of giving it time to ripen under care. Fred kept a few fruit until they were ripe enough, and then he tossed the seeds out on his terraces. One morning, after the seedlings had gotten a good start, he found that his neighbor's horse had gotten into the orchard through a hole knocked down in his stone wall. The horse had eaten the delicious leaves of the papaya and trampled all of the young seedlings. Fred realized that he would never be allowed to raise the trees. The neighbors, jealous of his orchard, would destroy it to prevent his having something they themselves did not have. The ancient ways were stronger than modern common sense.

Fred showed me a historic stone platform near his home. He told me the ancients stretched out their dead on the stone platform and anointed the corpse frequently with coconut oil until the flesh fell from the bones. The bones were then collected and put under a pile of rocks, while the skulls were taken up to a cave in the mountain.

Also nearby were the ceremonial poi poi pits. Breadfruit has two ripening seasons a year. During the seasons when more breadfruit ripened than could be eaten, the surplus was wisely stored in pits in the ground. It was not only emergency rations, but some of this fermenting dough-like matter made an extremely tasty cooked vegetable. Like Arctic sourdough, a small amount was added to fresh poi and gave it flavor. By itself it had a strong cheese-like taste. Most of the homes had poi poi pits nearby so they could still eat their breadfruit in the ancient way. I was told that every time a child was born, the family planted another breadfruit tree.

The captain of the *Vaitere* did most of his sailing at night under the broad band of stars, which had a special charm all of its own. I had never seen so many stars so clearly in my native New York. The plentiful phosphorous in the tropical water glowed in the dark when it is disturbed by the boat passing through it, leaving a trail of flickering lights behind in the wake. These were magical hours, except when it rained. The canvas cover kept us fairly dry, except for the occasional rain that the strong winds blew under the awning. The orange crates that once protected my claimed spot on the deck were gone when the fruit was left in the atolls. It made me aware I was traveling deck class. As passengers got off, I claimed their deserted area towards the middle position.

At sunrise we entered the great harbor at Taiohae (tie oh HIGH) on the island of Nuku Hiva. The bay drives deep into the island towards the center peaks and is protected from storms by hills. In 1813 an American, Captain David Potter, raised the

United States flag and attempted to claim the island for our government. However, nothing was done about it, and today there is only a lighthouse to mark the spot. This harbor is also where the hero of Herman Melville's novel *Typee* jumped ship to escape and live with the Islanders. The town of Taiohae is the administrative center for the Marquesan archipelago, though the town has only about 250 people. The French governor lived here in a very pleasant house on the hill. The local French teacher and his wife lived there also, and they welcomed all chance visitors. A small medical center, a communications office, and a jail made up the rest of the contributions form the outside world. Nearer the town, on the rocky beach, was the warehouse where the copra was collected and stored.

A footpath leading to the village passed through the shade of trees with magnificent red blossoms. A huge mango tree stood in the center of the settlement where the path divided. At this crossroads was the Chinese shop, freshly painted with a coat of bright yellow. This shop was important for two reasons. First, it had the biggest variety of items for sale. Secondly, because of its strategic location, it was the local meeting place. The porch was never empty of townspeople gathered to see the village life pass by.

Bob McKittrick, an expatriate from Liverpool, England, had his little shop on the path that follows along the shore. Bob's business was to dispense cold drinks, tobacco, and other earthly pleasures along with all the trans-oceanic gossip. The crews of most boats sailing across the Pacific stopped here to tell Bob what was new. He stored this information for the next visitors and exchanged items of interest. He was one of the few island subscribers of *P.I.M. Pacific Islands Monthly*, which was printed in Australia. It covered the stories of sailors plying the Pacific and related their successes, their traumas, and their disasters, so that regular readers could follow the course of maritime human events in this vast area. Bob could chatter on about all those whose names appeared on these pages. He advised and warned all those just beginning about the trials ahead of them. His favorite stories were of those who came to seek paradise and wrecked their boats, if not their lives, in the quest. It did not seem like a small percentage.

I had decided to spend a night ashore in Taiohae, as the *Vaitere* was scheduled to return the following day. There was no tourist facility, of course, so I found a vacant hut that was open to all the breezes. It was actually a social center with a solid wooden floor. I hung my clothes over the railing, which was all that offered me any privacy, and slipped into my sleeping bag. When I awoke in the morning, I was agonizingly surprised. My shorts were gone. These were only a pair of Levi cutoffs, but they were the only shorts I had. I was devastated. I knocked on the door of the Governor's Mansion. He was surprised to see me so early in the morning. He asked why I hadn't told him I was on the island and why I hadn't stayed with them in his house. It seems he always went down to the dock at the arrival of any boat to meet and greet whoever might have arrived. I had not come ashore with the first load of passengers, so he had no idea that I was on the boat or on the island. I told him of my loss and how frantic I was with no local money and no ticket for the boat. My passport, most of my traveler checks, and most of the other vital items were in a money belt that was safe with me in the sleeping bag. There was some radio contact with the *Vaitere*. The pants were easily identifiable, and I trusted that they would be found quickly by the Gendarme. I knew that it was the shorts that were stolen, not the contents of the pockets. The major problem was that the *Vaitere* was not going to return to Taiohae, and I would be stranded in the Marquesas unless I walked overland to the next port of call. So I had to start on my day-long trek over the mountain ridge. Fortunately I had left the backpack aboard the boat.

Back at the crossroads under the mango tree, the fork in the path climbed quickly up towards the peaks and into the center of the island. From a clearing on the ridge I had a magnificent view of the great harbor below. It was a treat to see so much natural beauty without the intrusion of banal man-made structures. During World War II the harbor had been used briefly by Allied shipping, but there had been no time for development.

Under a lone tree on the ridge, the trail divided again. One path led to the interior and came out on another side of the island at the settlement of Atiheu (ah tee HAY oo), a day's walk away. The other path led down a rugged trail to Taipi Vai (tie pee VIE). Fortunately, I met a man on a horse who stopped to chat a while. He assured me that I was on the correct trail, so I proceeded down towards a village on the harbor. From a clearing I could see the *Vaitere* below, so knew I would be able to get back on board. This time they would be expecting me.

I eventually entered the village from the land side, rather than coming from the shore. I surprised the residents. The first to notice were the children. Decades earlier, the hero in Melville's book was greeted the same way as I was. At first it was surprise. Then it was guarded interest, and finally friendship. Strangers just don't go walking around these islands alone surprising villagers. In times past, I could have wound up in an *umu* (underground oven), roasted, and served as "long pig."

Taipi Vai was a small town that seemed to be much like the ruins I had seen near Atuoana, but here, modern huts had been built atop the *paepaes*. That was the only remnant of their ancient traditional life that I saw, except for the underground cooking. I headed up to the temple compound. It consisted of a large stone platform, perhaps 20 feet by 20 feet. Apparently there was a large structure here at one time. It was the place where pregnant women awaited their time. Once they arrived, they were considered taboo. A quick survey of the area revealed half a dozen uninteresting weather-beaten tikis, further damaged by someone with a hammer and a vengeance towards the ancient gods. As I walked back through town, I passed between stone walls that surrounded each home, separating their private plots. These walls were the first such that I had seen in the islands so far, except for the one Fred Johnson showed me around his ill-fated garden.

I was welcomed into a home where preparations for the main meal were being made. A young man with a pair of bamboo tongs was removing the cover of hot rocks from the *umu*, which had been baking for hours. The tongs were made by folding in half a strip of green bamboo. Volcanic rocks are used because they retain the heat longer. Since there was no other kind of rock available, it was a lucky circumstance.

My host then removed some grapefruit-sized breadfruit from the oven. He had peeled off the outside rind with a sharpened bamboo blade before putting it in the oven. He mashed the steaming pale yellow flesh in a wooden trencher with a stone pounder. When the mass was the consistency of sticky mashed potatoes, he opened three leaf wrapped packets and mixed in the purple colored contents. These were the smaller wads of fermented poi poi that would add the tangy flavor. Men always made the poi poi. That was one of the taboos that had not been discarded. Men also did most of the traditional cooking, especially in the underground oven. The new-fangled method of using pots was considered women's work.

Another utensil at hand was a fist-sized cowrie shell, ground to a sharpened edge, for scraping off the tough outer rind of the taro root. There was also a store-bought, serrated metal coconut grater for making coconut cream. The other tools in his hut were two long poles used to pull the fruit out of the trees and a pick axe. In another corner were a saddle and a drum of kerosene. Hanging from the roof were leaves of drying tobacco. The young man told me that when the village was preparing for a feast, he would saddle up his horse and go out hunting for a wild cow, some pigs, or goats. It was here that I willingly traded a yellow nylon shirt for three old stone adzes in varying stages of development, a baseball-sized stone with a groove around it used as a fishing net weight, and an old poi pounder with a chip on the handle. Once I got back on board the boat, I was reunited with my cut-offs, to our mutual relief. The man on the horse I had met on the mountain had been appointed to catch up with the boat at the copra stop.

The part of the island of Ua Pou that we saw was drier than the other islands. It had been eroded into an extraordinary landscape, leaving soaring towers of bare rock. It had the barren look of having been hit with an atomic bomb. Near the rocky beach, scrubby bushes and plants held down the dust. It was noticeably hotter than the other islands due to its barrenness.

The *Vaitere* lay offshore, as there was no dock at Ho Hoi. The trip ashore in the longboat was fantastic. The open sea was relatively calm, but as the gentle waves approached the shore they were concentrated into ever higher swells. Fortunately there was little weight in the boat with only a few passengers, so we rode atop the crest of the chosen wave as if on a surfboard. We were carried right up onto the steep shore, where we hopped out. The surf crashed onto the stones with considerable force. All the stones were polished smooth from the constant pounding of the water rubbing one stone against another. A couple of crewmen had to hold the lifeboat in place. Meanwhile the island men formed a chain and carried bags of copra to the boat.

The whole loading operation would take about an hour, so I had time to do a watercolor of the scene. Before the whaleboat returned for the second load of copra, bags had to be weighed, recorded, and checked off. Weighing the sacks required the shoulders of two sturdy men to support the heavy, ancient, balance scale. Two sacks at a time were hung on the hook. The men stood tall, and the weight of about 130 pounds was noted. Then the next two sacks were checked off. A pile of these was made ready at the landing spot for the return of the rowers. Between loadings, the families relaxed in the bright heat of midday. There was no shade.

Two little boys played on the steep shore of fist-sized stones. One had a sheet of metal, and the other an old board of plywood. After a wave had surged up on the rocks, they ran and belly-whopped onto the wet stones, sliding into the swirling water. They scurried back up to safety just as the next breaker smashed onto the stones again. There did not seem to be any close adult supervision of their activity, which to me looked extremely risky.

With half a dozen others, I had to return to the schooner while sitting astride the last load of copra sacks. I had some concern for the size of the waves coming regularly onto the beach. A wave came with enough water to lift the heavily loaded lifeboat. The coxswain shouted "Now!" The Islanders gave a mighty shove and pushed us into the water as the crew dug their oars into the swirling remains of a big wave. The crew took two or three strong strokes. We had gained some forward motion. Suddenly, dead ahead of us was another high wall of water. It was the only time on the entire trip that I closed my eyes to prevent seeing the inevitable. If the surging water caught us underneath, it could very easily flip us end over end, crashing us back onto the beach. However, the sheer weight of the load and our forward momentum made our boat too heavy to toss. Instead, we went right into the crest of the wave. For a split second we were bathed in water and spray. I was certain that we had turned over. When we came through the other side we were all completely drenched. Quickly the crew rowed us beyond the breaker line to the open sea. The endurance that the seamen showed that day in the performance of their tasks, and their handling of the boat, won my undying admiration.

The *Vaitere* also acted as an inter-island school bus. It was time for a new semester to begin, so the children had to be taken from their homes to where the schools were located and where they would live until their next vacation. They all seemed to be excited about the voyage. As they were not to be on board for a long time, no one had thought to supply them with sleeping mats or bed clothes. In the morning, I saw half a dozen little girls, all in pink uniform dresses, huddled together in a corner of the cargo, chilled through from their night spent on the open deck. For breakfast they all received an enameled bowl of coffee and milk, a chunk of baguette, and a dab of jam. This meager offering, and the sun, soon warmed up their spirits. They all disembarked at the next stop.

Our last stop on the island of Fatu Hiva was at a little village called Omoa. The houses were all made from Canadian lumber and were the neatest and best cared for of any town we visited. I was shown a most interesting stone in the schoolyard. In ancient times this large stone had been in the river bed where there was waist deep water. Those people who had done wrong were punished by having to stand in the cool water and sentenced to grind adz blades by rubbing them in designated slots in the great stone. To begin, a piece of finely grained volcanic stone was crudely chipped into a general shape for an adz blade. It was handed to the wrongdoer who then had to spend many hours rubbing it into the groove until it fit. It was then ready to be sharpened by more rubbing so it could be used as a cutting tool, like a chisel. A chisel is hammered into the wood. An adz is secured to a handle and cuts into wood more like a hoe cuts into the earth. The grinding was tedious cold work, but blades were always needed for constructing homes or hollowing logs for *va'as*. Apparently human nature is universal, there never seems to be a shortage of wrong-doers.

A team of archeologists had been working in the interior, and because they were leaving, the town was putting on a dance. The performers came down to the beach dressed in their costumes. Both men and women had on kilts made of long, thin, dark green leaves with yellow blotches, much like aspidistra. Around their necks the men wore a traditional palm leaf or a banana leaf. The leaf had been split through the mid length of the center rib so that when put over the head, half of the leaf covered each shoulder like a wide floppy collar. The women had bras of yellow tapa cloth. All of them wore crowns of fern and flowers on their shiny black hair. They sat on the beach in several rows. The band began to play. It was a single musician with two sticks beating on a square tin can that once had held dozens of dry biscuits. In olden times, it would have been a small hollowed log of hardwood. He was good, and he was loud. Most of the dance was done while the group was sitting cross-legged on the sand of the beach, moving their upper bodies and their arms in rhythm to tell the story.

When the singing and dancing had concluded, a young *tane* and *vahine* stood up, and the others formed a circle around them and clapped to the tempo of the drummer. The pair danced their version of the rapid-fire Tahitian hula, the *papeo*. They had more enthusiasm than talent, but as entertainment it was great fun.

It was time to depart. As we walked to the edge of the shore, the villagers followed us to the longboat. This time there were no sacks of copra on which to sit. The passengers going on the *Vaitere* got into the boat, and then we saw two huge men coming towards us with a trussed-up live pig hanging from a pole on their shoulders. Another pair carried the largest sun-dried octopus I had ever seen, which measured close to five feet between leg tips. Others carried live chickens. Many brought baskets of coconuts, bananas, or breadfruit as presents to bid farewell to the visitors and the archaeologists. As the produce and the passengers got into the lifeboat, those staying on the beach sang their farewell song. The crew pulled on their oars through the mild surf out to the waiting schooner. It was not long before the motor chugged, and we were underway. Those left standing on the shore waved and called after the fading ship. We, in turn, watched the island sink into the eastern horizon. The *Vaitere* was again headed for the Tuamotus, and to Tahiti beyond.

I was the only passenger to make the entire cruise amongst the Atolls and Marquesas. On deck were the full compliment of new passengers and their gear. The animals that were to be our fresh meat supply were shoved into the space in the bow. Palm leaf baskets of oranges, papayas, and pomplemouse were stacked on the deckhouse roof. A hundred or so bunches of green bananas had been tied to the railings. We stopped at the same two atolls and left half of the fruit at each. When we returned to Tokopoto, the woman who had made the cruise around the Marquesas with us got off. She had disembarked at every stop and everyone seemed to know her. She seemed to know the members of the crew very well. Perhaps she was just taking a cruise to visit friends. However, with nothing more solid to go on but speculation, I guessed that she was making the voyage to further her career as an itinerant tart.

After three more days of ocean sailing with the benefit of "the trades," Papeete was a welcome sight. It brought to a close the return trip, which was rougher and wetter than I had expected. But for me, it marked the beginning of another opportunity to explore more of mankind's dream islands of the Pacific Paradise. I had plans to continue westwards below the equator.

Once on shore, my first stop in Papeete I stopped in to see my friend Mme Jacquimen at her tourist office. My next stop had to be the Police Station. I needed to get a document from them to show that there were no outstanding citations or warrants against me. I had to report to the British Consulate, which handled the affairs of New Zealand in Tahiti. My next planned stop was to be Samoa, which was a protectorate of New Zealand. Samoa is another group of Polynesian high islands to the west of Tahiti and just east of the International Dateline. Then I planned on continuing to Fiji, which was a British Colony. I needed to get my passport properly stamped for my arrival in Apia, Samoa. I also needed another stamp for a visa to visit Fiji. I had to show the Consulate that I had sufficient funds to cover my expenses while I remained in Samoa and Fiji. I had a plane ticket that would guarantee onward passage to someplace where I had a visa to land, which was Fiji, and New Zealand, before my visa to Samoa expired. I showed the Consulate my PAA ticket for a value of a trip half way around the world. The man in the safari suit flipped through my resources, and with a grumble said his customary, "I didn't know there was so much money in the world," and bid me "Bon Voyage."

Next, I went to the TEAL office to purchase my airplane ticket to Samoa and further on to Fiji with the PAA ticket, now that I had the visas. I stopped at the Banque de France to show them my visas, my onward bound ticket for the flights, and my clean police record. I collected the deposit I had been required to leave with them in November to guarantee my departure. With all the bureaucratic problems solved, I was now free to go to Punaauia to spend a final farewell with my friends there.

My friends had their same problems. They were still without solutions, trying to deal with a bureaucratic administration that would not bend in any way. They had not been granted permission to open a business in Tahiti, sell the copper, or sell the boat. They had to use much of their funds to repatriate the two Peruvian sailors who had accompanied them to Tahiti. Since there were only infrequent westbound flights out of Tahiti, the sailors had to make a circuitous route to Fiji, then to wherever a connection to Peru could be found. Not an easy, or cheap, ticketing job. My friends could not leave the boat in Tahiti and go back to their homes. With tears, kisses, and a lot of "Best Wishes," I caught my flight. As I looked down at the lovely jewel island in its surrounding lagoon, I realized that Tahiti is a tough place to make a mistake.

I boarded the plane on 22 February, George Washington's Birthday.

ILLUSTRATIONS OF THE ISLANDS OF TAHITI

PHOTO 1. AIR VIEW OF THE ISLAND OF TAHITI.

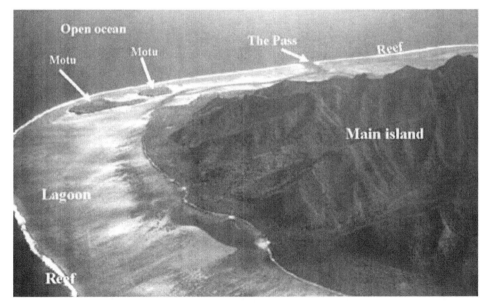

PHOTO 2. SCHEMATIC MAP OF TAHITI.

PHOTO 3. THE TWO-MASTED SCHOONER *TE VEGA*, AT THE PIER IN HONOLULU.

PHOTO 4. L TO R: THE BOATS *TRES DAMAS, YASMINE,* AND *HAPPY RETURN* IN PAPEETE HARBOR, TAHITI. (LARGE BOAT ON FAR R IS UNKNOWN.)

PHOTO 5. CHINESE SHOPS IN PAPEETE, TAHITI.

PHOTO 6. CAMIONNETTE OR "LE TRUCK," A LOCAL BUS, FOR AROUND
THE ISLAND TRIPS, IN PAPEETE.

PHOTO 7. OWNER PAINTING A TAHITIAN FARE (HOME).
A TYPICAL TAHITIAN FARE IS MADE OF SPLIT BAMBOO AND THATCH.

PHOTO 8. AN EARLY MORNING FISHING PARTY ON THE ISLAND OF HUAHINE.

PHOTO 9. AN OUTRIGGER CANOE AT UTUROA, RAIATEA ISLAND.

PHOTO 10. COASTAL AND INTER-ISLAND WATER BUSES, OR "CHUGGERS," AT UTUROA.

PHOTO11 MARKET SHOPPING HANGING FROM CHUGGER SHELTER.

PHOTO 12 CHRISTIAN COCONUT PLANTATION MANOR HOUSE.

PHOTO 13 AUTHOR GRATING COCONUT FOR COCONUT CREAM

PHOTO 14
ELIZABETH CHRISTIAN WITH SON CHESTER
AT THE GRAVE OF FLETCHER CHRISTIAN,
DESCENDENT OF THE FLETCHER CHRISTIAN,
AN OFFICER ON HMS BOUNTY, FAMOUS FOR
"THE MUTINY ON THE BOUNTY."

Photo 15 Mount Temanu, Bora Bora.

Photo 16 Home of the large Bora Bora family where I stayed.

PHOTO 17 FLOUNDERING CHUGGER ON THE WAY TO TAHA'A.

PHOTO 18 VILLAGE OF PATIO, TAHA'A.

PHOTO 19 MAMA!!!
(PICTURE OF A BABY IN A BASIN.)

PHOTO 20 FAMILY GRAVES BETWEEN THE TWO *FARES*, TAHA'A.

PHOTO 21 SEASIDE VILLAGE TAHA'A.

PHOTO 22 LOOKING TOWARD BORA BORA ON THE DISTANT HORIZON.

PHOTO 23. HEATING THE STONES IN THE *UMU*, AN UNDERGROUND OVEN, AND LEAF MATS TO COVER THE FOOD.

PHOTO 24. FOOD BAKING IN THE *UMU*: BREADFRUIT, BANANAS, AND FISH.

PHOTO 25. THE GROUP FROM THE BOAT *TRES* DAMAS. PUNAAUIA, TAHITI.
L TO R: PETER, DAN, SUSAN, ODETTE, ARTURO, AND BEA.

PHOTO 26 AN ANCIENT MARAE, (RESTORED) TAHITI

PHOTO 27. TOKOROA ATOLL IN THE TUAMOTU ISLANDS.

PHOTO 28. AN ATOLL BEAUTY WEARING THE
LATEST PARIS FASHION ON TOKOROA.

Photo 29 *Vaitere* delivering bananas to Tokopoto Atoll

Photo 30 The edge of the reef of an Atoll

PHOTO 31. THE VAITERE IN THE MARQUESAS.

PHOTO32. DECK CARGO ON THE VAITERE

Photo 33 Two of the crew soaping up for a bath at sea.

Photo 34 Butchering a goat for lunch. (Butcher facing port side of boat.)

PHOTO 35 THE GRAVE OF PAUL GAUGUIN,
HIVA OA ISLAND, MARQUESAS.

PHOTO 36 AUTHOR AND THE TIKI AT PAU MAU, HIVA OA.

Photo 37. Boy with model boat

Photo 38. 44-gallon oil drum used as bake oven for bread and fish

PHOTO 39 REMOVING FRESH COCONUT MEAT FROM THE SHELL IS A FIRST STEP TO MAKING COPRA.

PHOTO 40 WEIGHING THE SACKS OF COPRA.

PHOTO 41. LOADING THE SACKS ONTO THE LONGBOAT IN THE MARQUESAS.

PHOTO 42 CREWMEN ROWING CARGO OUT TO THE VAITERE.

PHOTO 43 VIEW OF MOOREA FROM COOK'S BAY

PHOTO 44 DANCE GROUP AT MOOREA LUAU.

PHOTO 45. WE HAVE LOVELY BUNCHES OF COCONUTS

PHOTO 46 DANCE COUPLE AT MOOREA LUAU

PHOTO 47 LARGE FISH CAGE TO KEEP BAIT FISH ALIVE DRYING OUT ON LAND.

PHOTO 48 FISHING NETS HANGING FROM TREE TO DRY.

PHOTO 49 A VANILLA VINE CLIMBING UP A COCONUT TREE.
(PICTURE FROM TAHA'A, SOCIETY ISLANDS.)

PHOTO 50 RIPE PODS HANGING FROM A CHOCOLATE TREE.
(PICTURE FROM UPOLU ISLAND, SAMOA)

PHOTO 51 TWO *VAHINI* IN PAREU, WAVING *"AROHA."*

PHOTO 52 TWO *TANE* IN SPORTS STYLE PAREU.

PART TWO

1.   The apostrophe (') between vowels in a word like "*va'a*," requires a quick stop between the sounds of the two vowels, "VAH 'ah," (as in "HA ha!") an outrigger canoe.

2.   In general, each consonant is followed by a vowel and makes a separate syllable, such as in the word for a Samoan hut, *fale. Fale* is pronounced "FAH lay." It would be similar to the two syllables, nearly rhyming with the English word "fol ly."

The Samoan alphabet had only 15 letters: A, E, I, O, U, F, G, H, K, L, M, P, S, T, V. Looking up something in a Samoan dictionary was not an easy task. Because of recent Westernization, the letter "n" may have become popular and currently included.

* * *

Some Instructions on Samoan Pronunciation

** <u>The Following Examples are for the Pronunciation of the Samoan SOUNDS only.</u> **
The letter "a" almost sounds like the English "ah" as in the expression "Ah choo."
The letter "e" almost sounds like the English "ay." Our word "be" would become "bay."
The letter "i" almost sounds like the English "ee." Our word "hi" would become "he."
The letter "o" almost sounds like the English "oh." Our word "to" would become "toe."
The letter "u" almost sounds like the English "oo." Our word "but" becomes "boot."

A Samoan faced with our simple word "pineapple" has problems. We pronounce the "i" in "pin" different from the "i" in "pine." To a Samoan "pine" would be "PEE nay." For "apple," we say "ah pull." A Samoan would pronounce it as "ah PLAY" or 'AH play." He might pronounce "pineapple" "PEE nay ah play," or, "pee NAY ah play," or, "pee nay AH play," or even "pee nay ah PLAY." The only difference to a Samoan is which syllable to accent. This is only an example, it is not a test.

For those who are interested, here are a few hints about the pronunciation of some special Samoan words used in this text. It might enhance your understanding to be aware of them. This is for sounds only. In the original alphabet the letter "g" makes an "ng" sound as in the English word "sing." For the reader's benefit, I will spell the words with the "n" before the "g" for the "ng." sound. But this is incorrect. Some examples: a'iga = a'inga, Palagi = Palangi, Siga= Singa, malaga=malanga, Pago Pago = Pango Pango etc. When the "ng" does not appear and the "g" stands alone, the reader will know that both ways are correctly spelled. They may have added the letter "n" to their alphabet since independence in 1962, as they were becoming more westernized.

Samoan Words Used in the Text and Their Meanings

These vocabulary words are from the memory of the author who apologizes for mistakes.

A'iga: A family group

Alu fe'a: Where are you going, Hello, Hi

Apia: Biggest town in Samoa

Au: The tattooing needle

Fa'a Samoa: Traditional way of life

Fale: A typical domed Samoan home

Fa lave lave: Too much trouble

Fale vau: Outhouse

Fafetai tele lava: Thank you very much.

Fiafia: A good time, a festival

Falese'ela: The village where I lived

Lali: Drum made from a hollowed log.

Lavalava: Most common garment, sarong

Malae: Village green

Malanga, (Malaga): A pleasant walking trip

Matai: Head of an *A'inga,* or family group

Maneuia: Nice, good, delicious, Cheers

Paepae: Stone foundation of a *fale*

Pango Pango, (Pago Pago)): Largest town on Tutuila, American Samoa

Palangi (Palagi):   Caucasian, or European

Palusami: Creamed taro greens, spinach

Pe'a: A man's body tattoo

Pisupo: Canned corned beef

Pu'a'a: Pig

Savaii: Second biggest island of Samoa

Siapo: Tapa cloth made from tree bark

Siva : Individual's own hula dance form

So'a: A young man's best friend.

Solulufinga: "Haven for the Abandoned"

Talofa: Aloha, Love, Hello, Good-bye

Tane: (TAH nay boy or man)

Teine: (TAY nay, girl)

To fa, soi fua. Good luck. Cheers, Here's to you, and, Good bye.

Umu: Underground oven.

Upolu: Main Island of Samoa

Va'a: A dugout outrigger canoe

Chapter XI
A BIT OF SAMOAN HISTORY

The Samoan islands are situated southwest of Hawaii and south of the equator. They are just east of the International Date Line and almost touching it. They are more or less halfway between Tahiti and Fiji. The modern nation of Samoa is made up of the two major islands of Upolu (oo POE loo) and Savai'i (sah VAI ee, as in Hawaii) and a few other minor isles. These two larger islands are where the following narrative took place in the middle of the twentieth century. Since sources vary on the history, I apologize for any errors.

Perhaps the islands were first settled as early as two thousand years BCE. At some point the Tongans, their Polynesian-Maohi neighbors and cousins located some 600 miles to the south, invaded Samoa and defeated them in battle. The conquest was followed with a harsh rule. However, the Samoans made an opportunity to defeat the Tongans, so their domination did not last long. The Tongan expedition returned to their own islands.

In 1722 the Dutch explorer Captain Jacob Roggewein was the first European to discover the Samoan Islands. The ships lay off shore, and the Dutch did not stay long. Apparently the Samoans canoed out to visit the ships. It was later recorded, "They are friendly in their speech and courteous in their behavior with no apparent traces of wildness or savagery. They are altogether the most charming and polite natives we have seen in all the South Seas."

In 1768 the French explorer Louis-Antoine de Bouganville also stopped. He named them the Navigator Islands. Apparently the Samoans canoed out again and there was a bit of friendly interaction, perhaps some trading in fruit and small ship-store items.

In 1787 another French explorer Jean François de la Perouse, apparently let some come aboard the ship, or some of the shipmates went to shore. A Samoan was suspected of stealing something, and was strung up the ship's mast. The Samoans were accordingly upset, and they attacked. A dozen on each side were killed. It was recorded, "(The natives) are a barbarous people, a stay of 24 hours and the relation of our misfortunes has sufficed to show their atrocious manners."

Obviously this was a severe case of culture clash. What the unreasonable French considered "stealing" the Polynesians considered "sharing," which was their custom. Due to this misunderstanding, a tragic event was recorded and long remembered by both sides. This was a common European reaction approach to natives everywhere the Europeans went. The Europeans always had guns at the ready. Where was caution when it was most needed?

In 1830 a missionary, John Williams of the London Mission Society (L.M.S.), arrived on the shores of Samoa and began preaching the word of God to the Islanders. He was dressed in tropical whites and, with his light complexion, he was a strange sight to the local people. They called him a *papalangi* (pah pah LAHNG ee, white cloud). This was then shortened to *Palangi* (pah LAHNG ee), which was the name the Samoans then applied to any Caucasian. The name "European" is also used for any light-skinned foreigner.

During the rest of the 19th and early 20th centuries the word was spread that the people of Samoa were in need of Christianization. Missionaries of a wide variety of sects flocked there and went on a conversion rampage like nowhere else. Among them were Assembly of God, Congregationalists, Jehovah's Witnesses, London Mission Society (L.M.S.), Mormons, Pentecostals, Roman Catholics, Seventh Day Adventists, Wesleyan Methodists, and others. How this herd of clerical bullies all managed to cooperate with each other is hard to figure. But amongst them they set up little dictatorships and created their Warden System of Storm Troopers, who enforced the Blue Laws, the rules of behavior. It is my personal belief that this heavy-handed control was for no other purpose than for the missionaries' own devotion to personal power. But as they say; "The first hundred years are the hardest."

Various mission schools were established to teach the English language, along with the doctrine. After World War II, basic public schooling was organized by New Zealand, their colonial overseer, and many of the fanatical rules were gradually being ignored.

In May 2008, I received a copy of "The Blue Laws" set up in 1879 by the Council of Ariki's (chiefs) of Rarotonga, on the Cook Islands, neighboring Samoa. Samoans also had to live under similar laws. Keep in mind that $1 was a considerable sum of money for a normal local farmer type person to earn in those days and was worth a lot more then than now. Here are some of the more interesting laws strictly enforced by the Wardens in each village.

"1. Should a person steal an ox or a plow, he will be fined $40, of which $30 will go to the owner of the ox or plow, $5 to the *Matai* (chief), and $5 to the judge.

2. If a man takes another's wife he shall be fined $20 of which the *Matai* shall have one half and the husband the other half. If a woman shall take another's husband, she will be fined $20 of which the *Matai* shall have one half and the wife the other half.

3. If a man steals a pig, the thief shall pay four pigs like the one stolen. Of these, one will go to the *Matai*, one to the warden, and two to the owner of the pig. All who have eaten of the pig shall each pay twofold. If they have neither pigs, nor goods, nor money, they shall be put to work on the roads, burning lime, cutting firewood, or any other work the owner of the stolen pig shall desire.

4. The fine for stealing bananas, kumaras (yams), or pineapples, is $4. If two people are involved the fine is $4 each. For stealing coconuts, sugar cane, oranges, or coffee plants, the fine is $4. For stealing other articles than money, he shall also return four-fold, two parts to the owner, one to the chief, and one part to the warden.

5. If anyone drinks bush beer (from oranges, bananas, or pineapples,) the fine will be for the maker $10, for the drinker $5. If drunk on the Sabbath the fine shall .be $15.

6. Sabbath observance: There shall be no trading on the Sabbath. All avoidable work is prohibited. The sacredness of the day is to be recognized and observed. No one is to walk about from house to house while the people are in church, except to visit a sick friend. He may strengthen a *fale* against a hurricane. If a pig dies he may go get it and cook it. If a canoe is carried out to sea he may recover it. He may cook food for those who come from the sea, or a journey (*malanga*), and bring water if there is none in the *fale*. People who travel needlessly from one place to another will be fined $5.

7. The woman who does not cleave to her husband, and the husband that does not cleave to his wife, let these be fined $5 each if they quarrel and separate. If they have no money, the husband is to burn lime, cut firewood &c. The wife in that case is to make 5 fathoms of matting (one fathom equals about six feet.) in length and 2 in breadth. They must not be divorced when thus separating.

8. Children who leave their home. When a father has lectured his child for this wrongdoing, and the child does not pay attention, let him be made to do 5 fathoms of stone wall a yard and a half broad.

9. Children who strike a father or a mother will be made to do 10 fathoms of stone wall, and be put for two months in the stocks. If they repent they may be released.

10. Card playing is not allowed in this land. Any who break this law shall be fined as follows: the owner of the cards $10, the players $5 each.

These are only a few; there were several more.

During the latter part of the 19th century, the Germans appeared in Samoa, while the British still had a missionary interest there. The United States became interested in the Samoan island of Tutuila with the excellent harbor of Pango Pango and did not want to be left out of the rush to gain colonies. By the end of the century, the Samoans had been up against the meddling European armies of Britain, France, Germany, and the United States. Each foreign nation developed loyal followers who then quarreled among themselves. This gained the Samoans a reputation for being savage and warlike. All they really wanted was to be left alone.

A rivalry developed among the three major powers. In 1889 several naval vessels of the three nations were in the non-harbor of Apia, the main town on the north shore of Upolu, A fierce typhoon blew in. The British commander ordered his ships out into the open seas. The Germans and Americans preferred to remain in the lee of the island. When the British fleet returned, they saw the other ships on the beach. The treaty of Berlin, signed by the "Big Three" in 1889, guaranteed independence to the islands. However, the international interference continued, so the Samoans continued to squabble among themselves. In 1899 a second treaty was signed again in Berlin granting Tutuila to the Americans and Savaii and Upolu to Germany.

One typical story concerning the rigid Teutonic occupation was their thoroughness at managing their coconut plantations. The foreign occupiers had been told that a typical tree would yield about 50 coconuts a year. This, they reasoned, meant one nut a week. Therefore, they planted their trees in rows of 50 and built the collection wagons large enough to hold 50 nuts. With the crop thus scheduled, the methodical but inexperienced administrators set out to regulate the rest of the economy. Unfortunately they had not considered the facts of tropic life, such as when a sudden storm can rip off many of the riper nuts in minutes, delaying the next crop for weeks.

When World War I started, New Zealand sent its forces to occupy Samoa. The Germans were stripped of their colony. Then there followed a loose New Zealand administration of the islands until the next international conflict. After World War II the self-declared Samoan leaders felt themselves capable of autonomy. Even though few of them had any experience, natural leadership qualities, or education beyond Mission School level, they sought the prestige of high office. They argued their case with the New Zealand Administration. By this time the islands had become more of a problem than a benefit to the governing nation. Samoa was gradually heading towards independence. The United States also saw an opportunity to rid itself of Tutuila by offering the residents of American Samoa freedom to join their cousins in a single nation. But they refused. They felt themselves to be more advanced politically and economically. They still remembered the period of terrible subjugation they had suffered under a former conquest by the larger islands of Upolu and Savaii before the Europeans had arrived. They chose not to experience it again. Through it all, the older and more rural Samoans on the main islands clung stubbornly to their traditional ways. The younger generation was ready for change. There the matter stood in mid 20th century.

From the sea, Apia appeared to be a line of colorful small buildings that stretched along the northern shore of Upolu. A few two-story buildings neighboring smaller ones gave a broken tooth effect emphasized by a long row of low trees, and tall spindly coconut palms, wherever they had found space to take root. There were no scruffy warehouses or docks to mar the quaintness of the scene. In the background, the long volcanic ridge was covered in green jungle-like forest growth.

A matter of trivia: because of a bend in the International Date Line which runs north to south through the mid-Pacific, Apia is the last town in the world to celebrate New Year's Eve. Its twin city of Nuku'alofa, (directly south) in Tonga, occupied by cousin Polynesians, is the first town in the world to celebrate New Year's Day 24 hours earlier.

The 5000 or so inhabitants of Apia found their amusement in the single movie theater, which showed mostly American Westerns featuring "Kaupois and Intienes." They also seemed to enjoy thoroughly attending religious services, and there were many from which to choose, all competing with services and social functions to attract the faithful. Apia was a missionary town, and everyone seemed content to be in the hands of God. I arrived after much of the extremely fanatical and restrictive rule of the missionaries had begun its decline.

The post office and the ice cream parlor stood on opposite corners of the main intersection of the shore road. Both of these corners became the centers of social activity while the monthly supply ship was in port. Since there was no dock for the ship, it had to stay quite a distance offshore. A barge would have to go out to the ship, be loaded with manufactured goods from the industrial world, and be brought back to shore. The cargo was off-loaded by barefoot stevedores, and the barge was re-loaded, mostly with cases of bananas, sacks of cocoa beans, and copra headed for New Zealand and beyond.

The New Zealand airline TEAL landed in the lagoon several miles west of Apia twice every five weeks on its way eastwards to Tahiti and returning westwards towards the Cook Islands and Fiji. On these days the town was full of people from the outer districts who came in for a double treat of mail and ice cream. The delicious frozen delight from the dairy land of the southern hemisphere was the popular subject of discussion. While waiting for the mail to be sorted, everyone offered their opinion as to whether it was better to unload the ice cream from the ship in the morning when it was cool, but gradually getting warmer, giving it time to melt. Or was it better to wait until after the heat of mid-day and unload it as the afternoon was getting cooler, as it might not melt as fast? To the best of my knowledge, there was never any practical test run to find out. But then, once settled, it would end the joy of speculating about the matter.

Near the center of Apia was "The Club" for "Europeans," as Caucasians were called. These were primarily temporary visitors and the New Zealand Civil Service people administering Her Majesty's wishes. They ran the public clinic, the government offices, and the schools. They managed the branch stores of the inter-island chains that sprawl over half of the vast populated area of the Pacific. Except for Aggie Gray's Hotel, The Club was the only place in the colony where liquor could be served. Liquor was available only to those with permits. Temporary visitors could get a permit merely by applying to the police station. A few Samoans felt they were also fortunate to have this privilege. Those of mixed blood, who had chosen to be considered "European" for legal reasons, did so at the cost of losing their native rights to land.

Church control was as evident in this, as in other matters of daily life, as I was soon to find out. To most of them, religion was the most interesting topic to discuss with any stranger. It was the one I preferred to avoid.

The first person I met after arriving from Papeete, Tahiti, was Sam. He was half Caucasian and half Samoan. Sam worked in one of the business houses in town, and he rented rooms in his home to girls from the Catholic Mission. We greeted each other with "Talofa" and "Talofa Lava," the second more informal than the first. I inquired if he would rent me a room for a few days until I got my bearings. He asked me, "What religion are you?" After I declared that I was not religious, I noted that it was with some pretended reluctance that he agreed to rent, confirming, "But only for a few days." When money entered the conversation, religion seemed to lose its preeminence.

The house was built with a large central room onto which opened several small bedroom cubicles. Meals were served in the main room, where we would sit and chat in the evenings. It was here that I had the opportunity to read Margaret Mead's book *Growing Up in Samoa,* which the islanders considered great fun reading. Sam told me that the informants "had only told her what they thought she wanted to hear." But at least it gave me some clues as to what I might encounter while I was visiting.

Sam had tried to lose his identity by wearing white Bermuda shorts, long-sleeve shirts, and occasionally a tie. This contrasted with ordinary native male attire of a *lavalava*, which was a two-yard length of wide material wrapped around the waist hanging down almost to ground level. Men were otherwise generally barefooted and bare-chested. Sam spoke English very well, but he did not necessarily couple the words he used with his real thoughts.

Sam's wife was of similar background and temperament. She dressed European, which meant she wore simple off-the-rack frocks from the trader's shops. The Samoan women wore an outfit with an ankle-length skirt and what could pass for a matching knee-length frock over it. She served tea every afternoon at 4 o'clock, sometimes with bread and butter, sometimes with slices of cold boiled taro. She only wore shoes when she went out in the street.

"If you want to see the real *fa'a Samoa*," (FAH ah Samoa, Samoan way of life), Sam said, "you ought to go to Savaii. There they still live their primitive way of life and you will enjoy it." I expressed my doubts about getting along without at least a smattering of the local language.

"No problem," he assured me. "I will put you in contact with friends I have over there and they will help you." In answer to my question, "Do they speak English?" he replied, "Better than we are talking now." Thus assured, I found out that there were two boats a week to Sala'ilua (sah lah' ee LOO ah), the village Sam had recommended I visit first. On the map it is located in the southern third of the west coast. I then bought a small Samoan grammar book and a pad of watercolor paper and got ready for the overnight voyage.

Sam wrote a dozen notes of introduction to his trader friends in Savaii villages, on formal note paper with matching envelopes in very nice handwriting. They all had identical sentences in English requesting they show me the usual hospitality and help traditionally offered to all travelers. Each note ended with a sentence in Samoan, which I assumed was a personal greeting.

In spite of his aid and his wish for a good *malanga* (mah LAHNG gah, a walking journey), it was not hard to say good-bye to Sam. He was a person who would be hard to like. Even though I was parting this way, with his best wishes, I had a feeling of apprehension for having accepted his offer of help.

Chapter XII
THE ISLAND OF SAVAII

The distance between the islands of Upolu and Savaii is only about 15 miles, but between the ports of Apia and Sala'ilua it was about 60. Every trip between islands meant another trying experience by boat. The large majority of these South Seas water buses were uncomfortable, unclean, and by all familiar standards, unsafe. Passengers and cargo were treated with equal unconcern for their well being. Everyone else on the boat was an islander, and as soon as they boarded they piled their bundles and children wherever there was space. There were no bunks, so every inch of deck space was jammed with great lumpy forms wrapped in colorful tropic print. It was hard to tell friend from freight.

The usual curious and well-wishing crowd had gathered along the quay to wave farewell. We left after dark and almost immediately were in rough water, where we were tossed around at random. It was to be another night of copra smells and belching black fumes from a cranky motor. I reflected back on the trips on the *Benicia* and the *Vaitere* out of Papeete, which now seemed like luxury.

The night air was clear but humid. This dampness was emphasized by an occasional far-flung spray of sea water that stung the face and made my clothes feel sticky. I had by this time been in the tropics long enough to become sensitive to the slight drop of temperature in the evenings. It was cold, and my teeth were chattering. It was going to be a very long night indeed.

The next morning as we neared the settlement of Sala'ilua, the water was smooth and clear. The white sands of the beach changed to pale browns as the weak surf spread white foam up to the roots of the coco trees. There were a couple of corrugated iron sheds under the trees. Jutting into the sea from the shore was a thin line of irregular black lava rocks barely breaking the surface of the water, to form a primitive jetty. I saw no other dock from which to load the freight. Barefooted stevedores trotted out on the slippery rocks carrying sacks of copra and returned to land with the cartons of cargo for the trader's store. When it was my turn to get off of the boat, I hoped I could be as sure footed as the others, or I would join the fishes I spotted in the water below me.

The only familiar-looking buildings were the crudely built trader's shop and his storage sheds, which looked more like garages. They had been painted at different times with different colors, apparently the leftovers from other projects. The only other structures in view were the neat thatch-domed huts of the islanders, their *fales* (FAH lays, two syllables). A *fale* is generally round or oval in floor plan, with a ring of posts supporting a roof that very much resembles a dome-shaped beehive. In fact, as I saw people stooping to go into their *fale*, it reminded me of the bees returning to their nest.

I had an instant of culture shock. Would I really be able to communicate with people so foreign in their ways as to live like this? Or should I return to Apia on the boat? Once upon the shore I put down my backpack, took some photos, and decided to give it a try. I noted a pair of parallel sandy tracks in the grass, which indicated that a vehicle of some kind was also on the island.

In an opening in front of the gracefully sweeping branches of a breadfruit tree, some men were at work building a *fale*. This offered me a chance to get out my water-color paint set and make a sketch of the framework already in place. To make the dome, the builders had set two poles, perhaps 15 feet tall, in the ground about a dozen feet apart and connected them at the top with a ridge beam. Onto this central beam they had attached three pairs of parallel slender poles that hung down in graceful arcs to within five feet of the ground. One set of three arcs hung down curving towards the water, the other set hung down curving in the opposite direction. Lashed to the outer surface of each of the three arcs on the same side were several horizontal cross pieces. It was reminiscent of a partial umbrella frame

On the ground nearby were two half-circle sections of roof framing that looked much as if they could be what supported a very large hoop skirt. They looked weathered, and appeared to have been parts of a previous structure. They had been carried here to this site by a team of five or six men. These would eventually be raised up and lashed with sennet to each end of the central beam, and also to the arcs already hanging in place. This would form the skeleton of a race track shaped oval dome. Sennet is the sturdy string made from braiding together small clusters of the fibers found inside the coconut husk.

Before any more could be done, a ring of sturdy posts about six feet tall would have to be set up in the ground to support the completed outer perimeter of the hanging dome frame. In reality, Samoans build their houses from the roof down, rather than from the ground up.

The next step would require the help of most of the other villagers. A lot of rocks, a foot or so in diameter would have to be collected to form an oval ring just outside the posts. These rocks form the *paepae* (pie pie) or outer rim of the raised floor level. The newly enclosed area will be filled in then with many basket loads of smaller stones to raise the floor level about a foot above the ground, to the thickness of the rocks. It will finally be topped off with loads of smaller pieces of white dead coral, or rounded black river stones to make a relatively smooth floor for the *fale*. The only source of rock available on the islands is from old lava flows.

The domed roof frame will then be thatched with hundreds, or even thousands of palm leaf shingles, each about a yard long and attached to the many cross pieces all around the dome. They will be layered for a thick rainproof covering. These shingles had already been made by the women during many evenings of group labor for the common good. The finished product will be a neat covering appearing to be in need of a slight trim around the bottom hem.

The final touch will be to hang a set of blinds between each of the posts. Each set of blinds consist of woven palm leaf panels about a yard long and a foot wide. Four or five panels are strung together in such a way that they can be raised or lowered easily by pulling a line of sennet, much like Venetian blinds. The *fale* will then be ready for the family to occupy.

I suddenly became aware that I had not been alone while sketching the construction site. It had taken no time at all for word to get around that there was a *Palangi* in town. This time I was the *Palangi*, and I had unwittingly gathered a cluster of children on-lookers on their way to grade school. Many of them greeted me with a giggling "Good morning," along with other odd bits of timid English such as "stone," "sand," and "water." I finished up my watercolor and put my stuff in the backpack. Much to my distress, the crowd of children jostled around me repeatedly shouting their few English words. I noticed that the little girls were much more eager to show off their language skills than the little boys, who appeared reluctant to get into the excitement with their classmates. Each child seemed to have learned a word that was special to her and they kept repeating it to me, pointing when they could to the object itself as they scrambled around me. Fortunately they soon tired of this game and dropped off and returned to their path towards the school.

As the group dissolved and went on their happily chattering way, I saw the boat depart and realized that I was now destined to stay on this island for at least a week. The town trader soon appeared. He introduced himself by saying, "*Talofa*" (tah LOW fah, Hello, love, good-bye, aloha.) I recognized that he was one of the people for whom I had been given a note of introduction by Sam, back in Apia. I handed it to him. He became most insistent that I accept his hospitality. He was, like Sam, a "half-caste" being only half Samoan, shortish, sloppy in dress, but reasonably well-spoken in English, which relieved me of some of my fears. We went to his store, and it became obvious that I was to spend the night with his family. I was somewhat crushed, as I had hoped to spend the night in one of the Samoan *fales*. Instead, I was shown a tacky room behind the store. In it was an ancient iron bed with a sagging mattress and an old wicker rocking chair. The rough wooden floor was still partially covered with well-worn and torn linoleum. Dirty ugly curtains sagged forlornly at the closed and cracked window. Cobwebs were everywhere. Dusty artificial flowers were stuck behind each of the pictures nailed to the robin's egg blue walls.

We gathered for dinner on the porch at a crude table and an odd assortment of chairs and benches. Instead of the fresh bounty from the land and sea, the trader's wife served *palangi* food unheated, directly from tin cans, onto enameled tin plates. The meal consisted of a can of *pisupo* (pee SOO po, New Zealand's corned beef, issued to their armed forces), a can of large sardines in tomato sauce, some uninteresting grayish mixed vegetables, and cold rice. They wanted to impress their guest that they had attained the level of modern day living of the outside world. I had come halfway around the world searching for a way of life that was different from that with which I was familiar.

Our evening discussion was on the general topic of American films and how bad they were for the Samoan people. The trader had a small generator which supplied the power for showing the pictures to the villagers. He owned the logs on which they sat to watch, and he collected whatever he could so he could rent the next film from the weekly boat. He told me frankly of the negative effect the films had on his neighbors. "It makes them want to leave the island and turns some into criminals, or at least made them want to be kaupois." He added, "You should make good pictures."

"And what do you consider a good picture?" I asked.

"Oh, films which tell the religious stories, and the story of Christ. Those are the only pictures I get for my people," he lied.

In the morning at departure time the trader stammered around the bush until he finally came to the point. "The note you brought from Sam said that you would be willing to pay a "pound" (New Zealand currency) for the night. Of course I don't want it, but perhaps something for the girls." I suddenly became aware of the little sentence in Samoan attached to the request for hospitality. This was the first inkling I had of the *fa'a Samoa*. I paid the price, but I was determined not to go that far over my budget again. I would use my sleeping bag from now on.

I got an early start along the sandy tracks northwards, which followed the shore line. The walk was very interesting, as all along the way I passed Samoans at their daily tasks. One group of three men were making a *va'a* by hollowing out a tree trunk. Two men, each with an adz, gauged at the wood, while one chopped with an axe. They had already done a lot of work so that the graceful lines of the *va'a* were quite evident. There was a nice covering of the fresh chips on the ground.

I asked them if I could take a picture with the camera hanging around my neck. Two of them protested, saying in Samoan and body language that they did not want to be photographed. One spoke enough English to tell me that it would bring them and the *va'a* bad luck. I showed them the paint set and paper and asked if I could draw them. That seemed to be a bad omen also. I suggested changing the colors of their clothing and that was considered to be all right, provided I did not paint their faces. I complied with their wishes, and when I was done, they came over to look at it. One of them asked me to give it to him. Unfortunately, these little paintings took an hour to make, and I did not want to leave it behind. He shrugged his shoulders and implied that it didn't really matter.

On the beach at the bottom of the cliff, some men stood motionless on the old black lava flow that stuck out into the water, their spears in hand, waiting for fish to pass. All of the men were dressed only in *lavalava*, (*pareau*) a sarong-type garment secured at the waist. These working men had folded them up into work-shorts length. Some were merely knotted to hold the cloth in place. Others were secured by a wide leather belt. I later learned that the belt was a social symbol, as it indicated prosperity and was an unchallenged possession of an individual in each family circle where everything else was shared common property.

The women were busy with more domestic chores, weaving mats, or baskets, or even wandering in waist deep salt water gathering up the creeping and crawling things from the sea bottom. Women also wear the *lavalava*, but they have different styles of securing it, depending on their tasks at hand. Some women had a curious large, black, circular collar-like thing around their neck and shoulders. It turned out to be the cloth covering of a broken umbrella. They had just made the hole in the center big enough through which to push their heads. Certainly no less restricting or more comfortable garment had ever been devised for the plump ladies who do their work in a tropic climate. Hats, a universal necessity in Tahiti, were noticeably missing here. Women near the water wore eyeshades, or a visor, made of woven palm leaflets. All work was divided into gender projects. Men catch, women collect. Both worked in the banana plantations and in the dry or swampy taro patches.

Chapter XIII
CHOW

It was getting near sunset, which I knew would be followed very quickly by darkness. A picturesque village was just up ahead out on a rocky cliff high above the surging sea, which was smashing itself on the solid lava rock. There was no beach. Almost everyone I had met so far that day during my hours of hiking had been most cordial in asking me to come in and rest, or stay a while. But now, with night approaching, I had to give the matter serious thought. From the shadow of one of the *fales* that formed a neat line along the track, ran a man calling; "Hey Joe! Come in for chow." For a second I wondered where the word "chow" had come from. I knew that a lot of young men who would otherwise not have had cause to leave their island, had been sent by their *matai* (mah TIE, chief, or head of the family unit) to Apia to earn cash while working with the Americans during their short stay in the early 1940s. This was a chance for the *matai* to command the customary obedience they expected from the younger men, and collect money at the same time. However, once free of the rule by the family boss, and with money to spend, these *tane* (youths) quickly learned that it was no longer necessary to obey blindly the traditional authority of their *matai*. Thus the breakdown of the social structure had begun. Their ability to maintain the new found freedom was graphically illustrated by their continued use of English, a foreign language that most of the *matais* did not understand.

I turned off the track and answered the call for chow. I was shown a post to lean against, in the front part of the *fale*, which was reserved for honored guests, and we settled down into conversation.

I must mention here that I was entirely dependent on having an English speaker present at any "conversation," although I was getting very good at universally understood body language. It would be a long time before I could use more than a dozen words of Samoan properly. I gradually collected a few basic words and let it go at that.

It was not long before an alarming rustle in a nearby frangipani, (a flowering bush) coupled with the screeching of a disturbed fowl, got my attention. It sounded as though someone was chicken rustling, but it caused no alarm and seemed to be forgotten. Perhaps a fowl had been having a bad dream and lost its balance on the perch.

My host asked me if I would like to take a bath. If so, we would have to pick our way down the cliff to the shore level where there was a freshwater pool fed by seepage from the rainfall on the mountain behind the village. Or, if I would prefer, we could go to the faucet in the middle of the village where I could take a shower. The small pipeline, which had just been completed, was fed from a cistern up on the hill. Although it greatly relieved the labor of the women who no longer had to go down the cliff to the natural spring to get every bucket of fresh water needed for the family, its main purpose, I was told chauvinistically, was so that the men wouldn't have to walk down, and back up again, to take their evening bath. During the daytime the women were also now doing the family washing at the faucet, which had so recently become the social center of the village.

The art of taking a bath at the public faucet, with no kind of privacy shelter, and with an audience of the most curious residents of the village looking on, was complicated. My host had loaned me a *lavalava* to wear while washing. To try to bathe in *Palangi* clothing would be hopeless. This facility put a new meaning for me to the term "public shower."

When we returned to the *fale*, we settled down again. Several men had come in and joined the circle sitting cross legged, tailor style, around a central kerosene lamp. Its golden glow highlighted the wonderful textures of rustic simplicity around me. In the center of the *fale*, I saw the rectangles of the woven pandanus leaf mats that covered the floor. Next, the ring of bare, lightly oiled upper bodies of the men glistened like new copper. Further back were the rugged black posts that held up the dome and the coarsely woven blinds that had been dropped to protect us from the cool evening breeze. High above, the exploring rays of light picked out the construction of the dome itself. There was nothing foreign to spoil this harmonious collection of evening patterns, except for the bright colors of the *lavalavas* that the men wore. I had at last found my Samoan *fale*.

From somewhere came the sound of a hollowed log drum. The group fell silent and an evening hymn was begun. From every *fale* the groups of voices blended into a pleasant choir beseeching only peace and praising the Lord for the good things life offered them. When the singing died down, a single voice rose up in prayer, and the responses echoed through the darkness of the night, assuring everyone that the entire village was unified in a common bond.

When prayers were over, a commotion in the rear of the *fale* made me aware that the women and children had been sitting there silently all the time. They were now preparing to serve the meal. Baskets made from woven green palm leaves for the food were pushed through the blinds, and the women selected pieces of roasted food and placed some on each of the woven palm-leaf trays in front of them. Meanwhile a youth passed around an enamel basin with water and soap, indicating I was to wash my hands and dry them on the clean towel. The water was changed continually as the bowl was passed around to all seated on the floor of the *fale*. The boy moved gracefully about his task, never rising above a squat. He had learned to serve without getting his head above that of the *matai* or any of the guests, nor turn his back on either.

When the washing ceremony was concluded, the same lad passed the rectangular food trays to each of the men present. On each tray there was half of a breadfruit and a baked green banana. Also placed before us was a tin plate with joints of the chicken that had recently been turned from sleep to stew. An extra tray of food had been fixed and was passed to the family next door in case they might have an unexpected guest. It was the duty of each family in the village to do the same as no one was ever to go hungry. We received a similar tray through the blinds on the opposite side.

After a short grace, the man next to me broke his piece of breadfruit in half and placed a piece on my tray. I realized that I now had to do the same for him. We had broken bread together and now we could settle down to the serious business of eating with our fingers. Breadfruit grows on a large tree and hangs from the ends of the branches. It is ripe even when still green, and picked. It is about the size of a cantaloupe, with a rough rind. It is peeled generally with a bamboo blade or large knife. It is cut in half when served. It is also mashed to make poi.

The breadfruit was hot and delicious. It is firmer, but reminded me of the fresh baked bread I used to savor at a New Hampshire farmhouse when I was a pre-teenager. The baked green bananas looked like charcoal and tasted like balsa wood. Inside the packets of charred green leaves there was something that looked like creamed spinach. It was very young taro leaves baked in coconut cream, which had formed into a custard. I found this *palusami* (pah loo SAH mi) to be one of the most delicious foods of the islands. Other packets of green leaves contained the entire bodies of lagoon fish, skin, head, guts, tail, and all. A deft touch is needed to remove the skin, scales, and fins. I listened to the sucking sounds all around the *fale*. The insides of the fish were relished by all, and the heads became mere appetizers for those inclined to suck out the delicious portions inside. I found that even the eyes had a delicate flavor. Well, when in Rome…

Glass cups were filled with a sweet watery brown liquid. It was native cocoa. The beans grew a few dozen in each pod, which had been picked from smallish trees up in the hills. The beans inside the pod were separated from the pulp, washed in the river, and then dried in the sun for a few days. They were then roasted over a low fire and coarsely ground so that bits of nut-like residue add something extra to the beverage. The only unpleasant aspect was that the job of adding the sugar was awarded to one of the children who always seemed to have an extra sweet tooth.

After a second wash-up, all the signs of food were removed to the rear of the *fale* where the women and children had been waiting patiently. They were soon satisfying their own hungers. There was plenty of food, but they were served last. The men had become focused now on the important business of becoming acquainted with their guest, while smoking their own hand-rolled cigarettes with locally grown tobacco. A light was obtained by calling a loud order to one of the younger children of the household who scurried out quickly to get a burning ember from the cooking fire. She carried it back in a coconut shell.

It was now my place to entertain the others gathered for the occasion. They asked questions to satisfy their natural curiosity on many points: my age (30), my wife (none), my family (parents and a brother and his family), my work (teacher), and why I had come to their village. All of it was friendly but embarrassingly probing. When they were satisfied that they had found out all they could about me, they asked me to tell them a story.

"What about?" I queried, ignorant about what they would most want to hear.

"About your island," the most fluent of the men suggested, as he translated for the others.

I reached over and pulled several colored postal cards out of my pack picturing New York City. As I passed them around, I told them about the buildings, the bridges, and various other indisputable facts about the city near which I had always lived. Each translation brought forth much mumbling. While looking at a postal of the New York skyscrapers, one of the men asked, "Why do you sleep standing up? Your houses are very tall, but not wide enough to lie down in." I then told them that each layer of windows was a floor, and that many of the buildings had 50 or 60 or more floors. Each floor is as high as a *fale*. That was followed with more doubtful mumbling. After several more parts of the story, they began to drift out through the sides of the *fale*. My surprise must have shown on my face, as my host said, "Don't worry! The old man says that you are a liar, and not to listen any more."

With only a few men left, the old *matai* asked me about my eyeglasses. Nothing is to be passed by hand to a *matai*, so I slid them along the mat to him. He put them on and then stared open mouthed at the wonders he beheld. He looked at me. He gazed at his friends. He stared at parts of the house. He examined his bare feet. He inspected his hands, turning them over and over again as if he had never seen them before.

The young man who had invited me into the house said, "My father wants them so that he may see. You will give them to him." My apologies were sincere, but I told him that that would be impossible. "He will buy them from you," he suggested. But reason won out in the end, even though the old man was gravely disappointed. It had been many years since the *matai* had begun to go blind, and the gradual decline of his vision had not bothered him until this moment when he realized it was possible that he could see again. I am quite sure that he never gave another thought to going to Apia and getting a pair of glasses of his own. Too much trouble, *fa lave lave* (FAH lah vay lah vay).

We retired into the mosquito net cubes that had been strung around in the *fale*. Catching the light from kerosene lamps or reflected from the moonlit sand of the path outside, these spooky rectangles seemed more like gossamer tombs over their sleeping occupants than shelters from insects. I was soon aware of the snoring of the sleepers from half a dozen *fales* and the yapping of a few dogs. The night noises also included the restless sleep of the semi-domesticated poultry, which clucked uneasily when the shadows of the flying foxes (large bats) passed overhead on their nocturnal raids for their favorite food, ripe fruit.

In mid-morning I was ready to continue my *malanga* (walk) through the villages strung along the northwestern shoreline of Savaii. All of the villagers had arisen at first cock's crow before dawn and had already done their domestic chores and some plantation labor in the cool and pleasant hours of the day. The first thing the men had done was start the fire in the *umu* (OO moo), the underground oven. Holes in the soil about a yard deep were lined with volcanic rocks. Dried coconut husks were lit to start the fires. When the rocks were hot, the leaf-wrapped packets of food were placed in the *umu*, and it was covered over and left to bake for hours, similar to a North American clambake. An *umu* was behind every *fale*.

About eleven o'clock the men begin to return home from their plantations up on the hill, or back from the sea. They were hungry for the big meal of the day, and the food was ready. After eating, the mid day was set aside for resting or more specialized tasks, such as repairing the fishing nets, community building bees, or tending to the drying of the copra or cocoa beans. By this time the women had already done the washing of the clothes and draped them all over the bushes to dry.

Around noontime I walked into the village of Samataitai (sah mah TIE tie) and was immediately spotted by a group of large women eating lunch in a large *fale*. This was the monthly meeting of all of the married women to discuss their part in the community projects for town maintenance. This day it was their pleasure to have an unexpected guest to give them honor and add some novelty to their meeting. I was summoned to come in and join them. Though their age range was great, I could not see one that had the attractive, more refined features of most of the Tahitian women. Size was a sign of wealth. It showed a man could afford to keep a woman who ate a lot and didn't have to work too hard. For some young man looking for a bride, a man with a large daughter was a good prospect for a father-in-law. Unattractive though this group of women was to my eyes, their hospitality and friendship were in proportion to their bulk.

I had to shake hands all around the circle and was pulled down several times into the laps of these buxom islanders as I continued the circuit. When meeting in the islands, no one rises from a sitting position. The islander's protocol demanded they stay seated and keep their heads lower than that of their guests. I noticed that a number of curious villagers were gathering around outside of the fale to see what was going to happen. It was probably the first time anyone ever had any interest in what the Women's Commmittee was doing.

Once I had been seated in the circle, a woven food tray was placed in front of me. Every eye was focused on me with an inquiring gaze to see what my reactions would be. I tried not to offend them. In this case, it meant I had to eat what had been put in front of me and say "*Maneuia*" (mah NOY yah, good, delicious). I tried my best to smile when I was eating a dish of soup made of the soft flabby flesh of shark's gum. There were still some tiny teeth in it. A swarm of ravenous flies tormented my delicate senses of sight, sound, and touch. A tawny *teine* (TAY nay, young girl) was quickly assigned to both my left and right side to fan the offenders away. Another pair reclined in front to fan my food. No potentate of an Arabian fairy tale felt his luxury any more keenly than I.

Another young *teine* was peeling an orange in a curious fashion that I did not think helped the orange any, but it took longer. She cut around and around with a great bush knife until an incredibly long corkscrew curl was obtained. The coil she draped around her neck, the orange she gave to me. She peeled a second orange and put the coil around my neck and she ate the orange. The many giggles that followed her coy peep through downcast eyes, made me realize how skillfully this *teine* had proposed a walk in the woods. Her selfishness had displeased some of the others, who rose and performed a *siva* (SEE vah, a Samoan hula). It was not long before I was pulled up onto the mats to perform for them. They are long used to entertaining each other, and I was obliged to do my part. Awkwardly I paid my debt to this gathering of the cream of Samataitai Society by attempting to do the role of the male partner of a *papeo* (Tahitian hula) I had seen just weeks before. Then I was ready to be on my way. I acknowledged their hospitality by saying, "Fafetai, Talofa," (fah fay TIE, tah LOW fah, Thank you, good-bye,) and departed Several of the young *tane* standing nearby on the sandy track who had been watching the gathering urged me in no uncertain terms to return and follow the lady of the oranges. "It's good. Betta try it," said one. After all, I hadn't had much ripe fruit since I had left Hawaii. I thanked him for his recommendation, and started down the track accompanied by several youngsters. I felt much like the Pied Piper.Gradually their interest faded. The first to drop out of the cluster were those children who had been given the responsibility of caring for a younger sibling and were carrying it on their hips. Soon I was alone again, strolling through almost jungle-like forested areas. I passed a deep gorge in the lava rock where the surf was being forced continually into the crevice, sending great surges of spray up into the air and making beautiful rainbows.

Chapter XIV
THE FALE OF UALOTU

A little further on I found I was entering another village, and the local warning system, the curious children, called attention to the fact that a *Palangi* was coming along the trail. As usual, the children gathered around, most of them fearlessly, to see what would happen next. I had spotted something I wanted to paint and settled down with my paint set to record it. I had hardly begun when I noted a middle-aged woman with a very pretty face supported by an awesome body shoving her way through the crowd. Her melon shaped breasts were only partially covered by a shrunken pink cardigan sweater straining against the safety pin that held it together. "Boobs" informed me that she had learned English because she had "married many Marines." Taking the word "married" to mean the loose informal relationships practiced by most Polynesians, I understood her point. Acting as interpreter for the gathering, she relayed all the information she got from me as accurately as she wished to the spellbound crowd.

With a suddenness that surprised me, she interrupted her discourse to order the boys to pick up my luggage and take it to the big *fale* nearby. The sky had literally burst open, and the shower had nearly soaked us all before I'd had time to get to my feet.

"This is the *fale* of Ualotu," (oo ah LO too) she said. "You can stay here, or please yourself." With the teeming rain, there was little choice. "Good, you can chow with us. Change, or you get sick."

I gave Boobs the two cans of *pisupo* that I had carried in my backpack to help with the dinner preparations. Without a word, she departed. The Samoans are so crazy about *pisupo* that after grace they often add, "Lord, we love you more than *pisupo* fried in onions," which is the supreme compliment. "Uma" (OO ma) means finished or done. "Uma lava" means really finished or completely done. "*Uma lava pisupo*" means as completely finished as a can of *pisupo*.

Ualotu, an elderly gentleman, must have been a very good man in years gone by. He came into the *fale* and seated himself beside me. In his hands were strands of coconut fiber and the coil of sennet on which he had been working. We had no conversation, as up to this time neither of us knew more than a word or two of each other's language. But friendship can be based on common interest. So, indicating that I would like to make some sennet, I was pleased that he was eager to teach me the craft. It helped pass the time and added to my storehouse of knowledge.

The making of sennet, or *afa*, was reserved primarily for the *matais*. As heads of the families, they were the ones more likely to have the time to produce inch by inch the miles of this essential cord needed in the daily affairs of the village. The *fales* and the boats would have been impossible without *afa*. It started inside the coconut. When the nuts were at a certain stage of development they were picked. The still-green fibrous husk was pried off of the hard shell of the nut itself. The green husk consisted of thousands of fibers, each about eight to ten inches long, which were mashed on a rock with a wooden beater. This separated the individual fibers. Bunches of the fibers were then taken to the sea and secured under a rock. They were left there for three or four days until they were clean. Later they were dried in the sun and, once cured, they were thoroughly separated and stored carefully until they were needed.

When a man sat down in the evening he grabbed a handful of fibers and placed them on the mat nearby. He picked up six or so, evened them out, selected another one, and twisted it around the small bunch, as he rolled it over his bare thigh. This little tight bundle was called a *"mui'a."* (moo EE ah) All of the older men showed a slight difference in their thighs. The one on which he rolled the *mui'a* was shiny. When there were dozens of these *mui'a* prepared, he would then proceed to braid them into a cord of *"afa,"* or sennet. Coils of *afa* were many yards long, weighed several pounds, and required months of patient work. These coils were the wealth of the village.

Among the visitors for dinner were two American Mormon missionaries. Leaning their bicycles against the stone *paepae*, or foundation, they entered the *fale* dressed in their uniform, of shoes, long pants, white shirt, and necktie. They were on Savaii because it was an inexpensive place for them to serve their two year pledge to their church. These islands staggered under a diversity of interpretations of the Bible by numerous sects of missionaries These two young men, vying for the attention and faith of the Samoans, were up against the professionals of the Catholics, Methodists, Seventh Day Adventists, Presbyterians, Baptists, the London Mission Society, and others.

One of the most numerous and plainly visible are the Mormon missionaries. They go to their appointed villages in pairs. (I don't recall seeing any female missionaries.) They cut quite a neat figure on the sandy shores of Polynesia. They come equipped with an adequate knowledge of the local language and their Book of Mormon. They were apparently encouraging another cycle of "dressing up the natives" as the missionaries did in the 19th century. It was not beneficial to the health of the Islanders, but it was a status symbol. It sets the convert apart from the rest, which was apparently the purpose. Because most of the Americans who were seen here were Mormons, the Samoans thought that all Americans were of that faith. When they asked me why I didn't dress like one, I felt it my duty to inform them that indeed the great majority of Americans were not Mormons and that most of us were ignorant of their beliefs. The Polynesians might well have thought that the *Palangi* culture was confusing.

These two were not the fine representatives of our people that I had hoped to find. Yet they had convinced the gathered villagers that they were outstanding students of the highest level of education that an American university had to offer. An example I would remember was when the more articulate of the two said to me, "We represent America in this here place, and I want you to act like me. We've got some of these here folk right where we want 'em. They're ours." The prospects of further conversation with them seemed grim, so I turned to speak halting English with the young attractive teacher on the other side of me. But I could not forget what the university student had said, and how he said it.

Boobs, the hostess at the party in the *fale* of Ualotu; was indeed doing a fine job. She suggested that I join her father in a game of "Sweepy." We played with a deck of old grimy cards of a vintage that I suppose dated them from the time of one of her "marriages" to the Marines. The object of the game seemed to be to match either the suit, or the number, of a previous card played, and yell "SWEEPY" with each victorious match.

Boobs asked if I would like to hear some Samoan music, and I agreed. Nearly a dozen boys came in through the back of the *fale* and began to strum guitars, ukuleles, a mandolin, a banjo, and two empty tin cans. One young man had brought two soup spoons that he clapped together. The music and group singing was a treat. The evening was progressing nicely. Everyone was mixing socially.

Eventually Boobs came up to me and cooed softly, "It is time to make your present."

"Make what present?" I asked, not a little surprised.

"Oh, you should give the boys each something, like a can of your meat. They have not yet eaten," she lied.

I well knew that no Samoan goes without eating at least once in the evening. My pack was empty of canned meat, as I had already helped to feed the family and their guests.

"Then money will do," she said with a note of disappointment.

"How much?" I queried.

"Oh, ten bob apiece would do." A "bob" was a shilling. That would have amounted to half a day's pay in an ordinary job in Apia. I reckoned that that was a little high with the entire group wanting equity.

"Oh well! Please yourself," she huffed, and strode away. I rejoined the players, and the music went on. Her own idea was to find out how much could be squeezed out of the American, remembering the good old days when the Marines didn't know any better.

In the morning Boobs asked if I would like to have some "pankaykees" (pan kay kees). Unaware of the adaptations that could be made on a word; I thought it a great idea. Watching closely to learn all I could, I saw blobs of a flour and water mixture dropped into a pot of boiling drippings. There they sat until they showed the slightest tint of turning brown, when they were scooped out and put on a plate to cool. The excess drippings congealed into white ringlets around the bottom of each pankaykeee on the plate. When properly cold, these golden globs of indigestion were served with some sickly sweet cocoa. Dunking them was the only way I could swallow them.

After breakfast, I had to go to the *fale vau* (FAH lay vow, outhouse). On the way, I picked up a freshly fallen breadfruit leaf that seemed to me to have the potential of being good toilet paper. It was soft and pliable. Before I could close the door, a young child came running out and handed me part of a coconut husk. I was supposed to use that instead. I had to think about it for a second and then realized that one takes some of the fibers from the husk and uses them for handy-wipes. Later I found out that the underside of the breadfruit leaf has thousands of tiny hairs that would have caused a great deal of discomfort if I had used it as planned.

Chapter XV
FALELIMA

The next town, Falelima (fah lay LEE mah), was seven miles away. The track, never very far from the shore, twisted its course through a bed of red clay, an overpowering growth of giant trees, vine tangles, and marvelous tropical plants. The very grandeur of this primitive jungle completely captured my imagination. Here was an island that had been inhabited for a score of centuries, and it looked even now as if people had only the barest foothold on the shores. The clearings that surround each village were the lands worked by the various families, though all of it was owned and controlled by the village *matais*. If cultivated land was not properly tended, it fell back into the village land pool. On the other hand, if a man needed more land he had only to clear it and it was his for as long as he wished to use it. But beyond the limits of these clearings, the forest is in control. The land belonged to nature.

I had reached only the first *fale* in Falelima when a young man called out to me. He offered me a rest and a cool drink, and we became fast friends. Faitalla (fie TAH lah, storyteller) was one of the two men teachers of the village who were living in the *fale*. The *fale*, their food, a boy to serve, a girl to wash, and a half a dollar a day, made up their wages. After finishing their free education course in Apia, they had been sent to one of the outer districts, where they must work for two years. Then if they wished to continue, a better post could be found. Many retired after this and settled down on a patch of land and followed the *fa'a Samoa*. But, for the time being, he was a light in the darkness of his country where compulsory education had only been instituted since the end of the World War II. The Department of Education was doing its best to teach its young people. If it stayed sympathetic with the traditional *fa'a Samoa* and could mix in some thoughts from the outside world, it would produce a contented society ... maybe.

The site of Falelima was wisely chosen by the ancient settlers. Placed on what was an ancient lava flow, the village had a natural protective seawall against the ravages of ocean storms. When the lava was in a liquid state, it formed a curved protrusion into the sea. There was a tiny cove behind it that offered excellent, if not expansive, protection for the storing and launching of every fisherman's *va'a*. The outer edge of the cove's barrier seawall was a natural feeding area for the fish, which could be speared or netted from the rock mass. But most important of all, on this peninsula of black lava rock was the outlet of an underground stream that flowed into several depressions, forming ever-changing freshwater pools.

In the late afternoon, the fleet of *va'as* was spotted on the horizon returning to the little cove. The first eight to arrive had been luckless. The ninth, some distance behind, was heavily laden with a rather large shark. Falelima was one of the few villages that still followed the ancient sporting pattern of the shark hunt. Equipped with only their *va'a,* a large sturdy noose of sennet, a bush knife, a small club, and a stick with a few halves of old coconut shells attached to form a rattle, the two-man teams paddled out into the open sea. At some likely spot, one of the men began to agitate the water with the rattle. If this failed to attract a shark, one of the men jumped overboard and flailed the water. Eventually the tiger of the seas, its curiosity aroused by the disturbance, prowled closer. Once a shark was spotted, it was up to the "bait" to get back in the *va'a* … fast!

They maneuvered the *va'a* into a favorable position. One fellow shook the rattle in the water, while the other one was ready with the noose. When the shark struck, the fisherman slipped the noose over the snout and pulled the fish into the boat. Instantly it was clubbed on the snout to knock it out. Meanwhile, the partner hacked at the backbone with the bush knife to sever the nerves and cut the muscles that control the tail. Otherwise, the shark thrashing around in the *va'a* would send them all into the sea. The shark was subdued in a matter of seconds, and the fishermen returned home victorious, one more time.

The others returned in convoy, as there was already enough food caught for that day. The catch would be divided amongst each of the families. The choicest pieces were doled out to those in the highest social position, and to the rest, according to their rank and need.

When a flock of a certain kind of sea bird was seen diving again and again into the water, the cry went out, "bonito." Every crew rushed for its *va'a,* launched it into the surf, and paddled furiously to where the birds were. This much-prized food fish was always accompanied by these aerial antogonizers that pecked their backs every time the fish surfaced for air. The only time the fish had peace was when the birds were scattered by the fishermen who tempted the bonito with hooks carved from mother of pearl shell that flashed enticingly in their midst. The sea provided, but the men had to prove to be cleverer than their prey.

At the end of the day, every *va'a* was carried up onto the tiny beach in the cove to dry out. The wives and mothers had come down from the town to greet their brave fishermen. Then the procession of villagers began towards the pools. The men got their soap, towels, and fresh *lavalavas.* The women had the same but with two or three children in tow. The lowest of the three pools was the least attractive. Though quite large and waist deep, the water was cloudy. The black rock of the side walls was stained with white streaks. This was the laundry pool, and a couple of chattering women were still squishing, slapping, and beating their clothes on the rock. Bare to the waist, they worked with determination. In spite of it all, the clothes always came out spotless.

A bit further up there was a nicer pool crowded with women scrubbing their younger children. Some ten yards in diameter, this one had the look of a public beach in summertime. Young children scampered around the edge, jumping in with glee, and climbing out again.

Bath time here was the best part of the day. However bath time for the very young came as often as four or five times a day. Whenever mother went near a water hole, the children, naked from birth to school age, took advantage of the pool. The less lucky older ones got a proper scrubbing with a handful of coconut husk fibers, sturdy as wire, but soft as a sponge.

All of the men stopped by the pool and greeted the bathers, patting their children, before walking over a few more yards to their own pool. It was a superb depression, perhaps five or so yards wide. The bottom was covered with white coral sand from the beach. A flight of several cemented steps led down into the chest-deep water, which was spring fresh and delightfully cooling after the heat of the day. This was one of the big rewards of being a "man" in Falelima. Traditionally, it was expected for a youth to get his *pe'a* (PAY ah, a, Samoan body tattoo) before he could be considered a man and be accepted in the men's pool. The rules had been gradually relaxed so that youths could graduate to the men's pool by becoming married and setting up their own homes. More recently, that had been modified so that they would be considered men when they left school and joined the men in their work. As a visitor, I was accorded this honor also.

The seclusion of the men's pool did not last long after I was invited to join them. Instantly there were the curious naked children squatting around the edge of the pool, their wet bodies glistening in the sun. Then a few of the partially draped women came to stare at the *Palangi* to watch how he bathed. The men remained draped in their *lavalavas*, which were uncontrollable in the water. It made washing themselves rather difficult. My walking shorts were rather immodest in their way of thinking, but more practical for the task at hand. The legs of a man were considered indecent unless they were tattooed Samoan style. The *pe'a* is a large project. It starts in the middle of the back, folds around the front of the belly, and covering the hips and buttocks, goes down covering the legs to just below the knees. When fully tattooed, boys became men. Theoretically, tattooed men were considered fully clothed even though they were wearing nothing else. (More later about the *pe'a* and tattooing, when we get to the island of Upolu.)

Back at the *fale*, Faitalla said that it was due time for me to become a Samoan and follow the *fa'a Samoa*. He handed me a bottle and told me to rub the light brown oil onto my skin, that it would feel good and keep me warm. The oil is obtained from the liquid of the crushed white meat of the coconut, which is mixed with aromatic barks and blossoms of many plants from the bush. Set in the sun to cook for several days, the semi-fermented fragrant balm is then bottled for daily use. Perhaps it was psychological, but I felt suddenly refreshed with a slight tingling glow all over.

Then I had a lesson in putting on the *lavalava* in the Samoan formal style. Faitalla handed me a piece of solid colored material some six feet long by about four feet wide. The longer top edge was folded under so that the width of the cloth fell from waist to ankle. Centered in the back, over a pair of boxers, with the two ends brought forward, and evened up, they were pinched together at the navel, and pleated from left to right two or three times until there was a panel of folds in the front about four inches wide. There were a few personal individual variations in the pleating, but they were all much alike. This would not stay on without a belt. Normally they wore a white cotton belt, which added a dash of contrast to the formal *lavalava*. "There! You are now a proper Samoan," Faitalla said with pride. The change of citizenship and race was comfortable and practical.

This Saturday evening we joined the other young men gathered on the *malae* (mah LIE, the village green). In the middle of the grass plot there was a long, narrow, rectangular cement slab flush with the ground where they played *kilikiki* (kee lee kee kee, cricket) introduced by the New Zealanders. Instead of a standard bat of wood, the trunk end of a coconut frond was often used to hit the pitched ball. I supposed the object of the game was to hit the sticks standing at the other end of the slab with the ball. In the cooler evening hours, this masonry slab radiated the heat it collected from the sun during the day and became a most pleasant place to sit and chat. Here important matters were discussed, fishing tales exchanged, and the girl situation assessed. This night the girls would have to wait a bit as there was an important visitor in town, and the young men had to learn everything they could about him.

They started with the religion thing, but by now I was prepared for their punch line, "Then you don't know God." It seemed to me that that was the only thing that they all had learned in common from the plethora of missionaries and their conflicting teachings. I often felt like challenging them by asking them "Well, what IS God?" But I was a guest, and I did not wish to start any kind of disagreement among the people who had offered me so much friendship and hospitality. Gradually as the evening chill became more noticeable, each one readjusted his sole garment so that it covered his shoulders and his back from the slight breeze. So draped like ancient Greeks, many of them drifted off, searching for whatever bit of good fortune they might find waiting in the shadows.

Walking back through the village, I was struck by the beauty of the scene; everything had been silver-plated by the brilliant moonlight. The waxy surfaces of the palm leaves glistened as they swayed in the trade winds, casting ever-moving shadows on the sparkling sand. The somber domes of the *fales* floated over the patches of light from the lamps within and appeared ready to snuff out each mellow glow. Inside, the hunched forms of family members sat on the floor. The men were talking and making sennet. Some of the women were using hand operated *Sigas*, (SING az, sewing machines) or pressing clothes with heavy irons filled and heated by lumps of burning charcoal, while other women were weaving mats. One by one the mosquito nets were hung, and the lights were put out. Night had settled on this beautiful little town.

"Pita, Pita, get up!" Startled from a sound sleep in the middle of the night, I crawled out of the covers and the net. Outside, Faitalla called again to come out. He asked me to take a picture of the full moon. I couldn't with my small camera, but I asked, "What are you doing up at this time of night?"

"I must cook. I have started the *umu*. The fire is heating the stones now, and soon I will put on the food, and then I will go back to bed."

"Couldn't it have waited until a decent hour?" I asked.

"Oh no! The village law is that no one shall cook during the Sabbath, and we must get all of the fires lit and covered before dawn. Then it is that we can have our food at noontime. If the Village Warden saw any smoke from the *umu* in the daytime, we would be fined."

As I looked around, I saw other pious, but scheming men were about the same task. They were all obeying the letter of the law, even the Village Warden.

The other teacher appeared and asked me if I had made any plans to go to church. I responded, "No, I haven't made any plans." This upset them and, and one said to me "Then you don't know God!" It was the *Palangi*s who brought Christianity to them and so we should all believe. Besides, it was the village law. There was no way out. I would have to go along with the idea. I could give homage to the stone walls raised by the missionaries, but there was no other meaningful way for me to be reverent. Moreover, they told me, they would be fined and lose honor if a guest in their *fale* did not attend. And so it came to pass that I got ready for church.

It took me longer to prepare than the others, as I had to shave. By the time I was ready, Faitalla had disappeared, and I had to follow the sound of the singing. I entered a rather small building, obviously a church, and sat down. Once accustomed to the dim light, I looked around for my friend. He was not there among the congregation. As I looked around, I saw some of the men were wearing pants. Something told me that I was in the Mormon chapel. At the end of the hymn, I slipped out. As long as I had to go at all, I might just as well go to the right one. Further along the track I spotted the unmistakable whitewashed walls and the red corrugated iron roof of the Methodist Church.

The contrast was striking. The joyous chorus was in full voice as I stepped inside the door. Everyone was dressed in purest white. The men were seated towards the front and the women with their children in the rear. All were sitting cross-legged tailor fashion on top of the benches like rows of chanting Buddhas. The surplus crowd and those with small crawling children were seated on the floor in the rear. My arrival created great excitement as the sea of wavering faces turned around to see the *Palangi*, dressed in Levi's and a blue nylon short-sleeved shirt. I had finally arrived in time "to meet God." But I was there, and that seemed to satisfy most of them.

I seated myself on the floor with my legs outstretched, leaning against the back wall. However, many of the women around me were more demanding. Several of them started using sign language that informed me that I was to tuck my legs under me, as they had been doing all their lives. For me that was impossible. I just couldn't do it. I made a couple of feeble attempts but was determined that my Samoanization was not going to go that far. Then the pickier of the women decided that the soles of my bare feet must not be aimed directly at the minister, which I had thought proper retribution for my having to go through this whole thing. Within seconds someone appeared with a floor mat and covered my legs and feet with it. This then seemed to be the perfect compromise, and the whole back section of the church settled down to the business at hand and joined in the singing.

When the service was over, they all streamed out into the glaring sunlight and filed down the steps. The men put up their huge black umbrellas, and with their family in tow, walked towards their *fales*. From the top of the steps where I was waiting for

Faitalla, the spectacle below seemed like a huge white caterpillar with black spots was invading our precious little village. Sabbath had begun, and everyone went to their homes and was now free to open their *umus* and have their main meal of the day.

No Samoan would have dared to break the Sabbath rules that I was about to ignore. I felt that it was time to leave Falelima and go on to Neiafu (nay AH foo) only a few miles along the track. The teachers had their work to do and did not seem anxious that I stay any longer. I not only had to walk between villages, an act forbidden by the rules of the Sabbath, but I also had to carry my pack. That was considered "work." I supposed that it served me right that the rain came down in torrents when I was halfway between settlements. The dense growth of trees offered little shelter against the shivering cold deluge. It was here that I discovered that it was really the wet clothing that made walking in the rain so uncomfortable. I stripped to my shorts. I stuffed even my shoes and socks into my pack. Then I grabbed a huge heart-shaped leaf the size of a manhole cover, from a *ta'amu* (tah' ah MOO, an edible plant stem), raised it over my head for some shelter, and sloshed my way along the trail, the red mud squishing succulently between my toes.

Chapter XVI
THE FALE OF VA'UNGA

The next village, Neiafu, was deathly quiet except for the splashing rain. The citizenry were all sleeping off their noonday dinner. Even the dogs had called it a day. There was only one *fale* nearby that was not sheltering people, and as I stooped to enter, I noticed a blackboard filled with music symbols. The alarm had been sounded before I could take more than a glance around me. From one of the *fales* a child had yelled "*Palangi! Palangi*!" With that, half of the village was aroused and rolled over to stare at my dripping body in their music classroom searching through my pack for some dry clothing.

Almost instantly a child obeyed a sharp command and carried a small crude wooden chair over to the music *fale*. He waited outside with it for my signal to enter. His broad, curious, but wary smile, assured me that I was to sit on it. "Chair for sit," he said, bursting with pride. I thanked him with a *fafetai tele lava* (fah fay TIE tay lay lah vah) and sat down as he left. It seemed the safest move at the time. I certainly couldn't change to dry clothes with the village all staring at me. The rain soon ended, and the boy was back with another child and an elderly, very dignified, portly gentleman. A few raindrops on his bare chest glistened like diamonds. We shook hands with a single downwards pump. With a kindly, but firm grip, he pulled me towards the outside, and said "*Sau!*" indicating that I was to follow. One child struggled with the pack, the other with the chair. A hundred eyes were focused on this strange procession as it crossed the puddle strewn *malae* and disappeared into a *fale*.

Refusing to use the chair in my host's home, I sat on the mat with many smiles of approval all around. Then started the unnerving period with the sudden realization that there is not going to be any verbal communication possible. In the rear of the *fale*, the family had pressed nearer and nearer to allow room for the assembling crowd of neighbors who were squeezing in with quiet curiosity.

A young mustached fellow inched his way to our sides. He said, "This is Va'unga, (vah UNG ah). He is the chief of Neiafu (nay AH foo)." Then he asked me, "You come from?" Then, speaking to the old gentleman, he acted as our interpreter. Pau (Pow) told me that he had originally come from Apia where he had gone through a mission school and then gone to New Zealand, where he worked in a meat packing plant. Therefore, he was the most able help that could be desired. The assembled crowd made their own speculations of the great event that was taking place before them. They interrupted their own disturbance with amused smiles, nervous whispers, and muffled giggles.

Following the obligations of Polynesian custom, the *matai* had to invite me to accept his hospitality. It earned him some prestige in the eyes of the others who were envious of his chance to entertain a foreigner. It also gave him a coveted chance to prove his wealth to provide for yet another, and unexpected, person in his household.

Suddenly the church bell rang, followed by a scurry of activity as everybody ran to their *fale. It* was a call for an afternoon service. Oh my! This time I knew I would have to attend. Now I had the chance to get out of my wet clothes and into dry ones, which would make me a lot more comfortable. I was ready and waited for Pau to take me to where I had to go. Pau showed up in the basic uniform of white shirt, jacket, and *lavalava*, accented with a black tie. He was far from being a respected *matai*, so he could not wear the broad leather belt or carry the large black umbrella. Together we shuffled through the sandy *malae*. I followed up the church steps with half of the village citizens. The Warden was standing in the doorway, checking to see that everyone showed up and was properly dressed to be in the House of the Lord. He stepped right in front of me blocking my way. Some quick words were passed, and Pau most apologetically told me that I would not be allowed to enter the church. I was not dressed respectfully. Inwardly delighted, though I tried to pretend great disappointment, I turned to walk back along the beach. A short-sleeved shirt and blue jeans had saved me from an hour of misery.

The afternoon hour was lonely and beautiful. The rain had refreshed everything until it all glistened and sparkled. The sand had all been smoothed out. The dogs were too lethargic to be dangerous, though they growled and yapped a bit as I walked along the curve of the beach. The reef that had formed off of Neiafu made it one of the few towns on the island that could boast a protective lagoon of a sort that made the settings of the Tahitian villages so attractive.

I could still hear the harmonious nasalized singing as it came from the church, and I had to concede some respect for the missionaries for utilizing the marvelous voices of the islanders in the services. It was an art form that had been handed down through the generations and was their chief form of amusement.

Unexpectedly, I saw a small group of men and women sitting on the verandah of a square wooden building raised up on stilts, which doubled for their store and their home. Painted a faded apple green with a rusted blue corrugated roof, this style-less structure was the only eyesore in the otherwise beautiful thatched hut village. Here, in open defiance of the local warden-enforced Sabbath rules, sat several members of a family on rocking chairs and stools basking in the afternoon sun. Spotting the lonely beach walker, they beckoned me to come to them with the now familiar hand signal; palm down and fingers bending towards the ground, as one might signal a puppy that had made a mess on the carpet. As I joined them in a squeaky rocker, I noticed that they were all dressed in *palangi* clothing, the men in pants and shirts and the women in frocks. All were barefoot.

They offered me a bottle of Lemon Squash and a glass. It obviously pleased them immensely that they were able to prove their westernization to such an unexpected guest. We passed some minutes in pleasant conversation, then they brought the talk around to the topic that most interested them. Knowing that I was an American, they assumed that I was also a Mormon. Pleasantly, but firmly denying this, I explained that in my own country the percentage of followers of that faith made up only a minority of our church-going public. I continued by saying that most of the rest of us were unaware of the teachings of their faith.

Exploding from her tight fitting chair, the largest of the women jumped to her feet shouting, "Then you don't know God! Go, and leave this house! We do not welcome you here!" This exclamation confirmed my point exactly. More amazed at the missionary instructors of all the faiths than their converts, I wondered about the rationalization for the divisive preachings of the Word of God. Whatever happened to the Golden Rule?

I turned towards the *fale* of Va'unga and noticed the church had become silent and the crowd was dispersing around town. Many stopped in their path to greet me either in Samoan, or English, or merely with downcast eyes that indicated something was troubling them. I finally met Pau, and he said that the villagers were upset because I, a *Palangi*, had not been permitted to attend the service. They were angry at the Warden. His job was to protect the church from profanity, but even the townsfolk could see the logic of making certain exceptions. Hard as I tried to convince my friend that I forgave them all and not to think further of the matter, he remained upset.

The sun was low but had not yet set. It was that time of day when the light comes under the low clouds and gilds everything with its fiery glow. Even the trade winds were taking a rest. The sea was completely tranquil. The shadows of the tall coco trees made stripes across the whole village scene. Everything was at peace. It was late Sunday afternoon. Every week at this time, the people changed their routine.

The villagers had left their homes and gathered in two *fales*, the women and children in one, and the men in the other. Every week they picnicked in this manner. The food is the same as always, and served the same way. But the pleasantness of the social division made it seem a little special. Every attempt I made at sitting cross-legged with the others in the eating circle was uncomfortable. First I had the sleepiness sensation with its tingles, then the numb feeling followed by piercing cramps. Custom demanded this position. It was difficult to be correct and comfortable without lots of practice. Since the food was placed on woven palm leaf trays in front of each person, a pair of uncooperative legs presented a real problem. But this was solved by Va'unga, who ordered one of the children to bring a couple of floor mats, and with these, my legs were covered so that everyone could pretend they did not exist. I was still sitting more or less side-saddle. I kept trying to sit properly, and gradually my time span increased. It was to take weeks of constant practice before my body became comfortable in the desired position. It did not come naturally to the children, either. Their parents constantly had to tuck their little legs under them as they were growing up. Soon they mastered the art and never changed. To relax at lengthy gatherings, some found comfort in slipping one bare foot onto the opposite thigh and wriggled it a bit, or manipulated it with their hands.

The talk around the picnic circle had been good, and the meal had made them all happy. They now knew all about me and considered that perhaps it was good for the village to have this stranger live among them. I was told that I was welcome to stay as long as I wished. I could join an *a'inga* (ah ING ah, a family group led by a *matai*). That, I knew, was an uncommon and great honor. To that I could only humbly say, "*Fafetai tele lava*," to express my appreciation for the hospitality.

Everyone began packing up their things and heading for home. Pau told me that the villagers had decided to have a special service in the church that night so that I could attend. What luck!

When the night was cool or the wind was strong, or when the residents were dressing, the blinds that are hung between the posts supporting the dome were lowered to the floor. With the blinds down, there was a real sense that it was a dwelling. Va'unga lit the pressure lamp that hissed loudly and brightened the inside of the *fale*. They all began to get ready for the service. Half of the Sabbath had been spent getting ready for church services. At first I was unconcerned at the repeated little whisperings and the rustling that went on in the back of the *fale*. Then I became aware of hands poking things under the blinds to the woman of the family. I was searching through my pack for my windbreaker. Va'unga came up to me, and standing tall, spoke to me in Samoan indicating with unquestionable meaning that I was to dress in the clothing he held out to me. The special service was being held to rectify the tragic error of the Warden for not permitting me to enter the church in the afternoon.

Many of the men in town had been asked to lend me their spotless clothes so that I might dress properly for the occasion. Trapped! So, removing my *palangi* attire, I began from scratch to don the uniform of the devout. I had been given a beautifully ironed white shirt and black tie. I then had to adjust the immaculate white *lavalava* in the formal manner with the neat folds down the front. I secretly gave thanks to Faitalla for teaching me how to do it. The lack of a knot to secure the *lavalava*, which is only done with casual daily wear, necessitated the use of my hand-tooled western belt with its silver buckle. But it was just the thing to complete the outfit. I put on the white jacket and took off my sneakers. Feeling like a million dollars, I was ready to join the crowd as it moved slowly through Neiafu. For the fourth time this Sunday, like it or not, I was on my way to church, albeit three different faiths.

As we walked on the sand, which was cool to my bare feet, I was delighted to be part of this procession of single-minded people. Carrying the hissing pressure lamps made them look like a file of fireflies. Above, the sky was black, but it was pierced with unfathomable numbers of tiny lights from the endless reaches of the Milky Way. The stars were so glorious that I thought perhaps I was really going to the right place after all. Halfway along, we passed the little store on stilts with the group still sitting in their rocking chairs. That family tried so hard to be different.

This time there would be no question of my being admitted to the tropic-gothic House of God. Inside it resembled a huge whitewashed cave. The floor was spread with mats. The increasing number of people settled where there was room with their hissing lamps. When the rows of people had all settled down the service began. I was struck with how much the whole congregation resembled a crowd of melting snow men as they sat like rows of tailors on the benches and the floor. The similarity became more perfect as the heat from the lamps turned the place into a steaming grotto. A lamp that emitted more heat than light, had been thoughtfully placed next to me so I could see better. It was the first time in the tropics that I'd had on a tie and jacket. I was literally liquefying into the mats.

My legs began to cramp, and the sweat began to ooze as the tie became tighter and the jacket clung ever closer to become an unbearable burden. The voice in the pulpit ranted on in verbal hieroglyphics. It was all most unpleasant. Finally I decided to solve the problem in the only way I could. Cautiously, I unfolded my legs that had become almost senseless, and stretched them straight out in front of me. It gave me great satisfaction both in comfort, and in knowing that I was getting back in my own way at the cause of the ceaseless torment coming from the pulpit. This caused great consternation among the congregants. A widening circle of advisers turned and indicated with their arms that I was supposed to fold the legs under. I responded with equal firmness that I would keep them straight. Their intolerance and my defiance were at stake. The rows in front turned around to offer their opinions about my disrespect for the Man of God. They were far more concerned about my posture than about the message of proper behavior coming from the minister. We had reached an impasse, and the ranting suddenly ceased. The brass band that had been in the corner suddenly struck up a lively bang-bang hymn, and they all started singing. Everyone was having a good time, and the *Palangi* had been forgotten. We filed out of the church as friends, and several approached me and thanked me for attending. I was very happy that we were going home and that I would soon be in bed.

Va'unga's wife showed me where I was to sleep as a member of the family, by placing a sleeping mat on one side of the *fale*. A sleeping mat is woven with much finer strands of pandanus leaves than the floor mats. It is often decorated with contrasting black strands woven in along the borders and with tufts of colored wool attached to the edges. The wife and the children would occupy the opposite side and the rear. Va'unga would be near the front, but leaving enough room should a chance visitor need a place to pass the night. Oddly enough, this part of the village did not suffer from the plague of mosquitoes that bothered other parts of town, so no nets had to be put up. I had heard that this was because these people did not take baths. But that was definitely not true. It was just jealousy.

It took no time at all before the village was quiet. I relaxed, knowing that I could stay a few days and get to know the ways of these very friendly people.

At some time during the night I was aroused just enough to know that I was not sleeping alone. There was a nice warm feeling behind my knees, along my back, and in front against my stomach. I could think of no reason for this unless I was surrounded. I stirred in the hopes of finding out what might be the cause, when the warm spot in front scurried away. It was very small. It ran away on all fours. I rolled over and the two warm spots at my back also got up, squealed, and ran off. Sitting bolt upright, I tried to wake from what I thought must have been an odd dream. Now awake, I felt the chill of the night, and reached in my backpack for a sweater. It wriggled, squealed, and ran out of the *fale* under the blinds. This time I saw what it was. A tiny piglet had been sleeping in my pack. Then I realized I had been keeping close company with a litter of baby pigs.

Laughing at the unlikely chance that this had happened at all, I settled down again and hoped that the sun would rise very late. Again, I was aroused from my sleep. My litter had returned. My reaction was quick, and with a few sharp smacks, they all dispersed and did not return.

I was glad to see the sunrise, as it meant the end of a rather trying 24 hours.

Monday was an interesting day I shall long remember. The *matai* of each *a'inga* went to attend the *Fono* (council) of *matais* at the large meeting *fale*. The *Fono* gathered to discuss the business of the village. They were responsible for local law and order. Their realm covered everything from taxes and fines to the problems of misbehaving citizens.

Having no form of writing, public speaking had developed long ago as a fine art. They had to learn to say things in a prescribed manner. Thus, when speeches are made, they are listened to with more anticipation for errors, than for the actual content. They talk long, phrasing and rephrasing their thoughts, weaving them into a complicated discourse that becomes incredibly involved. Armed with this pattern of speaking, they also tried to use English in a similar manner. Talking around the bush fulfilled their need for expression but created chaotic thinking in the translation.

This day the subject under exhaustive discussion was the church benches. New ones had been ordered from Apia sometime previously and were ready to be delivered. It was up to the *Fono* to decide how the delivery should be made. In any event it would necessitate an inter-island sea voyage and arrival at one of the few ports on Savaii, and then reshipment by truck along the sandy track to Neiafu. Thus it was only a matter to decide which port to use and arranging for the truck to pick up the benches and deliver them. There was much foot wriggling and manipulation during these hours of talk.

The mid-morning refreshment break was the ceremonial kava. At a pre-set time, the huge wooden bowl was brought in and placed in front of a man who had just arrived but who had not participated in the meeting. The sun-dried *ava* (kava) roots and stalks had been pounded to a light tan-colored powder that was put into the bowl, and water was added. After careful additions of water, the mixer placed a handful of fibrous material into the liquid, swished it around a couple of times and, wrung it out. He then tossed it over his shoulder outside the *fale*. A waiting youth caught it, and snapped it in the air a few times to dislodge whatever sediment had been collected in it. It was then tossed back. The whole operation was repeated three more times. Finally the *ava* was considered free of impurities. The young man brought in a cup made of half a coconut shell, blackened with age and use, and passed it to the mixer. The cup was filled, and the youth turned around, ready to serve it. A name is called out of the *matai* who had the highest rank and should be served first. If there was a mistake, the person entitled to the first cup would say "Here." The proper *matai* was then served, the youth keeping his head as low as possible. The back of the hand, like the sole of the feet, was never turned towards a person of higher rank. If the server was not sure, he passed the cup with both hands under the cup. The drinker takes the cup as handed to him, with one hand or two so as not to insult any noble person near him. The *matai* would pour two or three drops onto the floor to honor his ancestors, and salute the gathering with "*Maneuia*" (mah NOYE yah, good, cheers), and the rest murmur back, "*To Fa, Soi Fua*," (toe FAH, soy FOO ah), a greeting meaning: Cheers, good luck, and even good-bye.

It was at one of these *ava* breaks that Va'unga invited me in to join the group and placed me next to him. When it came my turn to have my draft of kava, I was invested with a Samoan name. I could use the name wherever I traveled in the islands. To be a guest at this kind of meeting was a special treat, as was the taking of ceremonial kava with the assembled *matais*. *Ava* is a dirty brown-colored watery drink that I found to have a slightly licorice-peppery flavor. I had been led to believe that it had an intoxicating quality, but alas, after other samplings, I can say it did not produce that effect in me. It is however, refreshing, leaving the mouth feeling very clean and cool. It did not take much time to acquire a taste for it.

About noon, the problem of the benches was still pleasantly unresolved. The main meal was brought in and served with much protocol. As there was little point in my staying longer, I apologized to "my" *matai*, excused myself from the gathering, and wandered out to learn what I could. I had now been accepted into Va'unga's *a'inga*.

Anyone can join any *a'inga*. It is simply an agreement between the *matai* and the newcomer to live together. Some may be related by marriage, or even, as in my case, total strangers. The newcomer is expected to join in the chores necessary for everyday village life, in exchange for a family with whom to live. In ancient times it might have been a matter of an offer of protection. It was a system that offered advantages to both parties. I visited one *a'inga* in which 74 people sat down for dinner together. One of the young unrelated men worked in the town for a salary, and his contribution was to spend his earnings on things the family needed. His shopping list each week consisted of such things as kerosene, sacks of sugar or flour, a case of canned food, or even a quarter of a cow, which was transported on top of the bus the evening he brought me "home" for the weekend. This particular *matai* was rich in the eyes of the village, as he had many able hands to work for him. My contribution was an eagerly received bag of powdered *ava*.

The meeting of the *Fono* of *Matais* continued with further lengthy discussions. Their extravagant use of time seemed incredible. Their hands were not idle during this time. They were plaiting the coconut fibers into *afa*. In the course of one of these days talking and listening, every man can make between 50 and 100 feet of this absolutely essential material. The rest of the men of the village, the untitled married men, and the *tane* are out producing food for their families. Some are at sea fishing; others are in clearings in the bush tending to their crops. Policy is the important thing, and the *matais* are responsible for that. In the end, the final decision was that the crew on the delivery boat should come as near Neiafu as possible and toss the benches over the side into the water and let the gentle surf carry them to the shore. But no one had discussed this with the ship's master, or would be able to predict the weather conditions on the planned day of delivery.

The married women were having a similar meeting without the ceremony of the *kava*. They had decided to go and clean up the cemetery. In short order they picked up their equipment, mostly bush knives, and headed out to the ancient burial ground. It was a lovely spot, not far from the sea. Each grave was marked with an oval or rectangular wall of black lava rocks about a foot high, filled in with bits of dead white coral. The grave markers were topped off with broken bits of pottery or old tin plates and cups, all broken or with holes punched in them. These had been implements used by the deceased and left on the grave so that he could have familiar things in the after life.

The women weeded the yard and spread fresh beach sand on the paths. The graves of the more important *matais* were a little bigger than the others, and a little higher, and the stonework a little more carefully done. The very small ones marked the children. There was nothing to indicate the name of any individual. There did not seem to be spaces for family groups. It appeared that each successive burial was placed wherever there was room.

The women made quick work of their task and returned to the village for lunch. They then disappeared into the bush and later returned lugging armfuls of dead palm fronds. Some of them sat down and began to weave the "shingles" needed when a new roof is to be put on a *fale*. Others disappeared to bring in more fronds. By evening their day's work had been most productive and impressive.

It was time for me to do some of my own laundry, so I headed for the washing pool with a bundle under my arm. I thought that this time of day the pool might be empty. When I arrived, I was greeted by four women who were about their own tasks. Without wanting to jeopardize my position in the village, or rocking the exalted standing of the men, and not knowing how to get someone to do the work, I was hard pressed for a solution. The group of half-bare laundresses beckoned to me to come in and join them. It was a big pool, so I tossed the clothes in as far from them as I could, and dove into the cool cloudy water. I stayed underwater a few seconds. When I surfaced I saw an alarming sight. The girls were scrambling for my laundry and had set about scrubbing it. By our combined efforts, and many a giggle at the unfamiliar garments, we were soon finished, and I was on my way back to hang it out on some bushes.

Out in the lagoon, a few of the young boys were wading through the chest-deep water herding a school of fish towards a shallower area. Soon they dove with their spears, and the chase was on. I waited no longer and went into the lagoon to join the group, even if only to go along for the sights. The sun was warm and the air cooled by the trade winds. The water was just perfect. The fishing was poor. With all their effort, there was nothing to show for it. The boys had not been able to fulfill the needs of the people who depended on them. Dinner for some that night was to be only baked green bananas and the dependable taro root, which tasted something like a gummy boiled potato and had a purplish tint.

I have to bring up this subject of outhouses sometime. There was, of course, no in-house plumbing in the Samoan villages. Each *fale*, or *a'inga*, has its own *fale vau* (FAH lay vow), which is always located at the edge of the sea. From the water, the first sight I could see of any settlement was a row of small shanties of incredible variation and construction. They are connected to the beach either by a walkway of rocks, or perhaps only a couple of logs on which one has to be very surefooted. Night trips are hazardous to one's well-being.

Tuesday was a big day. It had been decided to re-thatch the roof on the *fale* at the end of the town. Any project of this nature requires the entire population to be on hand to contribute their talents. The women had spent their time the previous days and evenings weaving the thatch shingles. Each one is about a yard or more long, and I think that they can make two shingles out of one leaf by splitting the leaf in half. Some 3000 would be needed for the job. Collecting 1500 leaves, or 3000 if needed, and dragging them to the *fales*, is not an easy woman's task. I assume that young agile men climbed the coco trees and whacked off a few leaves from as many trees as needed. They did it without safety belts. The *matais* had all been making sennet since the last project, so there was an ample supply to tie the shingles to the frame.

The project had begun at sunrise when the younger men had climbed up on the roof and started stripping the old shingles off of the frame. Some of the women and children were hauling away the old discarded shingles to rot in the coco groves. By the time this part of the job was complete, it was mid-morning, and they were all ready for the first break. The rest of the women and young children were collecting the prepared food, taro, breadfruit, and boiled green bananas. Some had brought large pots of boiled rice, others had brought cans of fish. The owner of the home contributed the *ava*, which was continually being made and served with little ceremony. The men gathered to have rice mixed with local chocolate and canned "*heligi*" (hel ING ee, herring) in tomato sauce, served on pieces of banana leaves. Little do the Scots, who put up the fish from their arctic waters, realize that their most appreciative customers are the natives of the South Seas.

After the meal, the real work started. The new thatch shingles had to be tied onto the roof frame. The more agile workers climbed up again to continue. The older men and older children were on hand with long poles to lift each new shingle up to one of the workers tying them to the frame of the dome. One or two played ukuleles and sang while they rested and to entertain the others.

The work on the roof progressed rapidly. In the early afternoon it was time for the next meal break. This was a heartier meal, with meat, taro, *palusami* (spinach in coco cream), and hot chocolate. The very young had spent the last hours doing what they could. One of their favorite jobs was licking the *pisupo* cans clean, which kept them out from underfoot. The flies were trying successfully to share with the children the good fortune left in the cans. This kept both of the most bothersome elements busy. It was a kind of holiday, a break in the normal routine.

During the break I was fortunate to see a few of the children's games originally played by the ancients, still being practiced. Young teenaged boys were throwing spears. The object was to run a short distance, throw the spear underhanded, as I recall, so it would bounce off of the hard-packed ground, and hit a pre-selected target. This was one of their fighting exercises. It required great skill that comes only from constant practice. It is something that has been passed down carefully from father to son over many centuries.

Another game was for much younger children. They were each given a two-foot length of the center spine of a palm leaf from which all of the side leaflets had been removed. A notch had been cut into the top, or rounded, surface. The under side is concave and has two slightly raised outer edges. These edges act somewhat as runners on a sled. A second stick, about a yard long is slipped into the notch and used as a pusher. The game part is to play with other children similarly equipped, and race around at full speed, running into the other players trying to force each other's sticks from the notches.

A modern adaptation of this was the clever invention of one child's father. He nailed a round, used, *pisupo* tin to the far end of the pusher stick so that the child now had a wheeled toy. This was called a *tavoli*, or car. This advancement avoided the determined body contact of the previous game as no child wanted his *tavoli* broken. The next advancement was to put a can on each end of a swiveling axel attached to a pusher stick. This was the Rolls Royce of island push-pull toys.

Another amusement was to walk on coconut shells. All that is needed is the top halves of two shells. To make these is very simple. One "eye" of each of the shells is poked out, and a strip of flexible bark or sennet is threaded through each hole. A knot is tied on both ends to prevent the bark from slipping out. The object is to hold one tether in each hand pulling up on it to have control. Then step barefoot onto each shell so that the bark passes between the big toe and the others. The challenge is to walk around on them, similar to walking on stilts.

In the late afternoon there was a whoop and a holler as a corrugated iron sheet was secured to the ridge section to keep the frequent rains from soaking through. The job was finished and everyone could call it a day. They all gathered for the last time to share a very special mixture of mashed ripe breadfruit and coconut cream called "*tau folo*." It is delicious and it is served to the village when they feel that they deserve it for having done a very good job. They are good workers when doing something for mutual benefit. But they had not yet grasped the idea of individual effort to improve one's own life.

Chapter XVII
LIKI

His Anglicized name was Ricky, but Samoan sounds could not manage the "R," so he was called "Liki" (LEE kee). Liki was a tall fellow, not yet 30 years old, with a body like a box. He had been totally blind for a decade. He had contacted some illness that dimmed his vision, but typically native in his thoughts, he did nothing about it until he was living in partial darkness. He had gone through the mission school system and was able to speak English very well.

He told me his story. As a protectorate of New Zealand, the Samoans could avail themselves of the medical facilities in Auckland if the local establishment was not equipped to handle the situation. When his case was finally brought to the attention of the proper authorities, it was determined that he merited this aid. He applied for an appointment to go to Auckland for an examination and treatment. The acceptance came, but Liki never went. His excuse was that his uncle, with whom he lived, would not lend him enough money to buy a suit so that he could arrive appropriately dressed. Refusing his opportunity for help and possible cure, he had become completely dependant on his uncle. He cannot contribute to his own welfare.

Liki's first question to me when we met was, "Can you teach me to read? I would be so happy if only I could learn to read the Word of the Lord. Is there anything you can do?" I considered the possibility of obtaining books in Braille in these islands. I suggested that with a lot of time, it might be possible.

"If you could only help me, my family would let you live with us, and we would take good care of you." He had just made a bargain that sounded mutually beneficial. I could continue my study of the customs of the people. He then said that as long as I was going to live with his family that it would be wise to meet them.

The following morning I told Va'unga I was going to try to help Liki, which everyone understood. I said, *"To fa, soi fua,"* to the family. Malosi, Liki's young cousin, was to lead the way and carry the little baggage we needed: a small cardboard suitcase, his cigarette makings, my toilet kit, their toothbrushes, our towels, and three fresh *lavalavas*. The three of us started out on another part of my *malanga*.

Our progress was slow at first. Liki was on the end of a short stick pulled by Malosi. Then the stick was abandoned, and Liki had to follow the tire track in the grass with his feet feeling the way. My feet were gradually getting used to being without shoes, but I was still careful where I walked. Malosi led without speaking hardly a word. He asked any necessary directions, then making sure I could follow, went on by himself. We followed an inland route over a hill.

We had a most pleasant walk the first day and arrived at our stop in the afternoon. It was at a small *fale*. There was a very nice young couple living there. Iosefa and Hina both spoke English very well so we had no trouble understanding each other. Iosefa, the husband, had a regular job, so he did not work the land. They had two small children. The thing that most interested me was that Hina had bought some green and white striped material. She was going to make a new dress. She laid the cloth out on the floor of the *fale*. Using only her eyes for measuring, she cut off a large piece and set it aside. That was to be the floor-length *lavalava*, or sarong, that women wear under their dress. She then turned the pages of a very old and much-used Sears Roebuck catalog to those showing dresses. I would have thought that she would have used a pattern, but I did not see signs of one. Hina stared at one of the pages for a while. She selected a picture of a simple frock, with a collar, an opening in the back, and short sleeves. She picked up the scissors and started to cut the fabric, again using only her eyes for measurement. She cut out the collar, the sleeves, and the other various parts, then neatly piled them to one side. She pinned all the pieces together, and I could hardly believe what I was seeing. Everything seemed to fit in its place. Then she got up and moved to her work area near her hand-powered *Singa*. She settled down again on the floor and began sewing the various seams. Incredibly, to me anyway, all the pieces eventually became a dress. To my astonishment, she wore it to the next church service.

Liki and I waited for Malosi to arrive in the morning, as he had stayed with another family somewhere in the village. We followed the dirt track a few miles and arrived at Falealupo (fah lay ah LOO po), a most picturesque town of about a thousand people, stretched along a magnificent palm shaded beach. It is located near the northwest corner of Savaii. It was obvious that the Council of *Matais* here had great civic pride, as all of the *fales* were in excellent repair. All of the *paepaes* had been carefully landscaped with base plantings of tropical lilies. Colorful hibiscus bushes grew everywhere. All paths and property divisions had neat rows of planting or were lined with large sea shells. There was not a dead palm frond or coconut husk lying on the ground. The *malae* and *kilikiki* court were neat and proper. There were no orange peels on the ground. In fact, it all looked just too perfect. The authority that controlled this town was doing so with an iron hand.

On a small peninsula I saw a group of rather large whitewashed buildings. The biggest was a tropic gothic church with drains leading off of the four heavily buttressed corners leading into cisterns. This was one of the original missions of the Germans, currently staffed by priests of several nationalities. It was one of the rare effective educating forces outside of the few main towns. The Samoans had not proven difficult to seduce to Christianity, so this was not a fortification. It had been a convent for some time and gradually converted into a boarding school for boys and girls who came from other districts of Savaii.

The priest in charge was a German who said that he had been there for 39 years. "I have been here long enough to have christened nearly all of the people in the town. I speak their language fluently, and I know their customs and their legends. I love them, but I do not understand them. I could be here for 139 years and not understand them."

I would soon begin to realize that he had a point.

Liki's Uncle Joe operated one of the three trading shops in Falealupo. Like the others, he was a representative of one of the large New Zealand trading chains in Apia. These overseas companies exchange the produce collected by the district trader for anything imported from abroad. The local trader exchanges these goods with the people for their crops of cocoa beans and copra. Some of them are cash transactions, others are on credit. Thus the industrious plantation operator can convert crops into pressure lamps, cloth, kerosene, soap, hair oil, or tinned fish.

Uncle Joe's shop was no different from any other. It was a ramshackle, neglected, weather-beaten box, with rusting roof, broken windows, and a sagging verandah with a loose step or two. These shops were the only commercial enterprises in town. They handled a most fantastic array of goods, poked in here and there without any order. On the floor in front of the grimy counter were open burlap sacks of flour and unrefined sugar. Every child who came in poked his hand into the sugar.

The local mixed-race traders met the needs of the islanders in a fashion that was completely satisfactory to all with the same unhurried unconcern. There was a surplus of nylon fishing netting in a box because it lasted so long, but a sewing needle would take weeks to replace. Long outdated canned goods collected dust. The best sellers were soft drinks, but there was no ice to cool them. There were no medical or first aid supplies, as there had never been a demand for them. They didn't know they were available.

By the time an ailment was worth attention, it was generally pretty serious, and the patient was taken care of at home or taken to a local care center called a "hospital." Once in a hospital, the family moved in also to care for the patient. They all camped on the floor. There was a place for them to prepare meals and serve the sick and themselves. To the *Palangi's* eye, these facilities were pretty primitive, and one never dwelt on being sick in the islands and needing to go to a local medical facility.

Behind Uncle Joe's shop was a padlocked shed where he stored the copra. Not only the sickening-sweet, ever-present smell of the copra, but also nasty little beetles, came from that shed at night. Next to that was a room furnished only with a small table painted a cobalt blue, On top of the table was a lace doily and an old powdered milk tin labeled "Klim," with a bunch of dusty plastic flowers sticking in it. On the patchily painted walls were pictures of religious figures, along with the elder members of the family, everyone with their arms folded in front. Yellowed pictures from newspapers showed a few sports stars from decades past. A couple of foot worn mats covered most of the rough board floor. The window, which had probably never been opened, was sealed with cobwebs. Three rusty nails served as clothes hangers. In one corner was a roll of sleeping mats. This is where we were to sleep while in the town. There was another small room with a door that led down a flight of treacherous steps. This room had a food safe, its four legs standing in tuna fish cans filled with kerosene to keep out the ants.

Uncle Joe, like Sam in Apia, was part Caucasian and part Samoan. His seldom shaven face was not nice to look at. His thick lips did not conceal his twisted teeth, his clumsy features were too heavy to be a *Palangi*, and his color was too faded to be Samoan. His dress reflected his features, torn dirty pants with no buttons on the fly, and a very soiled, unbuttoned shirt with the tails tied at the waist.

His wife Vi created an equally unpleasant picture. Fat and dumpy, she had lived through years of neglect with Uncle Joe. Her shrunken, unfitting cotton frock needed the attention of a needle and thread and a good scrubbing. Vi, at least, was a pure Samoan. It is not uncommon to see sloppy women in the districts, but they are generally working, doing their share for the family well-being. Vi and Uncle Joe merely tended shop for their occasional customer. His real business was trading in copra for the outside world.

Towards late afternoon, a few customers came to the shop for a bottle of soda or some other small purchase. Vi was lying on the floor as she asked, exhaustedly, what they wanted. She got up wearily after a while and seemed to use every last bit of energy to get herself to the counter. To her, working was just too much *fa lave lave*. The unhurried operation as she searched for the item requested created a backlog of customers, all chatting contentedly with each other.

Uncle Joe was talking with Liki, and so was unconcerned with the shop. His dozen or so daily customers kept him so tied down, he had admitted to me, that he no longer had time to go fishing or work his land. VI, bearing the whole load, went through each motion as if great weights were holding her down. She dragged herself here for a can of something, there for something else, repeating movements time and again with the greatest of effort. Each sale was calculated on a piece of old newspaper that was then thrown on the floor and scuffed underfoot, tripping her massive feet time and time again. Laboriously, she began to tally a simple two-item sale. Before it was complete, she broke the tip of the little yellow pencil stub. She gazed at it in wonder for a while as if in hopes it would grow out again. Then, with a heave, she straightened out her upper body, which had been lying on the counter, walked over to a pile of papers, and tried to write on them. Then she turned and scratched on a wrapper that had fallen off of some long-ago forgotten tin can. This did not work either. So, in her lethargic desperation, she ambled the length of the shelf, trying to write on every object.

Disgusted, she threw the pencil stub on the floor and called Uncle Joe. He called to a boy outside who was grating a coconut for chow. The boy came in and got the pencil, took it outside, sharpened it with his knife, and brought it back to the shop. Vi, by this time, had thrown the label on the floor. She stared for some moments as if wondering whether it was worth looking for it in the midst of the trash. Finally she decided to make a new one. The entire operation consumed better than 20 minutes. The other people, equally phlegmatic about commercial efficiency, waited apathetically for their turn.

One man paid for his items with a pound note. Vi crumpled it into a ball as she trudged to the far end of the counter, opened the drawer, and studied its contents for several minutes. Her stubby fingers pawed through a collection of small items of stock that Uncle Joe must have found difficult to store someplace else. In due time she decided that the drawer, with everything else, did not contain the needed change. She went to another drawer and explored there. She did find something that pertained to one of the other women who was in the shop, and they had a lengthy discussion over it. Finally she put it back, closed the drawer, returned to the man, tossed the crumpled money back to him, took the goods, and put them back on the shelf. The man thought about it for a moment, decided he wanted the items anyway, and she got them together again and wrote up a charge. It was quite some time before the store cleared of its customers. Uncle Joe went in to check the books.

This part of Falealupo had no adequate natural water supply like a spring or a stream. The shopkeeper had two petrol drums at the corners of his shack for the collection of water from the roof. In the wet season it rained daily, so anyone who wanted water was welcome to take it. In the dry season he traded the water for fish or taro roots. Behind the store he had a shower shack. The tank above was filled by rain, or by bucket. The spray head was a choice possession from Apia. A shower in the daylight is a wonderful stimulant, but when taken after dark, it can put a chill in the body. That evening I had one of the coldest baths I could remember.

We all gathered on the floor of the front porch covered with inadequate well worn mats for the evening prayers. A chipped bowl with washing water was passed around, and chipped plates were put before each one of us. A woven tray held cold breadfruit, cold taro, cold roasted bananas, and a single can of helingi in tomato sauce. "This cost four *siligi* (sil ING ee, shillings), grumbled Uncle Joe as he tossed the can on the floor for the boy to open. (There were 20 shillings to a pound.) Six people, three of them guests, and three family members, had to eat from the one can. At every meal thereafter, nothing went on the floor where we ate that Joe did not quote a price that it cost him. He was entertaining a *Palangi*, and he wanted the gathered onlookers to envy his fine social graces. He also wanted them to appreciate the cost it was to him. I assumed also, he was telling me what I should pay him for the privilege of his open hospitality. At the conclusion of our meal, Vi picked up the hem of her frock, wiped her oily hands on it, and, with the sound of a trumpet, blew her nose in it. Our demonstration of social graces was now concluded.

The next day we were there, I asked Liki about Falealupo *siapo* (see AH poe, tapa cloth) that supposedly was the best that was made in the islands. I had hoped to acquire some. It is made from beating inner bark until it is pliable, and meshes together with other pieces to form a kind of paper-like material. In ancient times, *siapo* was all the Polynesians had to wear. In more recent times, it had become used mostly for ceremonial occasions. The women did this tedious work, and when large pieces are made, they added designs with vegetable dyes to make it more attractive.

Liki said that he would go into town and, being a Samoan, he could get it cheaper than I. That sounded reasonable to me, so I agreed. He asked me how big a piece I wanted and I, not knowing how it came, said, "Oh, about four feet by four feet, or about six by six, something like that."

He went into town with Malosi and returned some time later. The piece was six by six feet all right, but it had been cut out of a bigger piece. At my utterance of surprise, he said, "But that is what you asked for." I later found out that it had come from a huge roll of *siapo* from Tonga, not from Falealupo. I asked him how much? He said, "It is very rare now, so you must pay a pound. It is a fair price." It seemed to be a good buy, but it wasn't at all what I had expected.

We got ready to depart to meet more of Liki's loving family. At this point Vi announced that our visit had cost them 18 *silingis*. She said that she had to go to a wedding and that she would have to take a piece of *siapo*. I should therefore buy her a piece for the wedding. She was lying, and I knew it full well, but I was trapped. It was the only time that I saw her in any but the most passive mood, and it was almost worth the price to see her face animated with avarice. I paid her the pound and thought how much my new "family" would learn to love me.

We turned around and followed a path along the shore back towards where we had started the *malanga*. Our next stop to meet Liki's family was westward around a point of land called Point Mulinuu (moo lee NOO oo). It is the most westerly point of Samoa, which is all just east of the International Date Line. A short distance westwards towards the horizon is "tomorrow." If a person was here at the right time of day, he could see the sun sucked into the sea this evening, and see the backside of the sunrise in Asia at the same time.

Liki's family in Tufutafo'e (too foo tah FOE ay) was delightful. One young man in his twenties had two dreadfully underdeveloped legs, so much so that he could not get around any other way but crawl. His sad story was not uncommon. Almost every village had one or more cases of this affliction. It was brought about as a result of a United Nations anti-yaws campaign several years priorly. I was told that a team of U.N. medical personnel came to Apia and taught several Samoans how to inoculate children with the vaccine. The new inoculators went off on their own and started to go to work. However, to gain social position and work less, they trained some other young people and told them to go out and do the job. Meanwhile, they basked in the prestige of being a "medical instructor." This was probably repeated by others. So by the time these meagerly trained people got to the outer districts, they were not vaccinating people as accurately as originally instructed. Vast numbers of children were inoculated during the project to stop the dreaded tropical disease. The malady was brought under control, but at great cost to some of the children. The government in Apia had tried to favor these victims by giving them employment in which they could deal with their handicap and still become worthy workers. I saw at least one girl who had become a teacher. Since everyone sits on the floor anyway, a teacher can do the same in a school *fale*. Others stuck at home learned to take over other needed family chores. Liki's relative had become expert at pressing clothes with the heavy charcoal iron.

Liki suggested that perhaps it would be possible to get some fine *siapo* in this town, if I should want any more. If so, let him know. He got some sellers together, and I saw the pieces they offered. Though they were not of fine quality, they were all priced at the one pound level. I selected several and closed the deal.

The next morning we had to wait for the rain to stop before continuing our *malanga*. The sky was swept clean of all the clouds, except a few caught on the horizon. We had hardly left the village when Liki asked me if I would like to buy the piece of *siapo* that the village had given him in appreciation of the sales he had made for them. He showed me the handsomest piece I had ever seen, his commission for making me a sucker. I bought it but was reluctant to see my personal treasury melting away so quickly.

Our *malanga* continued through a magnificent rain forest, occasionally passing little clearings where someone was preparing to start a taro patch or a cacao grove. We passed great trees whose high-up branches were dropping roots to the ground, fantastic giant ferns, and huge-leaved tuberous plants. It was a spectacle of variations of colors, shapes, and textures. The path was sometimes well-defined, but occasionally it became almost lost in the prolific growth of the dense jungle. Malosi would wait up until he could see us coming and then disappeared on his way. He was an odd sort, preferring his own company on a hike that was likely to take six or seven hours.

After missing him for an hour, we came out into a clearing. It was a neatly attended banana grove, and the young plants had recently been cleared from the entangling vines that seemed to grow overnight. It looked like a good place to rest. A moment later we saw Malosi emerging from the bush carrying a small orange-ripe papaya. He was followed by a teenaged *teine* who was carrying two ripe papayas, my favorite tropical fruit. Malosi peeled his papaya and sat down to eat it without thinking either of us might want some of it. Frankly, I was ravenously jealous of the fruit, as I had only had some unpleasant roasted green bananas for several days. But Malosi was eager to get on the way and left us.

The *teine* came up to speak to Liki and smiled, gave him a fruit, and waited. There was no doubt as to her expectations. It was not every day that so many men passed her plantation. They said a few words in Samoan, and she led him into the bush. Eventually she came out of the bush, leading Liki back to where I was sitting and put a papaya in his hand.

With a pleasant smile, she handed me the other papaya. I smiled and thanked her, but declined the offer. Both Samoans were quite perplexed. It was a question of discretion over valor.

When Liki and I had finally had our fruit, we started down the trail again. A man could be bought so cheaply! It reminded me of a little ditty I had learned in Hawaii.

"Princess Papuli (pa POO lee) had plenny papaya,
She love to give it away.
She give da fruit, but keep da root,
She like it betta dat way."

The first village we came to was to be our stop for the night. It was a most picturesque place on a stretch of wonderful beach. We stopped at a very imposing *fale* mounted on a very high *paepae*. In fact, it was so high it had the look of a temple about it. The two tiers of platforms each had a flight of steps to the next level. It had obviously been built for a very powerful and rich *matai*. Its position near the sea and at the end of the village gave it a commanding view of everything that went on. The interior woodwork was something to behold. Instead of ordinary posts, the builder had acquired about 30 trunks of the giant fern trees, a very hard wood. Liki said that these posts never rot, and they have the most unusual rough fibrous textured bark.

The workmanship inside the dome was marvelous. All the joints were dovetailed together and fitted in such a way that it was as fine as gothic vaulting. The beam that was attached to the posts all around had been carved with simple adz and axe so that there was no variation in its thickness. The same applied to each ascending ring of beams as each ring got thinner, making for a seemingly much higher ridge. All of the tubular shaped wood was completely wrapped in *a'fa*, giving the whole an effect of a series of ropes of varying thicknesses. This *fale* cost many *pu'a'a* (poo AH AH, pigs).

After my limited pleasantries with the host were made, I left to wander around the village by myself, searching around for any curiosities that I might find. I strayed behind the trading store. I was astounded when I was confronted with three clothes-lines stretching to palm trees a dozen yards away. These lines were blanketed with *siapo*. There was more of the tapa cloth here than I dreamed existed on the whole island. I scrambled through them frantically to see if there were any better than the ones I had purchased with Liki. They were all excellent in condition and design.

I turned to see the shopkeeper's wife shuffle her huge feet down the steps. "Wha you wan?" she yelled.

"Some of this *siapo*," I said.

"No for sale, I need it all," she responded.

"I know it's dear, but I want some. How much for this one?" I asked.

"Very dea'(DEE ah), fie' *silingi*." she asserted with finality. My face must have shown the awe I felt at the price I had just heard. At five shillings, it was only a quarter of the price of the others when I was getting "help" from my Samoan friend.

She was equally startled by my reaction, and rightly thought that I had probably considered the price extraordinary. She snapped, "Tole you it was dea', but I sell you fo' fo' *silingi*." I selected ten great pieces, gave her the 40 shillings (two pounds), and stormed off to find Liki resting. I told him what had happened and what I thought of him, of his help, and the "love" of his family, and his wanting only "to read the Word of the Lord." I picked up my things and set out to find my own way back to Neiafo. I was wiser now about the *fa'a Samoa*.

Chapter *XVIII*

SILAPE'A AND PAU

Again I had to pass through the forested land that separated the settlements. It had been a hot day, and I was getting very tired. Suddenly, with no warning whatsoever, it started to pour. I wasn't wearing a shirt, so I tore off my shorts, reached into my travel kit, and found some soap. Right in the middle of the track, I took a wonderful rainwater shower. As soon as I was soapy from head to naked foot, the rain stopped. There I was, standing in the buff, draped only in a cascade of soap suds. I went from one dripping leaf to another to try and get enough water to rinse off. Frantically, trying to get soap out of my eyes, I suddenly realized that I was not alone. I saw a group of school children coming along the track. Their giggles as they passed and continued on their way told me that this day would not soon be forgotten, by either of us.

Once back in Neiafu, I went right to Pau's *fale*. After telling him about Liki, he shook his head and said "Gotta watch Samoan fella. He pretty slick."

Pau was living with Meli, a girl that he had met in Apia when they went to a dance. She had been educated in a church school and spoke fine English. He liked her, and according to custom, he came back to her island with her. He met her father and agreed to work for him as one of his "sons" in exchange for living there. Pau was now a member of this *a'inga*. The boy can stay as long as he wants before he decides to settle or go on to some other place. Pau had been here for more than half a year, and although Meli showed no sign of ever becoming a mother, he confided in me that he liked her well enough to take her back to Apia with him. "Oh!" he added, "I might get married some day, but that is a lot of *fa lave lave*. Very dea'."

Silape'a (see lah PAY ah,) one of the teachers, complained about a splinter that he had lodged deeply in his foot and asked me if there was anything I could do about it. I told him that my stuff was at the *fale*, and that either Pau's beautiful wife, or I, might be able to do something about it. He came along and sat down with us. I gave the stuff to Meli, preferring that a Samoan treat a Samoan. Silape'a looked at me and said, "You said that she was beautiful. She is not!" Pau became enraged, not at what the teacher said, but at me for talking about his girl behind his back. Anything was all right to say in front of her, a woman's feelings were never considered. Though no goddess, she was certainly the most attractive woman in the village. No man would think to say nice things to a woman. It's only a woman!

Silape'a was a man in his mid-twenties. As with most of the members of his race, his male fitness surpasses female beauty. Physically developed by their life at sea and in the bush, their bodies often boast attractive proportions, perfect posture, and a supple agility. Perhaps there were no outstanding athletes in the islands, but they make every motion with grace and strength. On the other hand, from their earliest years, girls have been used to lugging water, carrying baskets of roots from the bush, or dragging palm fronds for weaving. Theirs is a life of unending toil that makes them valuable merely as economic possessions. They tend towards bulk and are apathetic about their grooming. After they are married, what's the use?

Silape'a had an urge to do something with his life and so had gone to school to become a teacher. He was, perhaps, a good one. At any rate, he was the only one who asked me to correct his errors. That is, until one day one of his pupils caught wind of what I was doing, and that was the last correction I was asked to make. It would be better to teach something incorrectly, than to admit an error.

Silape'a had invited me to have a meal with his father, a man of great importance as he was the Talking Chief of the village. These orators were responsible for the proper conduct of any ceremonial function in the town. They knew without error the history of the tribe and the genealogy of everyone in it. This history must also be recited at any function when a visiting *matai* from another village arrived. Each Talking Chief had a classic fly chaser to hold, which quite resembled a short tail from a white horse, attached to a carved handle. He either used it as a fly chaser, or sometimes while trying to emphasize an important point he might shake it at the listener, or he even just let it hold its place on his shoulder. At such a visit, the Talking Chief accompanying the visiting chief also recited the history and genealogy of the village from which they had come. It is a competition of accuracy and importance. It is a much respected, but an exacting position for which they are trained from childhood. Though rightfully the job should have fallen to Silapea, he was not interested in it. "What is its use? We are trying to create a new Samoa," he said to me.

I went with my friend to the other end of the village to the grand *fale* of his father. We had a pleasant meal. The aged chief sat one end of a long eating mat, and I at the other, with very few words passing between us directly. Silape'a did the translating when I was at a total loss for Samoan words. He rose to clear the food trays as he had been the server, and asked me, "Would you like to try some *afatu* (ah FAH too?)"

Always willing to try anything new that I see someone else eat, I answered, "Sure."

He went to the rear of the *fale* and put his hand in a basket. From where I sat, I could only see that whatever it was, had been wrapped in fresh green leaves. These were carefully opened and the concealed object was dipped into a bowl of water, shaken quickly, and put into a soup bowl. It looked like he was handling something too hot for his fingers. Again and again he went into the leaves and followed the same procedure, dipping them in water quickly, shaking them, and dividing them equally into two bowls. He gave one bowl to his father and then brought one over and placed it in front of me.

In the bowl I could see several finger-length white things that closely resembled thick pieces of chalk. Instantly I let out a yowl. "UGH! Take them away!" They were all moving around! The plate was full of a large kind of grub. Quickly, Silape'a removed the offending larvae as I had ordered, and said, disappointedly, "I thought you would have liked them." I chanced to look over at the old *matai* and saw that he was relishing the squeamishness of the *Palangi*. I realized that I would have to eat one of the loathsome things to prove to him that I was worthy of his esteem. I relented and requested that the bowl be passed back to me. Silape'a brought back the wrigglesome things and I stared at them for several seconds while I considered my fate. Gritting my teeth, I asked him how I should eat one. I watched the eyes of his father take in the scene, while he was munching his *afatu* with obvious delight.

My tutor picked up one and bit off the brownish yellow head, which he said I could eat if I wished. Holding the thing by the tail, he used the fingers of the other hand to squeeze out the interior contents, which looked like tobacco juice. He then swallowed the white flesh. Shuddering as never before, I had to make up my mind to try to eat at least one. I asked Silape'a to get one ready for me. He bit off the head and handed me the rest. Closing my eyes and all my other senses, I chewed the thing, and swallowed it. I was almost disappointed to find that it was not at all disagreeable. I picked up another, bit the head off as shown, squeezed it, and swallowed it. Bursting with pride, I ate a third one just to prove it had not been a mirage. No! They don't taste like chicken. Their taste was something like mild tuna mixed with whatever fruit they had been consuming. They generally come in banana, papaya, mango, and orange flavors. Actually, *afatu* amount to a fruit salad that crawls down by itself.

I was famished for any kind of fruit.

Afatu is also. pronounced "ah FAH koo," should you wish to request it sometime.

When we had finished, the old chief rinsed out his mouth and spat it out onto the little coral stones that made the floor. I winced at the sight of it before I realized that the ants that were everywhere would soon clean up any food particles that might be around. Still, my *palangi* upbringing found it most difficult to follow suit. On the other hand, I guess that the old chief was just as disturbed that I did not rinse my mouth out after eating. For a minute I thought that it might not be a bad idea to rinse out the entire problem of misunderstanding.

When I returned to Pau's *fale*, he invited me to join him in the music hut. The town's brass band was rehearsing for a competition they were entering in Apia, on the main island of Upolu. This event was in celebration of the Queen's Birthday. They were quite good, and what they lacked in ability, they made up in enthusiastic natural adaptation. Music has always been a part of their isolated lives.

From the darkness outside, a strange figure came up and sat next to me. "What about the lamp?" he asked. Not having the slightest clue as to the meaning of the question, I had to ask his story.

It seems that both the *fale* and the lamp being used by the band belonged to his father. One night recently this young man had come in and taken the lamp from the hut. It left the band in the dark and very angry. The *Fono of Matais* had convened and meted out a punishment of ten *siligi*. He wanted my evaluation as to the validity of his punishment. It was purely a case of native justice and communal rights, versus the new *Palangi* concept of individual property rights. The dispute probably could not have arisen in ancient times when all property was the produce of the land, and wealth was counted in working hands and *pu'a'a*. One of the early signs of the breakdown of their social structure had come with the introduction of work-for-pay and the ownership of manufactured goods brought in from abroad. Their life could neither run much longer in the familiar pattern, nor could it swing over quickly to a commercial society. There would remain sources of disputes with the misunderstandings of the foreign ways. Perhaps his punishment should have been to cut some of the grass on the public *malae*.

After the practice we returned to the *fale*, and Pau announced that some people were coming over to see me. Meli took several pillows out of the family cabinet and spread them on the mats. Each of these guest pillows had covers painstakingly embroidered with floral bouquets. When guests have settled down on the mats, they put these pillows on their laps to rest their arms, or put them under their shoulders when reclining. They are never sat on, or slept on. As a matter of fact, not infrequently, a short section of a bamboo log, about four inches in diameter, with little short legs, served as a sleeping pillow for them - but not for me.

Very shortly, three teenaged *teines* (TAY nayz,) appeared at the edge of the *fale*. They came in smiling, their glorious teeth no less white than the flowers in their hair, or their spotlessly white Sunday dresses. They had each taken very special care of their appearance. Their bodies had been lightly oiled and shone radiantly. Their hair was perfectly groomed, one had it combed out fully to the waist. The other two had braided theirs into symmetrical ropes. Their feet had been carefully scrubbed, and as they sat down I noticed that the deep cracks that are part of their leather-like soles were almost unnoticeable. They sat in the golden glow of the kerosene lamp glistening with the freshness of the frangipani blossoms in the morning dew. Our conversation amounted to little more than smiles and glances at each other.

They had each brought a piece of fruit. With each smile they muffled a giggle, the fruit was placed on the mat in front of them, and with more smiles and giggles, they rolled the fruit towards where I was sitting. It seemed to be a game among them to see who could urge the fruit forward with the coyest expression and the most amusing giggle.

Finally Pau said, "Take the fruit, they brought it for you. It is late, and Meli and I want to go to bed."

Following what I thought were Pau's instructions, I picked up the three pieces of fruit, and the giggling suddenly stopped. Pau turned to me and asked incredulously, "You want all three tonight?"

When I realized his concern, I smiled at them, thanked them for their visit, and asked Pau to explain that it was too difficult to make a decision. It was a "judgement of Paris" and I did not want to taste the fruit of discord.

I was surprised to realize he didn't think I liked fresh fruit.

Polynesian girls consider it very flattering if Europeans will have an affair with them. If this favor bears fruit, the honor is greatly enhanced, and the lucky girl becomes quite the subject of envy in the community. Everyone is jealous of a pregnant girl. Every baby is wanted. In fact, a girl who owes a debt to someone, will part with a child because she knows it will make the other person happy. She does it willingly as she knows that she can have another. Every child is brought up to think that anyone could be their parent, because they all love it. Children may leave their accustomed home and move into one down the track if they so desire. If this is done in anger at some misdeed of the parents, the new father must defend the child as his own. The real parents will do anything to get their child to return home. The parents are ashamed that in the eyes of the rest of the village they have so mistreated a child that it left. The Samoans can teach much of the rest of the world a thing or two. At first glance, the Samoan world seems to be so full of *talofa* (love) for their children.

But the Samoans also had a dark side when it came to their behavior towards children after the baby stage. As much as they were loved by all, they certainly had their unhappy times. Children were smacked, cuffed, slapped, whacked, dragged, snapped with a piece of cloth, whipped, and even stoned, on almost any pretext. One day I watched for about half an hour while a mother swatted her child a stinging blow with a handful of the central ribs of dried coconut leaflets. The mother kept yelling "Uma!"(Finish! Stop!) The more the child cried, the more it was hit, and the more it cried. I often saw kids sitting on the sand or on a stone sobbing. Others were tormented by neighbors or older siblings. In the villages, there was always some child wailing within hearing distance. So much for the *talofa* attitude towards the very young, it wasn't always practiced.

On dark moonless nights, a game called "night crawling" was frequently played. The girls had to be in their father's *fale* at bedtime. The youths often slipped through the village darkness and into their girlfriend's mosquito net. If she suspected some other disturbance to mean that her father or brother was aware of what was going on, she'd scream. Her suitor would flee with a good part of the village in half-hearted pursuit, almost as much in anger as in curiosity. If the offender was apprehended, he would be subject to a severe thrashing, not because of what he had done, but because he had been caught. Frequently the youths made clever preparations for these expeditions, including the stealing of another man's *lavalava*. If it was dropped in flight, the other fellow became the unwitting victim of the ruse. Even in the islands where so little is worn, a man's clothes were distinctive. When a woman was seen wearing a certain man's *lavalava*, it was considered as much a symbol of marriage as a ring. The village is then happy that the affair is settled.

The full moon had never seemed nearer, bigger, or so bright. It flooded every part of the ocean-side village with incredible radiance. Everything shimmered in the brilliance of the night. This was a very special time on Savaii. The nights of the full moon were celebrated with the lowering of the social barriers. These restrictions, though generally ineffective anyway, were designed by the missionaries to curtail the nocturnal adventures of the young.

On the bright nights of the full moon, the village was entirely different than on the darker nights. During the days before, the women had been out in the bush gathering pandanus leaves. These great leaves, some up to six or more feet long and about three or four inches wide were excellent material for making mats. Their fine qualities were much prized in the islands. They were slightly dried, and cured in the hot sun for several days. Then the leaves were rolled into large cartwheel coils. They still remained flexible and had a tough exterior surface. They also retained a spongy or springy interior so they could be walked on with bare feet without serious damage to the mats.

When the bright nights arrive, the women sat around in gossipy groups. The coils were unrolled, and with a thumbnail, the women peeled off the thorny edges of each leaf. The women worked through nearly all of the night. This single task was reserved for these two nights each month. The rest of the month the women devoted their talents to slicing the leaves lengthwise into strips. When each woman had an ample supply of this weaving material at hand, she began to make her mats. In order of increasingly finer quality and fine weaving, they were: floor mats, sitting mats, eating mat, sleeping mats, and "fine mats." The thinnest strips are reserved for the latter. They must be even in width, all the same color, and have many other qualities that only these experts recognized.

The fine mats were often decorated with colored feathers and were passed down from generation to generation as family heirlooms. They were believed to have some magnetic property that could absorb the spirit from the important people who had owned them. Each one retained a history of its owners that was recited at every ceremonial presentation. Sometimes, at exceptional ceremonies, weddings, funerals, and the like, one of these fine mats was often worn around the waist, over their clothes, just to show the importance of the individual. A woman who made more than a very few of these fine mats in her lifetime was extraordinary. The work was tedious, as a fine mat could take up to a year to weave. The reward was negligible, but as a family possession, they were exalted beyond any other material worth.

Around their happily working mothers were clustered the many children who seemed to come with the frequency of coconuts. The land was fertile, and their climate was protective. Even at their tender age, the naked children felt that these nights were something of a holiday for them too, and ran shrieking happily among the shadows until they tired and came home to rest on mother. Those who were older were chattering in the shadows or singing the lilting melodies of the isles.

The young adults had been entertaining each other in groups, playing the ukuleles, singing, and accompanying each other in turn as they performed their personalized steps in the *siva*, the Samoan hula. Soon they drifted off into the shadows and were not seen again until daybreak. It had been a long day, but the village was universally satisfied and contented while practicing their traditions.

It was with the memory of their ability to make so much from their limited resources, and the comfort with which they faced life, that I was to leave Savaii with my own directions altered. If we could make a compromise with both the Samoan and Western lifestyles I had now experienced, I was quite sure that some of our own problems could be resolved.

Chapter XIX
THE ISLAND OF UPOLU

After spending a month in the fascinating environment of Savaii, I was happy to disembark from the overnight chugger onto the shores of Upolu again. Apia was more than a welcome sight. My first stop was the ice cream parlor. As I placed my order, a priest standing next to me asked if I was an American. I responded positively and said that I had just returned from a wonderful *malanga* on Savaii.

"Oh, then you speak Samoan?" he queried. I laughed, and he invited me to sit at a table if I had time.

He introduced himself as Father Felix. "My followers call me *Patele Felise*" (pah TAY lay fay LEE say), he added. He was a Samoan-American, as he had been born in the town of *Pago Pago* (Pango Pango) on the island of Tutuila (too too WEE lah), which is American Samoa. He had decided to settle on Upolu in Western Samoa because he wanted to start some schools for the young adults who had grown up before the New Zealand Administration had established the public school system on these islands after World War II. The public schools would not admit students over 16 years old. Patele did not share the social discriminatory feelings of the traditional church schools. He saw changes coming. He wanted his schools to prepare the young adults for the new ways of life that would be inevitable.

"It would be ideal if I could have them learn to speak English," Patele said, "because no one is going to learn Samoan." He also wanted to teach them basic mathematics so they could function in the developing economy. He sighed as he expressed the unrealistic hope that they would still wish to continue to practice the traditional *fa'a Samoa*. I was eating all this up as fast as I was eating up my ice cream. The idea of staying here and teaching fascinated me, but I said nothing, … yet.

Felise had recently returned from a trip to the United States where he studied at a university in Boston for a year. The trip had been given to him by the Catholic diocese. He assumed that part of the reason was to get him out of Samoa where he had become something of a nuisance. He had established several educational centers on Upolu, which he administered as schools, for a single fee, and were open to all. Unlike the others, there was no religious teaching or requirement. These had become very popular with the young adults. It was becoming apparent that if he were left to continue this work of bringing non-mission education to his parishioners, his example would prove that it could be done if anyone in an official capacity really cared. The church was angry. The government was unhappy that he was hiring non-licensed teachers. At any rate, when he returned from the United States, he found that all his property had been confiscated by the Mother Church. He was once again assigned to mere priestly duties.

Not much time had passed before his parishioners had begun to ask him to set up some more schools. The government had set up schools for the young, but this left a large part of the population without any hope of getting any education. It was for these unfortunate but eager students that Patele had begun again to set up his little system of schools. He called them *Solulufiga* (so loo loo feeng GAH, meaning Haven for the Abandoned). One was in Apia, the capital city, with a population of about 5000 souls. Another was in Leulumoega (lay oo loo mo ENG gah), which was only a quarter the size of the capital. The third was in a little village some 40 miles out in the Lefaga (lay FAHNG gah) District on the other (south) side of the island.

Before World War II, Lefanga was a most remote area. It was isolated by a rather dense jungle that covered the central mountain ridge. It was only approachable by boat until the Americans stationed on Upolu built a dirt road over the ridge and down the other side. This road not only made access to the area possible, but it also opened up the interior for development.

The second big event in the lives of the people of Lefanga was the arrival of the motion picture company that filmed *Return to Paradise* starring "Gali Kupa." This was a spectacular occasion for the islanders, who earned money as extras working with their film hero, Gary Cooper. They already knew him from seeing so many of his *kaupoi* (Westerns) movies. Americans, when they came, seemed to bring good fortune.

Their prosperity continued with an ever-increasing demand from New Zealand for their bananas. It then became a matter of clearing more areas of their land to increase production. When a banana tree, which is more like a huge bunch of celery, bears a bunch of fruit, it is finished and is cut down. The root is then dug up, split into sections where small suckers have sprouted, and transplanted. The sprout on each section eventually grows a new tree. (I believe this practice still continues.)

It takes a full year and good luck from harsh winds to produce the next bunch of fruit. For weeks the saplings must be kept free of the rapidly growing vines that would encircle and strangle them. Each plantation has to be sprayed and cut constantly.

Eventually the fruit appears. When they are full grown and plump, but still green, they are ripe enough to be harvested. Each large bunch, or stalk, of fruit has an average of some one hundred to two hundred bananas. It then has to be carried to the village. In 1956 there was no port facility in Apia to handle the whole stalks. Therefore the women of the villages began the task of stripping the fruit individually from the stalk and pack it neatly in shipping crates. The crates were made by the villagers from bundles of slats and nails left by the pick-up truck. One case held about two hundred bananas, took about an hour to pack and earned two dollars. A hard working family with good land could ship out about thirty cases every two weeks.

Another main crop, and potentially the best paying, was cacao. It takes several years for the trees to mature. There had not been time yet for cacao to make a great change in the economy, but the number of plantations was increasing in the recently opened land. The labor involved was mostly in the collecting of the pods, which hang randomly from the trunk and branches of the tree like rose-colored elongated

Christmas ornaments. The fleshy pods were buried until the husk rotted off. Then the clusters of almond-sized beans inside the pod were removed, collected, and taken to the stream to be cleaned. They spent several days on mats drying in the sun, to become properly cured for either storage or shipment to town.

All this produce was brought to Apia and hand-loaded onto the barge, taken out to the ship lying offshore, and loaded on board. But it had brought a new prosperity to many of the villages in the outer districts. It would certainly be another push for change in the traditional *fa'a Samoa*.

It was because this new and unexpected income was coming to the District of Lefanga, which was in Patele Felise's parish, that they asked him to open a school for their young people. It might attract other young men and women from the area to come and join their local *a'ingas*. They had a need for more young willing hands to increase the labor force for the growing agricultural economy.

As Patele Felise and I sat overlong at the table in the ice cream parlor, I was amazed at the man across from me. He was almost six feet tall and probably tipped the scales at some two hundred pounds. He was shrouded in a well-worn, dreary black cassock. All that could be seen was a strikingly handsome face. Square cut and strong, he had finer features than any other Samoan I had yet seen. His ample hair was completely silvered, which added another aristocratic touch. In spite of answering the call to the cloth, one could see at a glance he was all man, and one deeply committed to his own people.

We took a jitney truck out to Felise's rectory in Leulumoenga, a nice trip of several miles westwards on the main road along the north shore. The shoreline and the beautiful lagoon with its transparent blues were seldom out of sight from the paved road. Added to the charm of this trip was the sight of the Island of Savaii on the western horizon. Along the way, on the mountain side of the road we passed a collection of neat little villages with traditional *fales*, and a few square wooden boxes that seemed so out of place. On the ocean side I saw an almost unbroken row of unbelievable variations on the general theme of outhouses. I could not believe the individuality of so many innovations. Since there was a *fale vau* for each home on the south side of the road, there were plenty of them to admire. Also it was interesting to note that there were sardine sized scavenger fish that took care of any waste problems, and they themselves are part of the piscatorial food chain.

Perched in the shallow water near the tidal lines, like cranes in their motionless wait for food, were these lavatories that the *Palangis* introduced in their drive for sanitation. While they gained in their purpose of cleanliness, they destroyed much of the natural beauty of the seascape for the passerby. Some *fale vaus* were painted, some were not, some had doors, and some had not. Some had bridges, some had logs, a few had ladders, and some had nothing. Some were perched on stone foundations and some were on frail posts. A favorite game played by the habitual traveler along this part of Upolu was to decide what to look for, and then count them. One search might be to find those in use with the door open. Next trip might be to see how many have at least one of their supporting posts missing. A few were without roofs. One had only a door in a frame, but no walls. There was nearly always someone who had forgotten the door key, but was in too much of a hurry to go back and get it. Meanwhile they unashamedly took advantage of being there anyway. The variety was endless, and the tabulated results of the search were amazing. If nothing else, native inventiveness was clearly demonstrated in their adjustment to the modern ways they were being taught.

We finally arrived at Patele's rectory, a leftover from the European occupation. The two-storied plastered building boasted walls as thick as a fortress. Now it was surrounded by bougainvillea, hibiscus of many colors, and frangipani bushes. It looked more like a rundown plantation house. A rickety verandah surrounded the second floor, offering us a wonderfully cool place to sit in the shade with a magnificent view of the ocean and Savaii beyond.

As Patele Felise and I talked, we discovered that each of us prized the attainment of knowledge for his people above everything else. We agreed that this must not upset their cultural patterns. That was most important, but was the least likely to come to pass. "We must teach them the new ideas, and yet instill in each the belief that their own civilization is worth saving," he said. We did not want to suppress their *fa'a Samoa* only to superimpose an alien culture. We agreed on almost every point. He told me that the only place he could place me was in the little village of Falese'ela (fah lay say' ay LAH) out in Lefanga, which I might find too isolated. It sounded to me like the perfect answer for my quest for something to do so I could stay in a village and study their ways. At the same time, I might be able to make some contribution to their general welfare. I was all set to go.

We rose to meet the head of the mission, an American priest from Maine who had been sent here years before to run this outpost. He wanted to show me something. We walked to the other side of the rectory, and there, almost blinding us with the reflected light from its white stuccoed walls, was the church. In any other community in the world, it would have been passed over as a tasteless adaptation of bad gothic architecture. Here it was impossible to pass over. It was far too bold. Its two massive towers rudely rammed through the pleasant green surroundings. The pointed windows, the crenellated battlements, and the many steps up to the front entrance, all of it, completely overwhelmed the village of *fales* that was clustered at its feet. It was truly the champion of the competition for ecclesiastic grandeur that had gripped this island. It seems that each shepherd had prodded his flock to construct something ever bigger to prove their superior devotion to God over that of the people in any neighboring village.

Nearly every village had two or more sects represented, and this divided the towns into groups as if they were teams. When we viewed this temple, which to me represented power, not love, I was ashamed at what our culture had brought to these islands. I felt only pity when the priest from Maine, with a grandiose sweep of his arm, boasted, "When I came here this was nothing but a basement. I built this." Compulsively, I looked at his hands and saw that he had never laid any of the thousands of stones that held this clerical cave together. True or not, he considered it his personal monument. I didn't care for it.

Patele and I got into a truck and headed westwards until we came to the new road over the mountain ridge. It was a wide dirt road that was beginning to need attention with repair machinery. This road had been cut through the impenetrable jungle to the south side by the Seabees who had landed in Samoa in April 1942. I believe that they also had constructed the base for the paved road along the north shore of Upolu. We turned south over the mountain and reached another smaller and more rutted dirt road off to the west. There was a sharp turn in the road and a clearing off to the south, and there below we could see a sapphire bay. Was that where I was to begin my own dream of living the island life?

We turned off of the main road and nosed down a mere track over rocks and ruts, between carefully tended coconut groves. We bounced and dove over the bumps and slithered through the sand patches, until ahead we saw the clearing that meant we were near the shore. Once on the level we could drive almost anywhere on the hard packed sand. It was so smooth. There was not a single piece of rubbish to be seen. It was about mid-day, so the palms cast their star-shaped shadows on the glowing natural pavement ahead. Every *fale* was in perfect repair. This was where the movie *Return to Paradise* had been filmed, because it was the perfect setting.

We continued on a few more miles and passed through a couple of settlements without stopping. By the islander's mysterious system of communication called Radio Coco, the news of our arrival preceded us. In a couple of villages the locals were standing in the middle of the track waving at the priest sitting in the cab with the driver. The greeters had to scurry to the side of the road as the truck passed, showering the happy jumping youngsters with a spray of dust. In front of a church, the driver came to a skidding halt, and the faithful ran to the side to greet Patele. After the excitement of the event cooled a bit, someone noticed the passenger standing in the back of the vehicle. At first they stared curiously, then affectionately at the *Palangi*. Each one surveyed me thoroughly, and on the basis of their findings, demonstrated their friendliness. Generally it was with shy gestures that brought tittering giggles and laughter among themselves. I felt like I was in the Popemobile at the Vatican. The braver ones stepped forward with a limp hand extended and offered one-pump handshakes. After the first ones had begun the shaking hands, the others pressed around as if I were giving out sweets.

The sun glistening on the water of the lagoon was dazzling. The reflections were blinding. Patele shuffled through the sand towards the church, its whitewashed walls gleaming as if they were made of snow.

I turned towards the beach and into the shade of the palms and sat, glad to be out of the jostling truck. I would be there for the next hour while the Catholic half of the village was having the service. Most of the rest of the residents rolled over and returned to their snoozing, which was the proper thing to do on a Sabbath afternoon. A few of the young adults gathered around to question the *Palangi* visitor and practice their mastery of a few English words or phrases that they had learned somewhere. Others just lingered and watched with fascination.

Chapter XX

FALESE'ELA

Eventually Patele returned to the truck and said that the next stop would be Falese'ela (fah lay say' ay LAH). This was where he was taking me to be part of the new school. The road gradually changed to two sandy tracks through the grass. It followed close to the shore so the beauties of the lagoon were never out of sight. Sweeping off towards the west was a long curving beach. At the far end I could see a cluster of tall palms. Under them, set on top of a *paepae* that jutted out into the soft blue water was the most picturesque *fale* I had yet seen. It had been built exactly like all of the others. The back porch arrangement permitted a man lying out there in the sun or in the shade under the thatched dome, to have a fishing line dropped over the side that he could attend with less effort than it took him to stay awake. He had moored his *va'a* to the few steps that led down to the water. It reminded me of a sleek gondola docked at the doorstep of some small Venetian palazzo.

As an aside; it happened later on that I visited this *fale* several times. We were never troubled with mosquitoes, as the smooth sea breeze nudged them inland all night long. It was the one *fale* in the village that received the low slanting rays of the morning sun that warmed the sleepers. The sun reflecting on the white coral sand under the water made it bright at mid-day when the coco trees overhead shaded the *fale* itself. In the evening every sunset could be seen by merely rolling over and watching the glorious colors, first brilliant, and then muted, finally blending into the encroaching nightfall. If ever there was a home that had been designed to give the family all the best the world had to offer, this was it.

In front of this *fale* the track took a sudden turn inland, and we drove through a hole in the curtain of thick green underbrush and trees. Once in the open again, the village of Falese'ela could be seen at a glance. Like all of the others, it stretched along both sides of the car tracks, which dissolved completely after another 200 yards and became a mere footpath through the grass. On the mountain side (east) of the track were two *malaes* separated by a stone wall and some trees. The smaller *malae* was in front of the first church, which was Catholic. The bigger *malae* was in front of the London Mission Society church. Fortunately for the village, both churches were modest in size and neatly whitewashed.

On the west side of the track, opposite, and constructed on a spot between the two churches, was a recently painted little store. The impartial trader named Tapo was taking no chances by setting up his shop any nearer to one church than the other.

All of the ground of this village was covered with grass that had been neatly and laboriously cut by hand with bush knives. Many of the *fales* were surrounded with hibiscus bushes, clumps of decorative sugar cane, and red poinsettia trees so high that a man could walk under them and not touch the blossoms. In a row behind the churches were several stark kapok trees, their arrow straight branches at right angles to their green trunks, looking more artificial than cheap Christmas trees. Behind them the hill rose to form a small shoulder of the main central mountain. Because of the dense growth around the village, I was not aware at first that Falese'ela actually sat on the shore of an inlet that like the track, had taken a sudden bend inland just beyond the *fale* with the fishing porch. I was already pleased with the people for the pride they had and the care they took of this settlement. It was a beautiful spot.

We got out of the truck and mingled with the surrounding crowd eager to greet their priest and the *Palangi* teacher he was bringing. We then walked across the rich green grass of the *malae*, now re-named "the school yard." We all walked up the steps of the *Fale Palangi*. It was a rectangular building about 60 feet long and half as wide, with a sort of long narrow porch running along the rear of the building. The outer perimeter of the corrugated iron roof was supported by a series of square cut Canadian lumber posts connected by a porch railing. The floor was an immense block of cement raised about a yard above the ground. The structure resembled a large park bandstand, or a picnic shelter brightly painted green and white with a red roof. It was the town social center. It was indeed a *Fale Palangi*, a half-caste house.

The catechist, who carried on the religious work of Patele Felise when he was not there, had taken squatter's rights to live in the *Fale Palangi*. Behind a floral printed curtain that ran across one end, there were two tremendous beds. Both were higher than a normal table. As a man of God, the catechist had slept higher than the rest of the village, to be nearer to God. Recently the *Fale Palangi* had also been transformed into a school by merely hanging up two blackboards Now that there were two male teachers, one a *Palangi*, the former tenant was moved to an ordinary *fale* next door. The teachers were to occupy the hallowed beds. I, for one, would need all the help I could get.

Patele went next door to the church to conduct the service. I strolled around the area getting my bearings. After the service in the church, everyone attended a feast on the back porch of the *Fale Palangi*. An ample barefooted young lady named Linga (LING ah) dressed in sparkling white, sat between Patele and me, fanning the food or serving that for which she saw a need. Linga was one of the teachers, and she had been assigned to take the lower school classes in a smaller *fale*. She asked me, "Why do you sit on the floor?"

"I believe in the *fa'a Samoa*," I answered

She sucked in a breath and responded, "Not me! I am a European girl. I prefer to sit on a chair." In truth, no pair of European-made shoes could ever be found to fit her ping pong paddle-sized feet.

Before us was a spread of various leaf-wrapped packages of fish, some chicken, an enameled dish of *pisupo*, *palusami*, and three hard-boiled eggs. These were the first three eggs I had seen in all the months since I had left Honolulu. Patele took one egg. He passed the plate to me, offering me an egg, and then he placed the plate in front of himself. Three dozen people stared at the lone surviving egg. After several minutes of urging from Patele, I took the third egg ravenously, in a delicate way, but ravenously. Linga looked as if she had been smacked. "OH!" she said with pique, as she snapped the fan on the mat, "I wanted that one!" The rarity of an egg made them available only to the clergy and visiting dignitaries. However, Linga soon cooed sweetly as we complimented her on a chocolate cake that she had falsely claimed in English that she had made. She knew the other villagers would not understand her. Short, dark, and bare-footed, she said with a smile that I was going to learn to hate "I told you, I am a European girl."

After the very serious business of eating had been completed, Patele introduced me to an assemblage of the Catholic faithful, saying that I had come to live with them and share their life and that they need make no concession to me because I was a *Palangi*. None, that is, except that they must make no attempt to force me to attend services, or force me to pay fines if I didn't. That, of course, was tantamount to breaking one of the most important and most sacred laws of the village that had been established during the harsh rule of the missionaries. I would endeavor to live up to all of their customs to the best of my ability. Patele explained to the gathering that, "In the *Palangi*'s country, they do things differently." That seemed to satisfy them. The introduction pleased them very much and appealed to their nationalistic feeling that here was one *Palangi* who was going to try to live up to their standards instead of continuing in his own irrational ways.

There was a traditional ceremony of welcome, including a bowl of ava and endless speeches in Samoan. A stocky young man of about my own age was sitting nearby. He rolled over towards me and suggested that we leave during the speeches and the religious instruction period. He introduced himself as Malaki (mah LAH kee). Malaki was a good-looking Samoan with obsidian eyes and teeth white enough to match the coconut meat on which he had thrived. He said that he had been teaching the upper classes. He was only going to be in the village temporarily until Patele found a more permanent teacher. He led me through town showing me everything of interest, being the bathing pools in the creek beyond the last *fale* and the huge walled-in village pig pen. The pig pen was where most of the *pu'a'a*, especially the larger ones, were kept so that they could run more or less freely. Occasionally a small piglet was kept around the *fale* of the *a'inga* as a garbage disposal. We checked out the creek and the bathing pools. We went to the shore and inspected the newest *fale vau*. It was not exactly like a tour of Rome.

As we walked, Malaki told me that he was the son of a wealthy storekeeper and had been running his own store for several years. Malaki's father had wanted him to go into the priesthood, but there was a girl who made him think otherwise. The store was the only answer. Patele lived in the rectory directly across the street from the store and had asked Malaki to come to the new school and teach English and arithmetic, which were the only two important subjects to be taught. He was glad that I had come, as he did not like the village. "It is poor," he complained. "All they eat is fish. I like the canned meat I get in my own town." Malaki showed his fondness for food with his prosperous belly. His inner man had expanded beyond the normal limits of his outer self. Size, to his countrymen, is an indication that he did not have to do physical labor and that he could afford the luxury of fine food and plenty of it. To keep up with the *fa'a Samoa*, one must count calories to make sure of getting enough.

Malaki showed me the *fale* where he was living and asked if I would care to share it with him. He did not like sleeping on the high beds in the school. He did not like it that many of the students who came from other villages also slept in the *Fale Palangi* on the cement floor. Inside his *fale*, I was introduced to his uncle Utai (oo TIE, as in necktie). Although Utai had silvered hair, he was still a good specimen of a once-powerful man. In his youth he had earned the name "Utai," which means "he who hits with the blow of a hammer." His advancing age only became apparent when he said that his oldest grandchild was 12 years old. He had the bearing of an aristocrat with an obvious noble background that stretched all the way back to the first canoes that carried the Polynesian pioneers to these then uninhabited islands. He could recite his family genealogy back for many generations. He was kind and gentle, and yet his courage and character could never be doubted.

At this point I will pause and introduce the family with whom I would live. Ponga, Utai's ample wife, was also of noble lineage. When she sat on the mat, she was a single confined mass with no angles, edges, or straight lines. She resembled a pile of melting ice cream. While in the *fale*, she most frequently wore one of the old black umbrella covers, the circular piece of material, with her head through the hole in the middle. This was set off with a broad brimmed white straw hat trimmed with colored crepe paper. Ponga could smile in such a way that a whole day of troubles could be forgotten in a moment. "Ponga," meaning "knot of a tree," was called that because she was crippled and moved with a severe limp. The day before the bananas were to be shipped, Ponga would sit patiently and pack one to two thousand of them in the crates that her son had put together. Clusters of the fruit had been removed from the main stem, but she had to separate them and pack them individually in the crates.

At our first meeting both Utai and Ponga were very warm and friendly. I knew that it would not take long to learn to love this family as my own.

Utai and Ponga had two sons, a daughter, and her close friend living with them. Petelo (pay TAY lo), Samoan for Peter, was the oldest son. He was about my age, and he was to become my close friend. Petelo lived with his wife Failili (fie LEE lee) and their four children in their own *fale* next door. Petelo's color came from the sun, his physique from hard work. I learned very little Samoan, but Petelo and I somehow could understand each other, and we could have short conversations. Failili must have been a beautiful girl, as her fine features were not commonly found among Samoan women. Her skin was clear, and she shared, with all the others around her, the perfect teeth that the Samoans have kept, along with their native diet. A woman's hard life had rounded her figure. Her hair was often left uncombed. Like most rural women, she spent little time on personal grooming. There was no point in it for a woman to try to be attractive once she was married. She was a life partner, a necessary economic unit to help the family survive and possibly prosper. Sundays were show-off occasions when everyone turned themselves out with pride.

Failili had been to a mission school in Apia, where she had learned and remembered enough English to make it easier for all of us to understand each other. Her two youngest children, Anna and Niko, were still at home, as they were only three and four years old and the sweetest children ever. Niko was almost as tanned as his father, and his head was always kept closely clipped. Anna had picked up lovely blonde hair someplace, and her glorious curls were the envy of every girl in the village.

One day a head clipped child came up to me and watched as I was making a watercolor of the *fale*. I turned and smiled and used two of my dozen words of Samoan and said, "*Maneuia* Niko." the rough equivalent I thought, of "Good Niko." The child burst into tears. Too late, I realized it was Anna, who had just been shorn of her golden locks. I found out later from Failili that it would be easier to keep her head clear of fleas.

There was no formality about moving in with Utai and Ponga. Two of their children, an adult daughter named Lua Au (LOO ah OW, meaning two days) and a son named Lua Po (two nights) lived at home. The entire time I was in the village, Lua Po, who was a student in the school, never spoke a word to me, except in class. His ability with the ukulele far surpassed his ability to handle arithmetic and English in the classes. He was in his late teens, but it seemed to me he would have to settle for life on the farm.

Petelo, the oldest son, was the obvious heir to the fine family line. With him and his children, it would continue. The Petelos ate their meals with us around the family circle in the big *fale*, but returned to their own *fale* for the night. From the moment I moved in, I tried as best I could to live their ways and never considered myself anything but a slow learning (of their language) member of their family.

I did have a personal interest in breakfast that the others did not seem to share. I had carried a large can of uncooked oatmeal and another of powdered milk, called "Klim." I had discovered that raw oats and this milk, which needed only water, no sugar, was a good and satisfying combination. The others could hold out until the large mid-morning meal. I could not, or at least I chose not to start a day on an empty stomach. I did dine alone in the early morning sunshine. At first I entertained the usual audience of onlookers, until everyone had satisfied their curiosity.

One evening after eating, Petelo asked me what would happen if I didn't shave. I said that I would grow my beard if he would show me his complete *pe'a*, body tattoo, so I could take a picture of it. He shyly shook his head, but I was determined to see it some day. Utai also had his *pe'a*, but I knew better than to ask my *matai* to show me something so personal. At that moment I decided to let my beard grow out again. Several weeks later, it became quite full. But Petelo was still not willing to show me his *pe'a*. The tattoo covered most men completely from the middle of the back to just below the knees. I imagined that it looked like a pair of black lace leotards. Although men were considered fully dressed once they had their *pe'a*, I never saw any man expose it, even in the bathing pools. Petelo was reluctant to show his *pe'a* to me, good friends as we had become. So in exchange, I refused to let him feel my beard. One night in the dinner circle he slyly leaned over and stroked my beard with his hand, and gleamed with pride at his sneaky achievement. In an instantaneous response, I leaned over and, grabbing the waistband of his *lavalava*, gave it a quick yank to at least expose that part of his hip that he was not sitting on. The family laughed, but Petelo thought it a great indignity. My quick glance did not satisfy me, but we'd had an intimate family moment.

During the following months I was to go to Apia every other weekend for mail and shopping. Only on those occasions did I don my *palangi* clothing and feel different from the community where I had chosen to live. I hope they felt that way also. Had I attempted to wear a Samoan *lavalava* in town I might have been questioned by the police or at the very least ridiculed by other Caucasians.

Returning now to the day of my arrival in Falese'ela and the reception in the *Fale Palangi*, it had already become late afternoon. Patele Felise had departed for his rectory. Malaki and I had returned from our orientation walk around the village. It was time for me to get settled in what was to be my new home. My backpack had been brought from the truck to the *fale* of Utai. It did not take long with Malaki's help to get organized. My backpack with most of my *palangi* stuff was stored up on the rafters under the roof. My shirts and *lavalavas* were put in the family chest. Everything in there was family property, and anyone could wear anything. Lua Au had the job of keeping it all in order, laundering, ironing, and storing it in the chest.

Ponga had decided to lay a stack of three or four sleeping mats at one end of the *fale* that was to be my area. It is possible that in doing this she had displaced Lua Po, causing him to carry the no-speaking grudge. The mats were beautiful examples of the weaving arts. Ponga had made them, and each had required many hours of tedious labor. All of them had a pattern of various colored wool fringe around the edges. There were also two pillows stuffed with kapok, in white cases decorated with colorfully embroidered flowers. The mosquito net was hung, and everything was made ready for me to spend my first night in the village in the most splendid *fale* in town. Thankful for my weeks of orientation on the island of Savaii, I knew the general pattern of domestic life. I was totally content with what promised to be a great experience, and before long I had dozed off.

For the first time I could remember during the past several months, it rained most of the night. It was a soft, gentle, steady shower. It made a most soothing sound as it fell on the thick thatch roof. The blinds had been lowered on the windward side. I felt very comfortable as I went to sleep on the mats in a place that was to be my home for a while.

In the morning, the *fale* was ablaze with golden light of the early sun as it shone over the ridge behind the kapok trees. The morning air was bright but chilly. It was a Monday. The rest of the household was already up and about. The thickness of the *pulupulu* (poo loo poo loo) covering me had been just barely enough to ward off the night chill. A *pulupulu* is made of two equal lengths of *pareau* sewn together along the long sides to make a big sheet. I had brought several yards of *pareau* cloth of different patterns with me from Tahiti. So I had my own, and unique, *lavalavas*. I did not have a minute to think about getting up at this early hour.

Malaki had already arisen from his net and was waiting for me to stir. "Come! We go to take our bath," he said, with an eagerness that I did not feel. Armed with towel, soap, and toothbrush, I stepped out onto the cold wet rocks surrounding the *fale*, and onto the cold wet grass. Icy green fingers shot between my toes and I began to think less and less about immersion in the river at the end of the village. The sand stuck to our wet feet, but it was brushed off as soon as we got to the end of the track. We passed all of the three dozen *fales* in town, while most of the dozens of pairs of eyes in the village were upon us. It was a novelty for them to see a *Palangi* enter into the life of the village so completely. In fact, I was told that no other had ever spent the night in the village.

As we passed the big *malae* in front of the LMS (London Mission Society) Church, I saw a group of boys and girls squatting on their haunches whacking away at the thick mat of grass, cutting it with bush knives (machetes). Malaki told me that every Monday morning; every family in the village had to send someone to help with the cutting. Utai had sent Lua Au, but she hardly smiled as we passed. The sun was beginning to glow over the treetops, and its welcome warmth dissolved the chill and felt so good on the skin. Each *fale* we passed had nice smells with the smoke coming out of their *umus* into the early morning air along with the ever-present wails of unhappy children, seldom spanked, but often scolded. The few dogs were curious, but not guarded. The trader waved from his porch. Children popped out of their *fales* and joined the procession towards the river. Children always followed me until they recognized that I fit into their own patterns and that my routine would not be worth the difference to pursue it so closely.

Today was a red letter day. For the very first time a *Palangi* was heading for the river with a towel and a bar of soap. Every child who could shout, scream, run, skip, walk, or be carried by another was crowding around us as the procession gradually passed through the line of *fales*. Every adult of the community was observing every move I made. Each step nearer the pool became more embarrassing. If I blushed, I blushed all over. Though I was used to being examined carefully in every village I had been in for the past months, I was only a temporary curiosity. I had chosen freely to live among these people, and any false move I made would supply the conversational mills with grains of humor for a long time to come.

The steps we had taken totaled up to a distance of less than a quarter of a mile. In time, it took several minutes. I had waved at every living soul in sight, and said some 100 "*Talofa lava*" greetings, similar to the Hawaiian "Aloha." Every person we met asked, "*Alu fea?*" (Where are you going?) It is the first thing anyone asks another upon meeting. It means nothing more serious than the "How are you?" we say in English, because the answer is just as unimportant.

Although regally attended by a noisy entourage as we walked through the curious community, Malaki and I were not the first to arrive at the stream. It was a large stream that began in the hills where there was often heavy rainfall, and it flowed through a rocky course under massive shade trees until it reached this point near the sea. The current was not swift, but there was more than enough flow to change the water continually in the pools every day, plus supplying all of the considerable needs of the village. Half a dozen large stones spanned the stream at the end of the path as stepping stones to the two *fales* on the other side. Upstream from the stones was a shallow pool about knee deep and big enough for more than a dozen men. It was full of curious *matais* this morning.

Above the men's pool was another smaller one formed by a small cement dam, which was the water supply for Falese'ela. The women and girls generally came with five-gallon cans to carry it back to their *fale*. Small children would go in pairs and hang the can from a pole on their shoulders. Older girls often balanced the cans on their heads. They all had to make many trips a day to supply the family needs. Several water carriers had collected there to watch what would happen.

The main pool was below the stepping stones. This pool was for the women and children. This water hole had been cleared of all of the removable rocks and the bottom covered with small smoothly rounded stones. It was about 50 feet long and not quite half as wide. The water was waist deep. It would be big enough I thought to have a short satisfying swim. This morning, however, it was crowded with most of the girls and young women of the village. When all of us reached the edge of the stream, more than half of Falese'ela had gathered there! They made a colorful display in their bright garb standing in and around the pools that, in turn, were surrounded by all kinds of interesting tropical flora. Shafts of sunlight filtered through the trees and made the place seem so festive.

In the lower end of the large pool, the children were frolicking with the sheer joy of being in running water. Many women had brought laundry to do and were scrubbing on the black rocks just below the large pool. One old man was washing out his cocoa beans in a wooden box as if he were panning for gold. Many were brushing their teeth. Several girls were washing their hair. Some were scrubbing younger siblings. A group of older boys were just sitting there watching the girls. Everybody was doing something to give them an excuse to be there when the *Palangi* came to take his bath.

As only the older men and chiefs were allowed to use the upper pool, Malaki pointed to the crowded one and indicated that that was to be ours also. It is no easy trick to try to bathe with two yards of cloth flapping around the body and trying to get a thorough cleaning. Some of the women just wear dresses when they go for their bath. In spite of the difficulty, everyone seems to have marvelous fun. And that may be the whole point.

We prepared to go in. Malaki walked to the edge and down the several slippery looking steps and entered gracefully with the bright red yardage of his *lavalava* floating on the surface for a second, baring his legs and embarrassing him. He had to push the unruly cloth down with both hands. To avoid this, and knowing that all eyes were focused on me, I decided to exhibit my athletic prowess, and dove in. The water was cold. No, after a second it was a glorious tingle on the flesh. When I came up to the surface I was even more embarrassed than Malaki. Frantically I fished around for the *lavalava*, which had come off during the plunge. It afforded the crowd great merriment and by joining in wholeheartedly, I saved the day. My audience was having a delightful laugh. All there was to do now was to apply soap liberally and forget the difficulties.

Second only to the difficulty of getting into the water is getting out. Swathed as we were from waist to ankle in what felt like adhesive tape, we had to climb out of the pool using the same slippery rocks, and then once upon the grass, dry off with a big towel. The towel is then meant to replace the wet *lavalava* for the walk home. With a deft movement of the wrists, arms and hips it can be done. However, Malaki, not willing to trust my ability to copy his practiced movements, made a shelter of his own soaking garment so I could change. Back we walked to his *fale* without the crowd. They were satisfied for the moment and had disappeared into their own *fales* to discuss every aspect of the day's event.

Chapter XXI
SCHOOL BEGINS

Malaki walked over to the *Fale Palangi* (the school) and rang the school bell, which was a long metal tank that had once held bottled gas. This was the signal for all that school would start sometime in the next half hour or so. Meanwhile I was shaving with a crowd of the local curious folk looking on. When he returned, we dressed for school in our school uniform *lavalava*, which was plain navy blue, worn in the formal style with folds in the front and secured with a white belt. The bare upper body was optional, but the teachers all wore shirts. Malaki gathered the notebooks and papers he had corrected, and we crossed the *malae* to the school. The beds had been dismantled the evening before when it had been decided that Malaki and I would not sleep there. They were moved into the Catechist's new quarters so he could again sleep "closer to God." We hung each of the two blackboards at opposite ends of the schoolroom. We were ready for the classes to come. Malaki was taking one end of the classroom for arithmetic, and I was to have the other for English.

Malaki had already divided the students into two groups after his previous weeks of working with them. I was only going to watch for the first day or two to get the hang of what he had been doing and what sort of routine the students expected. He busied himself writing something on the blackboard that looked like something from the Bible.

"Why are you attempting to teach them English with such prose that is so hard to read?" I asked him.

"That is what they like to read and can understand." On the other board he wrote several problems, and then went to ring the bell again.

In a short while the students arrived and played around in the *malae* as they do every place. They were, to my surprise, all ages and all sizes. Many of them seemed to be too young, others seemed too old. Many of them could be parents, I thought. Some had brought cardboard suitcases with extra clothing. They had been back to their own villages over the weekend and would stay with their *a'inga* in Falese'ela during the school week. Some just brought their lunch, a couple of boiled or baked green bananas wrapped in a breadfruit leaf, or just a plain roasted taro in their hand.

The taro plant has a large bulb-like root that sprouts great big arrowhead-shaped leaves. When the top of it is removed and put back into the swampy soil, it will grow another plant. The bulb turns purplish and sticky when it is boiled, and it turns tan when it is baked. It is similar to a heavy potato, or perhaps a turnip without the strong flavor. The most common type of Hawaiian "one-finger" or "two-finger" poi is made from the mashed boiled taro. There is also a dry land taro; both are staple starches of the islanders' diet.

When the third bell sounded, all the boys and girls lined up in two formations, the smaller ones in a separate group. Once in neat rows I could see that the enrollment was about six dozen. First they sang "God Save the Queen." Then, with far more vigor, they sang the Samoan anthem, which for hearty voices is second to none. One boy dropped out of formation and sat on the ground near a five gallon tin can, and with two sticks, began to beat a rhythm. The rest did marching formations at Linga's commands. Dressed in spotless white, and her hair glistening from an overdose of coconut oil, she became radiant at the smooth show the children were putting on.

One young man named Pepelo (pay PAY lo) tried successfully to make things go badly for Linga for the sheer joy of it. He was called down several times, but no serious attempt at discipline was made. He was obviously a teacher's pet. I had met Pepelo the day before in the town where Patele had stopped to hold a service. I had asked him in English, "What do you do?"

"I work in my garden," he answered

"What do you grow in your garden?"

He thought for an instant and said, "Airplanes!" Along with the rest, I had to admire his sense of humor in both languages.

When the marching was completed, the students re-assembled in the *Fale Palangi* in their assigned groups of English or arithmetic. I noted a considerable increase in the number of older ones as the latecomers took their proper places. Many of these had already spent the early morning hours up in the bush taking care of some plot of land to pay for their room and board while living in the village attending school. The student body had grown to just over 100.

Malaki called the roll: Au (tattooing needle), Au Vai (chin or jaw), Faiamasofa (ocean), Faitala (storyteller), Leuma (unfinished), Meli (Mary), Olive, Paepae, (foundation), Pati (claps), Pelenato (Bernard), Pepelo (liar), Povi (cow, and the cutest child I had ever seen), Ta'ase (wanderer), Tai Fela, (weary of seeing you), and so it went. The translations of the names were given to me, as I had no way to know them. There was only one repetition, we had two Melis. It is interesting that a child is labeled by some whim of a parent. The father may have a special interest as did the village tattooing artist. Maybe the parents were building a *fale*, and it was not finished. Perhaps they wanted a cow, or the child began to tell falsehoods, or walked with a limp. Recent *Palangi* law required that they each have two names, and the second name was to be the father's name. By following the law they developed another problem. In the case of my family, as previously mentioned, the names would work out something like this: Utai chose to name his son Petelo. So, the son would be Petelo Utai. Petelo had a son he named Niko, so he was Niko Petelo. Modern laws attempting to straighten out traditions for legal reasons did not work out right away.

When I arrived in the village I carried a small blue flight bag with the logo "PAA" of Pan American Airways on the side. From that moment on I was called Pa'a (PAH AH). The word *pa'a* in Samoan means crab, the kind from the sea. When it was discovered that I was particularly fond of this seafood, the name was even more appropriate. So Pa'a was the only name by which I was ever referred by the villagers amongst themselves. When they greeted me face to face, many called me Pita (PEE tah), or Pita Pa'a, Peter the Crab. *Poto tele* means "very clever." I was one of the teachers in the town, so therefore I must be very clever. Eventually, that was added to my name. One day I returned from a trip to Apia to find that my school uniform *lavalava* of rich navy blue had been embroidered "Poto Tele Pita Pa'a." My name was to be drastically changed one night, at which point the Pa'a thing would be completely forgotten. But that was still, mercifully, in the future.

After the school roll call, about half of the students, mostly the younger ones, followed Linga to a smaller *fale* next door. The other half, mostly the older ones, turned and walked into the *Fale Palangi*. The youngest was 11 and joined the older ones because he had spent a few years in a regular school. The oldest was 29 years old and went with Linga. He had come from another village where there had never been a school. He had no idea how to use a pencil. He wanted to learn so badly that it was heartbreaking to see him sitting in with such youthful competition. I had to rely on the 11 year old youngster to translate for me.

They all settled down cross-legged on the floor mats in neat rows. One boy had brought a little box, about the size of a portable typewriter and placed it in front of him. It was a little desk made from the wooden case for canned *pisupo*. Every pupil could have made one for themselves, but none bothered, *fa lave lave*.

Malaki indicated a passage he had written on the board, and he called on one of the students to read. It was read haltingly, but clearly. The reading was fine, but I suspected the student had no sense whatever of what he was reading. Another reader took over with the same pronunciation. I was very impressed. Again he selected, and again it went smoothly. Another and another read to me, and I could hardly believe that there were so many good readers in the group. I had been in Falese'ela only a few hours, and I hadn't heard any of them speaking English. Generally anyone who could boast a word or two got into the thick of any group near an English speaker, to show off their vocabulary. The mystery was cleared up when I stood in front of the board while one of them was trying to read. She kept right on in spite of not being able to see the writing. They had all heard it once or twice, and instantly memorized the passage. That is only one example of the fantastic memorization process developed by the Polynesians over the centuries by repeating their legends and genealogies.

They were fooling Malaki, but they weren't learning English. They were performing according to their customary pattern. When the reading was completed, he instructed them to copy what he had written. They had been sitting on the mats like Egyptian scribes while reading from the blackboard. When it came time to write, they took out their pencils and paper and doubled over lying in their own lap, in order to write on the floor. It seemed to me to be an impossible position in which to accomplish anything.

Many of them could not form their letters, even the 15 letters of their own alphabet; which goes: a, e, i, o, u, f, g, h, k, l, m, (n,?) p, s, t, v, An early missionary in the1830s put the language into writing. He thought he could teach everything from his one textbook, the Bible. Why he re-invented the order is uncertain. It was a huge error.

As for teaching arithmetic, I found that would be impossible for me. Most of the problems were practical enough, based on consumer needs for purchasing material goods. However, they used the Sterling system of pounds, shillings, and pence. I had discovered previously that even having been in a Sterling area for a month that I still couldn't handle it. For example, how much would one pay for a yard and three quarters of material that costs "one pound nine and sixpence" a yard? That is: one pound, nine shillings, and sixpence.

Here is a brief explanation of the Sterling system then in effect. There was a large coin called a penny. Three pennies equal a thrupence. (I am not sure I ever saw one.) Two thrupence equal a sixpence, which was quite small. Two sixpence, or 12 pennies, equals a shilling. Twenty shillings equal a pound, which was sometimes called a quid. A pound plus a shilling equal a guinea. A guinea had a higher status than a pound and was used most frequently in luxury English shops, but it was not used in Samoa.

Malaki and I divided our work. He took the numbers, and I took the letters. Our system worked well, and I had great hopes for the future. One day, Malaki announced that he was going back to his store, and I was going to have to do the whole thing by myself. He had told me that Pati, one of the students, could handle the numbers.

In the early days, the group was alert enough as they sat on their mats repeating sound for sound what they heard. We dropped the religious readings and began with easier sentences. These proved too hard, so we worked on simple phrases. We did not have a text. Again, there was little response. I finally got them down to the single word "mat." This they knew. From here it was a step up to indicate "I." "I am sitting on a mat," was a major accomplishment that required a great deal of cooperative effort, even though all of the sounds were familiar in their own language.

They struggled with the sounds that were strange to them such as "b, c, d, g, j, qu, r, x, and z" ("z" is "zed," in New Zealand speak). All were beyond them. This could not be done in a class so large and so varied in ability. They couldn't grasp supplementary nonsense syllables for the sounds, thinking they should be words. The "th" in mother and father was a tongue and face twister. They tried, but I couldn't get most of them to do it. What I didn't want was to settle for the substitute that their peers used, the "dd" sound as in "mudder and fadder," their parents. As they say, English is easy, when you know how.

The next challenge was to get them to say: "I am standing on a mat." I had them stand up. I had them sit down. We worked on it, but it didn't come easily. So we went back to "I am sitting on a mat." That always seemed to work. For all I know, a half century later, they are probably still saying it.

We had a chair and a table in the classroom, and I tried to get them to say, "He is sitting on a chair." I had a boy do it. They could repeat, but they didn't understand. I had another stand on the table and coached them to say, "He is standing on the table." Nothing seemed to get through. The context of grammar in both languages was so different. I tried to learn some Samoan from the small grammar I had bought, but it didn't come to me either. So, we went back to "I am sitting on a mat." Their smiles showed they were back on familiar territory, and were willing to try again.

Not too infrequently, our classroom was traversed by a chicken, a dog, or a pig, all of which had the run of the village. In those moments I had them try, "I see a chicken," and point to it. They pointed beautifully, but what I heard was "I see a shiken," or a "dok," a "pik," or even a "bik pik," if it was large. I began to prepare lessons with drawings on the blackboard. At first I did a drawing of "One dog is sitting, two dogs are running, three dogs are eating, four dogs are sleeping, five dogs are barking." This was necessary, as their concept of numbers was explained to me as "a single, a dual, a triple, and then a mob." A consecutive order was foreign, and so counting, or a numerical designation, had to be learned. Without my use of their language, it was overwhelming. We soon returned to "I am sitting on a mat." I could well understand their difficulties.

I wanted to teach them enough so that Patele, who was paying me my $14 a month, would be getting his money's worth. One afternoon, a month or so after we had started, one of my girls was sitting on a *paepae* with me watching the people go by. With a smile that could have swallowed me whole, she said brightly, "I see a girl. She has a basket. She has bananas in her basket." These were the three most beautiful English sentences I have ever heard.

I was caught by surprise after class one morning when one of the older boys approached me and quietly asked: "Would you teach us the Sex Well Interest Course?" I had to think about what the question meant before I could answer such a serious request in a serious way.

One day I thought I would test the more able ones on their sense of the outside world. Here are some of the results. They knew about the United States because that was where the *kaupoi* movies came from. When they sang "God Save the Queen," it was for the Queen of New Zealand. New Zealand was where they sent the bananas, which were turned into cans of *pisupo* and sent back to their island. The Islands of Tonga beat Samoa in a war, but they were later defeated and returned to their own islands some 600 miles to the south of Samoa. Hawaii was the home of Waikiki and the ukulele. The Tokelau Islands were where the white woven straw hats came from. Tahiti was the home of *papeo*, the incredible Tahitian hula. Palestine was where the Bible came from, so at least the catechist had done his job well. All of these places are a ring of very small islands around Samoa, which is in the center. Geography 101, Samoan style.

Pati, on his part, was doing very well with the numbers at the other end of the room. He was a very clever fellow with a very enthusiastic manner. He had been a diligent student in Apia. He spoke very well and wrote very understandably. Pati was able, but he was a Samoan. I wondered how he would profit from all of this. Apia was a small town and was likely to remain so for the rest of his lifetime. There were few jobs of any value available to the Samoans except teaching in the districts. They could work as clerks in the big trading stores, or in the Post Office, or as orderlies in the hospital. Most of the supervisory positions were held by New Zealanders who preferred these upper status jobs be kept for them. Those of mixed blood, who lived *palangi* style, were granted the middle level posts. What could Pati do with his education and his enthusiasm? The Islands were slowly headed for independence, so that might eventually create more opportunities.

We divided the best readers into four sections of not more than six pupils each. I then took each group in turn out into the shade of a giant poinsettia tree. Patele had sent us some reading books for the elementary level of English. Unfortunately they had been printed for the British colonies in Africa. The stories were about people who lived in mud huts or desert tents. The animals were lions, elephants, and zebras, not chickens, dogs, and pigs. The only thing the students had in common with the characters in the books was the generally warm climate. Much of our time was consumed trying to relate the foreign life and difficult words to their own needs.

Teaching English would have been so much more satisfactory if someone in authority had cared enough to prepare a text relating to life on the Pacific Islands. They needed to work with every day vocabulary and patterns of behavior that fit into their lives. Therefore, they had a difficult time being saddled with an alphabet that had only half the letters of the English one that they were now expected to use, a difficult system of counting, and handling money. I had nothing but sympathy for the terrific struggle that was forced on these enterprising young people.

Linga had not shown any patience with her elementary classes. She was attempting to teach English with platitudes like, "A faithful friend is hard to find." When her children stumbled over these, she hit them a stinging swat with a stick. When that split, she used a board that could have broken a bone with her fury and her weight behind it. In her sadistic way, she reveled in her triumph of ruling by fear and force. Often with a lesson that was slowly learned, she would hold the class two hours beyond closing time to give them what she called "big punchment."

One morning Linga left her group and strode into my class while I was conducting English and told the students to stand up.

"What do you think you are doing?" I asked

"I am going to teach them "God Save the Queen," she announced.

"Not now!" I said. I was furious at the interruption.

"But they don't know it. They must practice," she argued.

"Get back to your classroom!" I shouted loud enough for the fishermen in the lagoon to hear. Later she held the group while they practiced for two hours after the arrival of the afternoon bus, which was our normal quitting time. Finally I sent two boys into her classroom to remove the blackboard. Linga turned purple with rage.

When the girls accused Linga of letting the boys win the pasketpall game that she was umpiring, she took the ball away. There was no way to understand with this woman.

There was to be a "lukapi" (rugby) game one afternoon, and Linga told the boys to wear their school uniforms, which for most of them was the best *lavalava* that they had. Those that showed up without uniforms she beat with a stick. She hit one so hard he couldn't walk for two days.

Linga excelled at the commands during the morning marching exercises. In the evenings she drove the youngsters successfully through practice for the completion of a dance program. But, I don't think that she taught a word of English that meant anything to the children. Her vengeance at not being the top teacher in the upper school was taken out on the young pupils.

At this point, I requested permission to attend the next meeting of the *Fono of Matais* where I asked them to try to find someone with more patience for the job of teaching the younger and slower pupils. I had brought one of the sticks she had broken when striking a child. The *matais* took note. Soon the school seemed to be running more smoothly after someone spoke to Linga about using force and weapons.

Our faculty increased by yet another when Maunga (mah UNG gah) arrived. She came on the afternoon bus and stepped barefoot onto the warm grass of the *malae*. She had been sent by Patele to ease our growing troubles with Linga. Maunga was all happiness. Her smile was almost continual, as every small thing seemed to have its good side, and she was the first to see it. She was delighted to have a chance to teach, even though she had no training. She wanted to share her good fortune of having learned something useful with all of the eager younger ones she knew were waiting for her. Maunga was 20, old enough to have settled down and have a family. She was more interested in all of the things there are to do before being resigned to life in a *fale*. She had been all around her own island of Upolu. She had also traveled to Savaii, which in itself was not too common among most Samoans. The only two other places she wanted to go were Tahiti and Heaven, which she was quite sure was on the beach at Waikiki. Maunga was prettier than most of her Samoan sisters, perhaps because of her smile. In fact by the time her luggage was off of the bus she was well established as the belle of Falese'ela.

A few mornings later, Tupe (TOO pay) arrived. She was quite tall, slim as the lines of a *va'a*, and straight as a mast. She had walked with a brisk pace into the village from somewhere down the road. She opened up her suitcase and took out a blue uniform and cap. Right in front of my class, Tupe changed herself into the district nurse. Without warning she had descended on us and halted all proceedings while she held an inspection. She was looking for signs of yaws, ringworm, or any other thing she had been trained to diagnose and treat. The pupils were lined up, and no record of student, ailment, or treatment was kept. They passed through one at a time. She had the boys strip to the waist Male modesty was much more noticeable than that shown by the girls. All but the most mature girls had to take off their dress, which they then held in front of themselves.

On this day Tupe discovered several cases of a peculiar fungus that caused round, light-colored blotches to appear on the chest, shoulders, neck and face. She slathered coats of red or purple liquids on some patients. Tupe buttered several of them with a yellow salve that caused them to perspire freely, making something of a surrealistic painting as the melting salve oozed down the blotched skin. With this, we declared recess. It was time for breakfast anyway.

About ten o'clock every day a child came into the classroom and announced that the food was ready. Each day, one of the families in turn was responsible to feed the teachers. The men had started the cooking in the *umus* at the crack of dawn and then had gone to the plantations to work. As the day grew hotter and the flies where they were working became more bothersome, they returned to the village for the regular mid-morning break. With a clang on the school bell announcing that recess had begun, the young people went out on the *malae* and chased each other around. The boys picked teams for some "pasketpall." Others gathered in groups to chat.

The teachers went to the Catechist's house and compared the delicacies prepared by today's competing village chef. My favorite was crabmeat baked in coconut cream. Chicken or pork prepared the same way was almost as good. I liked breadfruit cooked any way. Fortunately it was in season twice a year. Taro root was a second choice. It was heavier and had less flavor. It takes a while to develop a taste for it, but boiled or baked it is acceptable. To me, the least desirable of the starches, which were served at nearly every meal, were the baked or boiled green bananas. They were green when picked, and very tough. They must be peeled with a razor-sharp piece of split bamboo. They were tasteless with a dry texture, and tough to chew. There were ample greens, which I liked very much. Fresh meat was almost never served unless a pig had been killed. Yet with the variety of seafood available, which included many kinds of fish, crawling things, and rarely some fresh turtle, I was perfectly satisfied. With an occasional switch among the starches, I found Polynesian cuisine no less varied than our own. Exotic foods are interesting at first, then, an indifference towards them develops, which quickly leads to boredom. After the first couple of weeks, after settling into the routine, I found that it was like any other food, and it was all wholesome.

During the time of recess, the Catholic children had to re-assemble in the *Fale Palangi* for lessons from the catechist, who kept them for about half an hour of the break. When they were released, they joined the others and munched on whatever they had brought from their *fale*. Several of the youngsters ate sitting on the edge of the *paepae* of our dining hut like expectant puppies waiting for handouts from the teacher's food trays. Often they would suggest that they would like a certain thing. Sometimes they got it, sometimes they didn't. But, they never stopped trying. Most of them respected the teachers and just waited patiently for whatever tidbit might come their way.

Generally, after our morning meal, we returned to the classroom and worked again on English and arithmetic. It was the slow part of the day. The heat would be getting worse and there was little breeze to cool us off. Many had been sitting on the floor trying to write or calculate while bending over yoga fashion to work in their notebooks. It was a time when it was hard to discipline, as many became uneasy. Several tended to fall asleep. It was a natural carry over from their traditional rest after a meal. The habit was too ingrained to break. Besides that, some of the older students had already done much of their work for the day.

During the few minutes before one of these after meal sessions was to begin, I noticed one of my favorite students Pepelo (liar) talking with some of his friends in the doorway. He had unfolded a neat little pocket he had made in the upper corner of his *lavalava* and had taken something out. He held it up to his ear and listened to it. Then he held it against the ear of his friend. They both admired it once again, and he replaced it in the little pocket. A moment later I saw him approach another friend. He unfolded the pocket. They both admired the object and placed it against the friend's ear, and replaced it in the pocket. A moment later I saw him approach a third friend and go through the same routine. Realizing that Pepelo had somehow become the owner of a new watch that he was so proudly showing around, I thought I would use this as an opening to chat with him in English. "Pepelo," I called, "What time is it?"

He leaped upon this opportunity to converse in front of the class, and beaming, he unfolded his pocket. He took out the prize, examined it, held it to his ear, looked at it again, and said. "I do not know. It has not legs." He led the class in a unanimous burst of laughter. His act had been a complete success.

When the bus arrived in the afternoon, which could be anytime between 12:00 and 2:00, school automatically came to an end. It was a good stopping point. The bus sometimes brought friends or family from other villages, or at least interesting news. So when we heard the grunts and groans of the ancient vehicle, and the squeal of breaks as it skidded to a jerky stop, spraying sand and passengers in every direction, we called it a day. It was not long before the classroom was empty and the pupils had all returned to their *fales*. For some of them, the workday was now beginning. They had all signed up for the school with the agreement to pay ten shillings a month, and they had to earn it. In the hours before school began, and in the afternoon, they would have to work for the school and their room and board where they were staying. Many of them went up to the bush to get the big bunches of bananas that the owner had not carried down. Others put on an old *lavalava* and went out into the lagoon for some hopeful spear fishing. The girls generally went to the river to do the laundry. Some went into the bush to collect the long pandanus leaves for the making of the mats that had to be woven almost continually. There was work for everybody and everyone knew exactly what was expected of them.

Chapter XXII
OUR *FALE VAU*

Tuesday afternoon was an exception. It was the time set aside for some school project that had to be done. The first one that needed attention was the building of an outhouse, or *fale vau*, for the school. Up to this point everyone in need had just walked into the water to a chosen depth and accomplished their wish. It was not an unusual sight to see in any village. Linga was ashamed that the school did not have this basic facility when all of the schools in the other towns did. In fact the school in Leulumoenga had access to a huge "twelve holer" with two doors one for boys and one for girls. Therefore Linga volunteered to design our *fale vau*. She drew up plans in her own mind and announced that ours was to have four doors; one for men teachers, one for women teachers, one for girls and the other for boys. We would have to build a long causeway out into the water "at least a hundred yards" to ennoble further this grandiose scheme. When it was all finished, Linga wanted four locks on the four doors so that she could have the four keys on her belt.

When each Tuesday afternoon came around, our work teams gathered and began to collect stones. They then had to carry the stones to the construction site. There was one thought to keep in mind. This village had been here for many decades. Most of the readily available building material had been gathered and utilized long ago. The crew that was working on the causeway now had to go farther and farther each time to find suitable rocks and stones, which they could manage to transport. There was no mechanical equipment or work animals to help them. There was not even a wheelbarrow. The larger stones had to be rolled to the site. The older boys were assigned to fit them together to make the footpath stretch out to sea. Children just able to walk did what they could. Pairs of older ones shared their load by suspending it from a pole on their shoulders. Most of the girls busied themselves weaving palm leaf baskets and filling them with smaller stones. Gradually the tons of rocks added up to a considerable project. After four Tuesdays of hard labor the enthusiasm began to wane. So were the *paepaes* of the neighboring *fales*.

Part of the problem was solved by deciding it was not necessary to make the causeway so long. A hundred feet would do. They next decided that if a tree was cut and if its trunk was laid across to bridge an open span of water, that we could save even more work. Someone brought an axe and felled the nearest coconut tree, which dropped into the water with a majestic splash. Coco trunks do not float. However, they are much easier to maneuver in the water than on land. The trunk was chopped in half. With a great deal of effort, the gap was spanned with a pair of logs. The trunk was not much thicker than a muscular man's thigh and it took a surefooted native to balance their way across the swaying and bouncing bridge. The boys trotted over it with loads of rocks, their experienced toes grasping the textured tree trunk like talons. I was immediately disqualified.

Finally we had the triumphal causeway completed. In total, it was about 50 feet long. The basic foundation upon which to construct the *fale vau* itself was in place. It was really only a square foundation with three sides reaching just above the surface of the high tide level. The fourth side, the rear, was open to allow the water to change constantly.

The next Tuesday we all followed the streambed up through the dense forest. We climbed past small waterfalls, through thickets of tall scratching grasses, and tangling vines. It was not a long walk. It was about a mile. We finally reached a point on the ridge above the coco trees where the vista opened up so we could see the inlet below and the reef far out in the sea. It would have been a magnificent spot for a picnic. Behind us was the grove of huge bamboo trees, at least 20 to 30 feet or more tall. We entered this very special place, and as in the bamboo grove on Raiatea, I was awestruck. It was a fantastic sight to me. The dried fallen leaves had turned a silvery tan color, and covered the ground like a silken carpet. The dark green stalks, so perfectly similar to each other, reached heavenward until there was a feathery ceiling far above our heads. In this magical cathedral I was only aware of a complete silence, in spite of the chatter of the children.

The sturdy older stalks were unsuitable material for weaving together to make the sides of our proposed *fale vau*. The work crew needed to cut down the younger still flexible shoots, only about half as tall as the mature ones. With their bush knives, the boys cut several dozen poles that were then divided up for the group to drag back down to the village below. On the way down, we stopped at a little cascade. Taifela stepped into the stream and felt under the ledges of the shiny black stones. Suddenly he stopped, stood up, and showed us that he had caught some small shrimp-like creatures. With that, every stick of bamboo was dropped as all the youngsters rushed into the stream and began turning up stones in the search for the little crustaceans. "Good for eat," he said, as he handed me some. And they were, once the vicious-looking head was bitten off.

After our shrimp break, we continued to the village *malae* where the walls of the *fale vau* were to be constructed. First the bamboo had to be crushed with the back end of the axe so that it split lengthwise. Then very carefully, the more skillful among the group began the work of weaving the shredded stalks into mat-like squares for the wall panels. Every edge of shredded bamboo is sharper than most knife blades and must be handled with great care. In a very few minutes there were three walls ready. Earlier, Maunga had taken a group of girls off to collect coco leaves and had woven them into large shingles for the roof. Uprights of sturdy trunks of saplings for the corners of the building had been set up while the stones were being put in place. The basic frame of the structure had been tied together with yards of *afa* contributed by the *matais*.

When everything was apparently ready we all went into the water, or along the viaduct in groups, carrying the three pre-fabricated sections out to the frame to construct the *fale vau*. It was finished in a few minutes. It had all been so perfectly worked out in their heads. I never saw anyone take a measurement. No one had seemed to be in charge. They all knew their part in the project. There had been no disagreements of which I had become aware. The end result amazed me. It left a little bit to be desired from my conception of the original plan. But who could object that we now had our "school only" *fale vau*. Not only had we failed to complete a four holer, but it was merely a short perch. Not only had we not provided for the four doors, or three, or two, or even one, but they left the opening squarely facing the village *malae*. That was not objectionable.

The neat bamboo shelter stood proudly at the far end of the walkway, with no key, no lock, and no door. Nor, had it any clients. Before the *fale vau* had been built, there had been no noticeable modesty to the problem involved without the structure. Everybody simply walked into the water and then returned to class as if nothing had happened. Now everybody complained that the bamboo had been too immature and shrank so much upon drying out that the two end walls and the back wall offered little privacy. The fact that there was no door was never questioned. In a few days, it turned to a golden yellow. For the rest of my stay in Falese'ela, it stood there in its shimmering solitary splendor, a monument to the enthusiastic efforts of the young; abandoned while still a virgin.

The *fale vau* for Utai's *fale*, where I lived, was the most substantial of all of those that lined the inlet. It was a sturdy structure made of odd boards from an old trading store, and it had been put together with nails. The roof did not leak, as it had been neatly cut from a piece of corrugated iron. The door fit tightly, and it was locked. The key was threaded with a piece of wire onto a block of wood that had the owner's name burned into it. It hung from a nail in the cooking *fale*. The *fale vau* was roomy and equipped with a two-holer that had been carefully carved out of a large part of an old door. Just inside the entry door was a box with several dried coco husks. A cluster of the fibers is a more comfortable tropical substitute for corn cobs.

Impressive as the *fale* was, the walkway that led from the land was the main deterrent. Though I noticed that there was seldom more than a two foot rise or fall in the tide, it was nearly always low at midday and midnight. Early in the morning and in the evening, the tide was full and covered the walkway. During the years of use, no one had ever completed the stonework to raise it above the water at high tide, a matter of six inches or so. Therefore, an evening visit meant wet and chilled ankles as the walkers picked their way carefully over the slippery submerged stones. When the tide was low, and the stones were exposed, they were treacherously slick. It was much more satisfactory and safer to walk in the water on the sand beside the footpath.

Another major work project at the school was to erect a *fale* for the teachers. The others wanted to live a more independent life away from their *a'ingas*. They had asked the Council of Matais to construct a home for them. It would be near the school on the *malae* and could be used as a classroom in the daytime. The men agreed and it was no time at all before they collected the smaller tree trunks for the framing. This structure was not to be made as a regular *fale*, as no one was paying for it. It would follow the lines of a cook house, simple and easy to put together. The hip roof was assembled on the ground, and several of the women were assigned to the task of making the palm leaf thatches, which they carefully piled in stacks so that their work could be tallied and credited to the proper family. The upright posts were selected and stuck deep into the ground. A few sturdy poles were fastened to the tops of the posts to keep the frame steady and firm. Rocks had to be found to follow the traditional custom to make the *paepae*. The women and children made many trips to the river to gather rounded pebbles to fill in the floor space. This raised the living quarters, and greatly facilitated the house keeping. A *fale* never had to be swept out, as the ants took care of the crumbs and the dust sifts down through the smooth stones that were constantly being shifted when someone walked upon them.

When the floor was ready and the roof thatches were all tied in place on the roof frame, the word was passed around the town, and there was a happy gathering of the students, the teachers, and many members of the community. Each took a place around the rim of the roof, which was still on the ground. At a given signal, all bent down, and together lifted it to their shoulder. For a moment I considered that everyone was a pillar of the community as they raised the roof. It was only another moment before it was in place and lashed to the uprights. Again I had not seen anyone taking measurements. By nightfall three of the teachers had moved in and were settled as if they had just returned from a weekend. There was no need to build a cookhouse as the village would continue to supply their meals. There was no need for Maunga and Linga to think about making more mats, as now, all they had to do was ask, and the mats were immediately supplied. With this, their salary of $14 a month could stretch and cover all of their anticipated expenses.

I frequently took walks in the afternoon when the rest of the town was occupied with their domestic chores. One Saturday as I walked along the beach passing another village, I chanced upon a large party in progress. I heard the music coming from a brand new *fale*, and I strolled up towards it to satisfy my curiosity. Inside there was a large barefoot crowd standing on the new floor mats. Some were dancing. Most of them were doing a Samoan *siva*, while one pair struggled with western couple-dancing. I paused to take some pictures. It was a wedding. The service had been earlier in the morning. One of the guests spotted me and insisted that I come in and join the festivity. I was certainly not dressed for the occasion, but everyone greeted me warmly. The groom, dressed in a one-size-fits-all white outfit, urged me to dance with the bride. She looked most unhappily embarrassed but the musicians struck up a danceable tune and I reached out to hold her. She responded shyly, and we shuffled around a bit, to the delight of the rest of the crowd. I kept stepping on the bottom of the shapeless ill-fitting bridal gown that hung so forlornly on her slight frame. When the music stopped, I requested that the couple come out so that I could take their picture. The bride picked up her bouquet, which was more like a floor-length muff. I noted that the white flowers amongst the green ferns were made of ordinary tissue paper.

Beside the new *fale* they had set up a narrow sun shelter of a few poles stuck in the sand with a covering of fresh green palm leaves. The sand was covered with mats and down the center was a row of fresh banana leaves. Roasted food was being placed on the leaves. Three women carrying cakes arrived. I was not sure whether the iced delicacies were made in an *umu*, or if they had been purchased from a bakery, which seemed equally unlikely. The fancily decorated bridal cake had its own little stool to raise it above the level of the mats. It had three square tiers and a little floral arch on top. This one surely must have been acquired at a bakery, and the nearest one was in Apia.

Eventually the guests settled down for the wedding feast of roasted breadfruit, bananas, and taros, packages of roasted fish, and chunks of pork. Pork is special. Somehow through custom, certain parts of the *pu'a'a* are assigned to the various families according to their social status, and that part is what they take. Some of the guests sat under the shelter, perhaps they were family. For those who sat down on the mats, there were no plates or place settings. The men sat on one side, and the women on the other. They were all sitting tailor fashion. They soon reached out with bare hands and grasped at the food before them. I was invited to sit and join the party, but I gave my thanks, wished them all well, and went on my way. I had so enjoyed the discovery of this social event that was a blend of the traditional and the modern.

Something ought to be said about the wedding presents. I was told that the bride's family makes and collects mats and *siapo*. The groom's family collects money. All are essential to begin housekeeping. However, it seems to be more a contest between the two families as to which one can amass the most. It is that prestige thing again. Any of the guests who brought presents, which might be anything minor, like a mirror or a kitchen pot, is entitled to take a basket of food. It has been a memorable party if there is a lot of food to take home.

After several weeks of living in the village, I was accepted as a member of the community, at least to my face. Everyone treated me courteously, though I could not chat with them. In the morning I would be walking towards the river for my bath with soap, a toothbrush, a towel, and a clean *lavalava* folded over my arm, and everyone would ask me, "*Alu fe'a?*" (Where are you going?). It is the equivalent of English speakers asking "How are you? Or, "How are you doing?" (But don't tell me.) It is best translated as "Hi!"

I answered a dozen times, "*O te alu ta'ele*," "I am going to bathe." (An explanation: "alu" roughly means "going," "fe'a" roughly means "where," "ta'ele" roughly means "to bathe").

On a day when I was going to take the bus to town, to Apia, and I was dressed in my *palangi* clothes, shoes, jeans, and a shirt, and headed in the opposite direction toward the place where the bus stopped, I would be asked a dozen times "*Alu fe'a?*"

I would answer patiently, "*O te alu Apia*."

Eventually I began to think it was time to alter the dialog. I had really given up learning the language from the little grammar I had, as it needed a teacher with it. I could not get any of the friends I had in the village to teach me some different sentences. They didn't understand the concept of teaching by repetition, since few of them had been in school. So, I tried on my own to be clever. My first attempt was the following.

One morning when I was headed toward the river with soap and towel, I was asked, "*Alu fe'a?*"

I responded with, "*O te alu Apia.*" The other person was stunned motionless. No one had ever answered in such a silly way. Obviously I was going to the river to bathe. Later when I was headed toward the bus stop in my *palangi* clothes, I was asked the usual, "*Alu fe'a?*"

I responded, "*O te alu ta'ele.*" There was utter silence, and I kept on going.

I don't know what took place while I was away in the town, but when I returned to Falese'ela, the following afternoon every child in the village rushed up to me, and sometimes in groups of two or three at a time shouting, "*Alu fea? Alu fea?*" and then giggled loudly with their hands over their mouths, running off in all directions.

The following day when I was headed towards the river to bathe, the first person I saw asked me "*Alu ta'ele?*" I was stunned! We both had a good laugh.

During my frequent visits to Apia, I met several young Samoans who were glad to be friendly as it was a chance for them to practice their English. One young man asked me if I would like to go to a dance, and I readily agreed. When we got there, I saw that the price was two shillings sixpence, which would have been about the price of a normal candy bar. But it would have been a good percentage of a day's pay for any Samoan with regular employment. He asked if I had enough money, as he had none. I willingly paid, and I had a very good time. The music was made by local players. I danced with many of the local girls. Surprisingly, several of them wore shoes. The next time I was in town, he invited me to go again, and when he asked if I had any money I said, "No." I suggested instead that we go to a rehearsal of some show.

He was put out that I didn't want to go where he wanted to go. His response was a flat "No!"

On my following visit he suggested that we go to the dance again if I had the money. I said, "Yes, I have some money."

He responded enthusiastically, "Then we should all go." He and his wife got dressed and all three of us went. He asked for the money, and I told him I did not have enough for the three of us. "How much do you have?"

"Only about six shillings," I answered. He suggested that he and I go. I did not agree, because then his wife would have to go home.

"OK! Me and my wife will go, and you can go to the movies."

I was learning that they will try any trick to get something for nothing.

By this time I should have known better, but they were a friendly bunch, and I liked being with them. One weekend the fellow asked if I wanted to go to a party. I decided to go, and then the family announced that they wanted to go also. There was another girl present, and they urged me to take her as my date. We walked to the place and all went in together. It was a gathering of people celebrating a wedding. I did not know anyone there, so I just stood around for a while talking to whoever came up to me. Not long after we had arrived, the food was brought out. The group I came with filled up a basket they had brought and all began to leave. They had what they wanted, so I had to leave too, as I was staying with them. It certainly was not very gracious of us, or any of the others who followed us out.

One weekend when I was alone in Apia, I went to see a play. Of course it was to be done in Samoan, so it really was not going to mean much to me, but I was so hungry to be back on Broadway, New York, I would go see anything. The play was titled *The Albino*. It was to be in the Tivoli Theater, a hall with wooden benches. The audience perched on the benches as in church. The play was about a poor man who went out searching for food for his family. Instead, he found an abandoned bundle all wrapped up. When he opened the blanket he saw that there was a baby inside. It was an Albino. He didn't know what to do with the child, so he brought it home to his astonished wife. The play continues about the following years.

In between the acts the curtain did not close, and the cast remained on stage. The enthusiastic audience tossed money onto the stage. At first the young child, hearing the tinkle of the money, just stared at the shower of coins. The cast tried to resume their roles. The child just stood there. The longer he delayed the show, the happier and more generous the audience became. He began to bend over and pick up the money as the play continued without his participation. His stage mother grabbed his hand to pull him back into the act. The child stretched as far as he could, picked up a stick that was one of the props, and started raking in some coins. The audience was on their feet cheering this action. A true Samoan, even a very young one, knows the value of a "thrupence," and he struggled through the act to pick up the coins while the audience was in hysterics. The small Albino created a shambles of the show. It was a fun evening for everyone except the cast.

During another visit to Apia, I felt I ought to take the opportunity to have some medical attention. Before I had left home in New York, I had paid regular visits to the dentist for two decades. I'd had years of braces, before starting with fillings and eventually crowns. A dentist's office was one of my second homes. Since I had been away for almost a year without a checkup, I thought I better go to the public clinic, the only appropriate medical facility in these islands. It was staffed by a variety of New Zealand specialists. I had no trouble getting an instant appointment. When I opened my mouth, the dentist exclaimed, "Oh MY!" I was shocked! He then asked, "Would you mind if I brought in my colleagues to see your dental work?" I agreed, and four men appeared in the small room. Proudly the dentist said to them, "I want you all to see REAL dentistry!" At that point I became concerned. Yes, he recognized the fine work, but no, he was not likely trained to do it himself. I realized that Island dentistry meant extraction, not repair. Fortunately there was nothing that needed attention. So far I had avoided the possible reality of medical problems that could develop in an undeveloped part of the world. This experience kept me on my toes regarding my own health.

I met a real European named Hans Zimmer. He told me about his experience while working on a cultural research project similar to mine. He stayed with the family of a village *matai*, and they promised Hans that if he would stay with them and help them with their English, they would get him some fine mats, an *ava* bowl, and some *siapo*, all for free. They decided to take him on a *malanga* to meet the other relatives so that he would get to love them as much as they loved him. They were correct that at each stopover he would get a present. His collection of fine mats and *siapo* was coming along nicely. Someone else carried the *ava* bowl. The problem developed when he found that all this "family love" was costing him more than he expected, because the *matai's* wife kept telling Hans that he would have to give something to their hosts. That something was a pound note a night. A pound was two days wages for a Samoan, but more than a traveler would budget for a night.

When Hans and the group arrived back at their *fale*, he went out to continue with his painting. When he returned, he found that the fine mats had disappeared. When he asked where they were, he was told that they had been stolen. The wife had cut up the *siapo* to make covers for her mats. The bowl was nowhere to be found. One day Hans discovered that someone had also robbed him of ten pounds. The next day, five more were missing. The following day he saw a pile of three coils of wire in the *fale*, each with a tag of five pounds on it. Hans asked his host where he had gotten the money to buy the wire. The *matai* said, "Oh, I sold some copra today." Hans knew that was a lie because no one had made copra for several weeks.

On my return from these trips to Apia, I would bring a present for Utai, my own *matai*. The bus from town would arrive in Falese'ela sometime around mid-afternoon on Sundays. One time I brought a large can of *pisupo*, thinking it would be a great treat some evening. I knew that the family had eaten a Sunday meal after the church service around noon. I could see that all they wanted to do was sleep the afternoon away. On the special Sundays when Patele Felise would be coming, they attended his service after their nap. Utai woke up when I got to the *fale*, so I presented the can to him. He was delighted and ordered that the can be opened right away and to bring in a breadfruit for him also. He could not wait for dinner; he had to eat it then and there. The next time I brought a can of *pisupo* I suggested that the family hold on to it until one day when they didn't catch any fish. These days did not happen often, but they did occur. When I had finished my speech, Utai said in a manner that made me realize that I had made no impression, "That's a nice can of meat."

I left it on the table, and within minutes I saw him eating it. The others in the family went without any of it. I never dared to bring him a bottle of alcohol, much as he wanted me to do, as the government did not allow the Samoans to drink. I realized that the bottle would be opened right away, he would drink it down like water, and it might possibly kill him. I was learning, slowly. Apparently there is no concept of tomorrow.

The man in the next *fale* to ours had a fairly large orange tree that was just coming on to bear ripe fruit. Not that the oranges were getting yellow, as no fruit was ever given that chance. The green orbs were getting round and fat. Every time one of the villagers went by, he or she helped themselves to the oranges. Not only did they take what they wanted, but they left the peelings all around. As often as not they broke the branches in trying to reach the coveted prize. Not many days later I noticed that the tree had been cut down and was lying on the ground looking most dejected. No other family had bothered to plant a tree of their own as long as this one was available. The Polynesian custom of sharing what one wanted with someone who had it was stronger than their desire to have their own supply for their own needs.

Everyone who raised *pu'a'a* had to keep them in the village pig pen. This was several acres, and was enclosed by a high stone wall. Each man had a spot along the wall allocated for his own use, and where he had to feed his *pu'a'a*. As they are smart animals, they can be trained to come to a certain spot to be fed and will come when called. Each man had a different call. Petelo had a tin can that he beat with a stick, to get his pigs to come to their accustomed spot. Another man tapped on a wooden block, while a third whistled in a distinctive way. A man had to know his own pigs and feed only those he owned. By tradition, he must shoo away those that didn't belong to him. Generally there was no problem over this, as the *pu'a'a* did their part and went to the right place. I had been told that in another village a man did not shoo a strange *pu'a'a* away from his trough. In the eyes of the village, this amounted to stealing the food from another family. The owner of the stray had witnessed the act and threw a stone at the thief and killed him. There was no repercussion, as all agreed the owner was within his full rights. In fact, the case had never reached the Palangi Court, as no one in the village had ever reported it to the authorities who would certainly not know how the *fa'a Samoa* worked.

One afternoon I thought that it would be nice to have a small project of my own on which to work. I wanted a garden. It would offer me some productive exercise and a chance to see how things really grew in this climate. I also thought that it might set an example to the rest of the community that with little trouble, their own garden plot could supplement the rather narrow vegetable part of their diet. Many village women walked along the shore to the Chinaman's store in the next village and bought his foot-long string beans when they could easily have grown their own. I selected a spot near the school where everyone could see it as they passed by. I began to clear the space of the vines that had taken over. Obviously this spot had been cleared priorly.

Utai came out and joined me in the heat of the day and insisted on putting in his full effort. In a way, this was defeating part of the purpose, but he was determined. He was not happy with my selected spot and suggested an alternative. I could see his reason, and so we got to work. My plot was not to be very big, just an experiment. When the vines were all thrown over the stone wall for the pigs to eat, I discovered that the soil was full of little sharp stones, which were quite rough on my not-yet hardened bare feet. We tossed hundreds, if not thousands of these stones to the side. Then I discovered that the place was swarming with biting red ants that seemed determined to defend their terrain from any and all intrusion. It was discouraging, and after working a couple of afternoons, I realized that I did not have the seeds. I would have to wait at least another week to get the seeds before I went again to Apia for the mail. It was then that I learned that it was the start of the rainy season and they would not grow too well anyway. So, the good example I was going to set fell by the wayside like so many of their own projects had done. During the week of waiting, I watched the vines re-sprout and re-conquer the empty place. I settled down and began to enjoy the taste of taros and roasted green bananas. My desire for working in a garden to make a point began to fade when I considered the hot sun and the rain. Rather than fight nature, when I wanted to have some fresh green vegetables, I found that the walk along the shore to the Chinaman's store would be much more pleasant. Was I becoming a Samoan?

Chapter XXIII
THE *PE'A*

As boys grew up, each one picked an especially good friend to be his *so'a* (SO'ah). They learned to fish and work together. They often shared families, moving back and forth between them when they wished. A young man's *so'a* was responsible to be a go-between if a boy had a dispute with his own family, and wanted to return. A *so'a* was the one who approached the other's girlfriend to ask if she would marry his friend. A *so'a* was indeed one's closest confidant.

When the two boys faced maturity, one could challenge the other to see if the other had the heart to get his *pe'a*, or tattoo. Any man could present himself independently to the artist, or *tafunga* (tah FOONG ah) if he wished. Some didn't even begin the ordeal until they were well into their twenties, or older.

Theoretically, two young men, would go together to see the village *tafunga*. He could be an itinerant professional, or the village carpenter. He looked them over and evaluated the work to be done as he formulated what he wanted to do to each particular part of the body. He considered the body contours and the bone structure. A bargain was made for a number of pigs, or fine mats, an amount of kerosene, or even an amount of cash to pay the artist for his many hours of work. He instructed them about not eating or drinking before he started his work each day as they would not be able to answer the calls of nature. A date was set for the boys to appear. They were told to come on alternate mornings.

A *pe'a*, or a *tatau* as it is also frequently called, is the venerable Samoan body tattoo covering most of a man's skin between his rib cage and his knees. This is a Samoan tradition that has been carried on for more than a thousand years. Only males with the *pe'a* were considered to be men and deserve to have rights and privileges that the untattooed could not enjoy. In olden days it was not unusual to exile any male from the village without a *pe'a*, if he refused to submit to the village *tafunga* and his sharp fearsome *au*. The exile was no longer being practiced, but the untattooed must still wear a shirt and never show his bare legs. An untattooed male would not have rights to land. Many young women would not marry a boy without a *pe'a*, as he would never be considered a man in the village. It was an ordeal that tradition had established for social acceptance. It was expected of all. It was a process with a challenge to bravery, and it was a physical risk. Death by infection has always been a factor.

The reader should understand that this information was gathered a half a century ago. Except for what I witnessed, much of what follows was told to me when I was there, by various men who had been tattooed and knew what it was all about.

Come with me. Let's walk together down the beach to explore the next village. Along the way we see a group of people sitting on the sand up near the tree line by an old weathered–thatch, lean-to shelter. When we get there we find that a young *tane* is getting his *pe'a*. We receive a friendly greeting and are invited to join the others.

It is something you may not wish to see. I am going to stop and watch for a while. If you wish stay with me, we can watch the process together. If you prefer, you can keep on walking. I will catch up with you later.

I never thought I would actually see a *pe'a* in the process. Although there is a general formalized pattern, the design itself allows for a limited choice of variations, depending on the skill of the artist. I was told that a *pe'a* can relate the heritage of a family. Each part of the pattern has a special name and meaning to the wearer and the viewer.

All *pe'as* feature a large, more-or-less rectangular black area across the lower back. The top line is extended so that it frequently goes along the lower ribs and comes around the lower part of the chest to a point where both ends can be seen in front. I was given two different explanations about this black part of the design. The first was that it represented a fruit bat, or flying fox. The second was that the shape represented the canoe on which the earliest settlers arrived at the islands. To me it appears more likely to be a canoe, as each end is slightly curved as are the lines of the traditional *va'a*. It is placed high enough so that the canoe will show above the *lavalava*.

Below the canoe there is a broad triangular pattern that points down between the buttocks. These in turn, along with the hips, are also covered with varying patterns of several fine lines between thicker lines. On each side of the stomach, a fan-shaped design curves downward from the canoe, around the belly, to meet in front where the legs divide. Each leg is also completely transformed to just below the knees to appear much like a pair of tights, or some masculine form of black lace body suit. Lines can be wide or narrow. There are saw-tooth-like triangles that are inked solid black, contrasting with the bare light-brown skin areas. Further decorations can be added, such as crosses or stars, to give some individuality. The general overall design has been worked out in the mind of the artist before the first needle is applied. There is nothing haphazard about it at all. I have been told that a *tatau* can take as few as ten days for a most courageous youth, or a month or longer for a less ambitious and more cautious *tane*.

The first day the boy brought a few old mats to lie upon, and spread them out in the shade of the crude shelter. With him was his girlfriend, and members of his family who wanted to keep him company. This was a family affair, not something done in secret. They brought along their ukuleles and planned to play and sing and have as good a time as possible to try to distract the youth from his trial. Completely nude, he lay face down on the mat, his bare back towards the carpenter who had studied his physique for a final time to set the pattern for the contours he was going to cover. The boy tried to relax, but he had heard too many stories about the ordeal he faced.

The *pe'a* had already been started before I arrived. But, the process began something like this. The artist had a supply of black ink made from the oil of burnt lama nuts. The tools used looked much like back-scratchers. A tiny comb-like blade was attached perpendicularly to the end of a wooden stick about a foot long. The blades were made of human bones, boar's tusks, shark's teeth, tortoise shell, and even sharpened pieces of other seashells. The blade was carved into a single straight row of tines, as in a dinner fork, numbering from a single tine up to 20. This was placed on the outer layer of the skin, the epidermis. The stick holding the blade was then tapped with a second stick sharply enough so that the tines of the blade pierce the outer skin down to the dermis, and deposited the ink into the piercing before being lifted and struck again. It was rare that a blood vessel was pierced. Once the ink was under the epidermis, it caused a permanent coloring of the skin.

Each blade strike made a thin line of tiny dots. To make a line without dots, the blade had to be moved slightly and struck again. To widen a line, another row of dots next to the first one had to be added. To blacken an area completely, the blade had to be struck repeatedly, until there were no "dotless" spots. A spotted area would show that the master craftsman had been careless. It must have felt like being stabbed repeatedly with a dinner fork.

The master did not work alone. He had assistants. One was a "stretcher," whose job it was to keep the skin taught so that the designs being engraved in the flesh would be true. Another assistant kept wiping the work area with a rag of tapa or old cloth to keep the area clear of the oozing fluid, the mixture of expelled excess ink flushed out with blood. The skin had to be clean for the *tafunga* to continue his work. There were other assistants or apprentices present who helped to hold the body still during the procedure. A modern procedure is still much the same as this.

Once the artist had begun, he probably would not alter the pattern in any way. He put the *au* in the ink, placed it in the middle of the lower back, and gave it a smart tap with another stick. The skin is thin over the back bones, so the needle probably jabbed right down to the bone. This was followed by an involuntary lurch from the body of the victim. The trial had begun.

The boy grits his teeth in anguish. He wants to groan with pain but does not dare, as the needle is the challenge to see if he has the heart to continue. His girlfriend has his head in her lap and tries to sooth him by stroking his hair and mopping his face. She too now realizes the dreadful time that is ahead. The youth tries to keep his body as quiet as possible so the lines of the *pe'a* will be clean and true. The pain continues as the needles keep biting into the skin. Getting a *pe'a* has frequently been compared to a woman's ordeal during childbirth. However, neither of them can testify as to which is more painful. Certainly the *pe'a* takes longer to accomplish. Many women also had tattoos, but not as massive as a *pe'a*.

Within minutes the needle has been dipped again and again into the black ink and tapped several times into the young clean flesh, making a long line following the curve of the ribs towards the front of his body. Each strike of the blade leaves a short thin line of inked dots.

The boy begins to sweat and tries to hold his breath. His mouth is as dry as cotton. There is no relief. His face is mopped with a cool wet rag. Nothing seems to help.

The pain never lets up as the increasing length of the line is seared into the flesh. "Over," urges the artist. The body before him moves and suddenly it feels to the youth as if he is being cut in half. The black line is continued on the other side along the lower ribs. For one it has seemed like a dreadful eternity, for the other it has only been a few minutes of painstakingly careful work with a practiced eye.

With the initial line drawn, the tattooer really begins to go to work. The first part to be done for the traditional design is the canoe, or flying fox, which is attached to the line already in place. The oblong shaped va'a has to be a solid black area without any skin showing through. To be perfect, it must be gone over again and again. He works back and forth, tap, tap, tap, tap. One of the assistants wipes the area clean so the artist can see his progress. Another stretches the skin to keep it taut. The tafunga then continues, tap, tap, tap, tap, each time sending electric shock-like pain into the flesh. A mixture of ink and blood is now seeping out of thousands of tiny openings in the skin. To an average non-Samoan eye, it is sickening.

The tafuga stops for a second and wipes his own face. It is hot, and the work requires his closest attention. The once-rugged boy is wilting, but he knows he cannot utter a sound. To help distract him, the girl whispers sweet things in his ear. She says that it will be the most handsome pe'a ever made. All the other men will admire this one. The village will be proud to have such a brave man in their midst. His mother is wiping his face. His friends are singing love songs to give him courage.

Finally the needles stop. The tane no longer hears the tappings. The boy feels himself rising from the ground. He suddenly becomes afraid. If the work was not finished, it may have been that he yelled out to "Stop!" But it was fine. He had done nothing wrong. His two uncles are lifting him and supporting him as they lead him, step by painful step, away from the shelter, towards the sea.

The boy is moving his legs one after the other slowly and reluctantly. He knows that there was more pain to come. Years before when he had cut his arm his mother brought him to the sea to soak the wound in the water. How well he remembered how much it stung. He could recall that day as if it was this morning. A few more steps after his ankles get wet, he will begin to feel that sting again over a far more vast and painful area of his lower back. He feels himself being lowered slowly into the water. The sting is sudden, but not as bad as he had feared. The sea is cool. It is the coolness that helps the most at this moment. He sits there with his uncles, and is comforted with the knowledge that they, too, had suffered the same when they each had their pe'a applied. They could understand what he is going through.

After an hour or so, the bleeding stops, and the surplus ink and blood have been washed away. He is gently lifted to his feet again, and they walk towards the shore. Waiting in the shade are his mother and elder sister who, unaccustomed to his nudity, are none the less proud of his achievement. They had been in the forest collecting medicinal leaves to apply to his wounds to cool the burning. For long moments they stay, none wanting to move. Finally an uncle braces the lad on his shoulder and walks him slowly into the cooling deep shadows of the forest. Here they will meet no one and can begin the long hours of walking that lay ahead. They walk for an hour or more and then they will return to the sea for another soak.

This was only the first of dozens of hours of walkings and soakings by which he would pass the next several days. The newly tattooed must walk continuously to keep the blood circulating to prevent poisoning and to prevent boils and scabs from forming too early. These would blister and leave scars that would ruin the perfection of the *pe'a*. Not once did he meet his *so'a*, who was having a day free of the *au*, but probably walking and soaking at the other end of the village. It would not be good for them to meet each other until it was all over.

The next time the boy returns, the tafunga starts to work where he left off. At the bottom of the canoe, he creates the broad triangular design that points down into the cleavage between the buttocks. As he gets to the lower part of the spine, the *au* strikes the bones again and is intensely painful. The next areas are the hips and buttocks. The boy wants nothing more than to jump up and flee from his skin. The carpenter says, "Roll over." Gentle hands roll him over onto the other side. Then as before the sensation of wasp stings begins again.

The girlfriend whispers: "I am so proud of you. I can't wait to marry you. The other girls will be so jealous."

The needle continues to dig into his skin. The sure hand of the tafunga never falters. The work continues relentlessly. The boy tries to think of something other than his misery. "Is this really making me more of a man?" he wonders. He hopes her love is increasing with each jab that is turning his body into a permanent record of these days of agony.

On a following day, the youth is weary from restless nights. He has found no relief as fatigue fuses with pain. The artist continues the design he had worked out on the boy's mid-section. He must create the fan shaped segments that cover the sides of the belly and drop into the area where the legs divide. After several hours the uncles led him step by painful step away from the shelter, towards the sea.

The wounds of the days before are bothersome. The scabs that had formed itch as if thousands of ants were crawling over his body. There is no way to get relief, as scratching would destroy the scabs and ruin a part of the *pe'a*.

One day the work begins on one of the thighs. With the new work continuing, there are more places for the persistent flies to bite. While the carpenter works on the leg, it begins to twitch uncontrollably. An uncle holds firm. The needles and the tapping continue. The leg is all muscle, and the stinging has been bearable, but suddenly the leg cramps unmercifully. The needles are being tapped down to the bones of the knee. He cannot move. He cannot cry out.

Once more he feels himself being lifted and going towards the sea. This time, however, it will be a slower walk. He has not one muscle functioning voluntarily in his messy, bleeding leg. The first days he was lucky that he could not see the results of the tattooing. But this time he can't help staring at the wretched gore that was once his thigh. This day, more than any other so far, he feels his nerves and muscles. The very

sight makes him go mercifully limp, so that he can be carried quickly to the water. No one speaks. The cooling water brings him around. When he opens his eyes all he can see is his dreadfully mangled leg stretched out before him with little wisps of black ink and red blood hanging like storm clouds close to the ugly skin. Gradually the blood and ink mixture drifts off like smoke, clearing the water in which he is sitting. He wants to cry at the sight of his outstretched limb. Would it, could it, ever be the same again? There was still one leg yet to be done.

The mother was so proud of him now that he was more than a boy. He was almost a man. This night was no less long, as the walking and soaking continued. The work of the past several days was itching terribly, but there was to be no relief from it for days to come. During the following sessions the second leg will be covered.

In earlier times, there was complete tattooing deep into the groin, around his anus, and covering the genitalia, I was informed. More recently this intimate part of the *pe'a* has gradually been discontinued.

Finally, it is the last day. He is still *leuma* (lay UU mah, unfinished). There is still one detail left to be completed. The final touch, considered the most painful of all, is the decoration of the navel. Stretched out flat on his back, with many hands offering friendly but firm pressure, he braces himself for the pain that would end his boyhood forever. With his stomach in knots, he awaits the last taps of the *au* as it incises a tight circle around the navel and that is emphasized with a four-pointed star. Theoretically this cuts his final tie with his mother. His suffering was now over. He is the proud possessor of a traditional *pe'a*. He is now a "man."

That night he was allowed to walk lamely through the village. He was able to meet his *so'a*, and they could walk together, brothers in misery. Now they were allowed to drink and eat all they wished, but neither had much interest in food anyway. They were forbidden to scratch their itching body. But walk they must, and soak, they must. They needed their friends as crutches as they slowly paced their way up and down the sandy lane that went through the village. The cool night air felt good on their flanks and legs. Never before had they dared to even think of walking naked through their village. However, the entire village was with them in spirit, as the town had gained two brave men.

It would be several days before they would care to lie down for very long, or even choose to sit with any comfort. It could be weeks before they will even fall into a sound sleep. It will be a very long two to four months before they can comfortably go back to their work. They have deserved the privileges of manhood. They can now bathe with the men. They can marry with pride. They can own land in their own right, and they can go anywhere without a shirt.

How did this tattoo thing come about? One source told me that many years ago a Samoan princess was taken to Fiji and married to the king. She tried to kill the king's son by another wife. This attempted assassination so infuriated the king that he took his Samoan wife to an uninhabited island. There he tied her to a tree that he set afire. Huge Samoan flying foxes saw the fire and their princess in the tree and flew over and put the fire out. Some Samoan men landed and rescued the princess and took her back to her homeland in their canoe. Two Samoan girls then living in Fiji, decided to go back to their island of Savaii. They had learned a song that they wanted to teach to the people of their village indicating that all Samoan women should be tattooed to honor the bats. All the way home they sang the song. Eventually they saw the village of Falealupo, their hometown, at the western tip of Savaii. When they arrived their first thought was to have some time in their own lagoon to relax from the voyage.

When the girls finally waded ashore much to the pleasure of the townspeople who were glad to see them back, they remembered the song that they were supposed to sing to honor the bats. They sang the song to the entire village, but by chance they said that it should be the men who must be tattooed to honor the bats. The chief of the settlement, wanting to be the very first to honor the bats, immediately submitted to have the abstracted design of a bat carved into his flesh. In those days (perhaps one to two thousand years ago) there was no sharp needle, or au. The artist probably used a shark's tooth or a sharpened piece of shell to engrave the skin. Too late for the chief, and indeed for all men, the mistake was soon discovered. It could never be rectified without shaming the chief, and so to this day, men are still being tattooed.

However, this custom, like other traditional aspects of the fa'a Samoa, was dying out in the mid 1900s. Many of the young men were refusing to yield to the custom, preferring the jeers to the jabs. Creeping urbanization, income opportunities, and new Palangi laws establishing land rights, were breaking the customs and weakening the fa'a Samoa. This breakdown of the once strict social structure comes when the young decide that anything that is disagreeable or inconvenient to them is "useless." The pe'a for many of the young men is useless. It is a danger to their health, and it is probably advisable to eliminate the ordeal, even with the new drugs that might stop a dangerous infection.

In the early years of the 21st century, after all of the above was originally noted and written, there has been a resurgence of cultural pride in Polynesia, particularly in the Marquesas, Tahiti, and among the more activist Maoris in New Zealand. Some of the young men and women are again heading to the local parlors to get their pe'as, or "tribal" designs applied. Many of the more recent "tribals" are symbolic patterns, bolder, and nontraditional. These are personal proclamations of pride in heritage and boasts of nationalism. They no longer have to undergo the lengthy suffering as before. Now the artists can use modern electrical tattooing equipment under more sterile conditions. However, for the traditionalists, there are still artists who will use the old ways if the customer wishes, at their own risk.

In the year 2005, a half a century after my visit to the area; I heard a sad story. The 20-year-old son of a Samoan living in Southern California returned to Samoa for a two-week vacation. He wanted a pe'a, and he went through the ordeal. His father told me that his son died of an infection shortly after returning to California.

Chapter *XXIV*

LATE AFTERNOON IN FALESE'ELA

I generally spent the late afternoon hours correcting the school papers. It was an interesting time to be in an open *fale* watching the daily village patterns gradually coming to a close. The women had spent much of the day sitting inside in the shade weaving mats, or sewing clothes on a hand powered Singa. When the sun began to shine through the *fale* from the water side, the women gathered up their young and herded them towards the creek. They all knew that they would be going for their evening bath. It was a time for the youngsters to have more carefree play with their friends in the wonderful moving water. This was forbidden to them when they were not with a parent

While the women and children were busy at the river in a happy mood, their places in the village were taken by the men who were coming down from the bush with the evening supply of food for the family. Most of them carried palm leaf baskets over their shoulders and their long bush knife. Occasionally one carried a rifle and a few wood pigeons he had shot. From the beach where the va'as were being carried to dry out, came other providers with their catch of lagoon fish strung together in colorful bunches. Some had boxes of eels or crabs they had trapped. Some had nothing. The older men would go to their *fale* and rest a while, sorting out and repairing their equipment. The younger men began to prepare the *umu*. When the *umu* task was completed, the young men were free from their daily chores.

Gradually the women and children would return from the river as most of the men were on their way to bathe. It was a time for all to socialize and enjoy themselves. At this place there was no conflict of religious beliefs, every person was a friend. The shadows were deep near the river due to the big trees overhead. As the sun sank further behind the hill across the bay, it became quite dark. There were no more children around. The only sounds near the pools were the voices of the men telling tales of their day in the bush, or out in their va'a.

From the village came the sound of the big *lali*, the wooden drum made from a hollowed tree trunk. This was the first warning and the men finished their bathing quickly in order to get back to their *fale* before the complete curfew for the evening began. This is a part of the missionary period that still had a hold on village life.

By the second *lali*, everyone must be in their homes gathered around the kerosene lamp ready to pray. Both faiths in our village took the curfew seriously as wardens from both churches were on patrol ready to slap a fine on any offender. On the third signal from the *lali*, prayers began in every *fale*. From the homes of the LMS people came the soft singing typical of the a cappella voices heard throughout Polynesia. The night air carried the tunes and mixed them with the recitations of the Catholics. The evening mists settled in the valley blending with the wisps of steam from the cook-house. The mingling of these sights, sounds, and smells brought every day to a pleasant close.

As I had been excused by Patele from participating in the prayer time, it was this time that I could go to the river to take my bath. Each evening I stopped by the store and met Tapo. We went to the river together. His reasons were different from mine. Born and raised in the Ellice Islands, he had come to Samoa during the war to get work. While he was in Apia, he met and married a girl from Falese'ela. When the war work was finished, he decided to stay and live with her *a'inga* and open up a little trading store. He was accepted as such by the village, but no more than that. He had known that in order to become part of the village with all of the rights and privileges, he would have to take the final step to becoming a man. So he went and made arrangements with the local tattoo artist for his *pe'a*.

He lay down on the mats under the tiny shelter one hot day and felt the thousands of jabs of the vicious au. That night he did the walk and soak, and walk and soak. He did not go back the next day, or the next, or the next. In Samoa, a man without a *pe'a* is not a man, regardless of age. Men are tattooed, boys are not. But one who starts and does not finish it proves that he has not the heart, and he is considered so low that no one wants any association with him. Tapo was "leuma," and by definition could have been so ostracized that he would have left the village. He had, however, the good fortune to be an Ellice Islander. Tapo, being from another place, naturally meant that he could never be a real Samoan anyway. The others realized that his failure was only natural, and so they gave him credit for trying. His failure to reach Samoan manhood only reinforced their opinions of themselves and their low regard for others. Tapo, by this act of fate was not permitted to bathe with the men, as he was not a man. He was also deprived of the use of the big pool when the women and children were there, as he was not one of them either. Tapo had to sneak off in the dark during prayers, which was the time allotted to him. It was because of this that both of us, Tapo and Pa'a went together.

One evening on the way to the pool, he told me about one of the *matais* in the village who had sent his daughter to the shop to get some canned fish, tobacco, and soap. Tapo told the girl that her father had already reached his credit limit of three pounds and until he paid that off he could have no more credit. She went back and told her father. The *matai* sent her back again with the message that if Tapo didn't give him the goods, he would never pay the three pound debt. Tapo then reluctantly gave the girl the goods to take back to her *fale*. The next day the girl was back again with an order for a can of *pisupo* and baking powder.

The father of Tapo's wife was named Vaufusu (vow FOO soo). He was a big slob of a man. Tapo worked hard at his storekeeping and was gradually beginning to make something of it. He was willing to pay a little more for the dried cocoa beans, so more people in the area brought him their harvest. One day he was sick and needed supplies to replenish his stock. He asked Vaufusu to take the sacks of beans into Apia and sell them. They were worth about 50 pounds. Vaufusu took the beans to the trader, sold them, and got some of the needed items on the list. Sometime later he returned to Falese'ela with only two sacks of flour and a carton of canned fish. Tapo asked about the rest of the goods. Vaufusu said that he had gone to Molenu'u (moe lay NOO oo) where the local big wigs meet, and treated them all to lunch. He was a little man from a little village trying to impress the city boys.

Often when Tapo and I went to take our baths, the blackness of night had already fallen and the stars were out. At other times, the sandy path reflected the bright moonlight that silver plated the entire village. When we got to the river, some caution had to be used, as the rocks were slippery. Worse than that, they were covered with small nocturnal snails that had three little horns sticking up from their shells. Though not dangerous, they were most unpleasant to step on, or sit upon. The little spikes often broke off in the skin and presented a small problem of extraction. This was the only thing that marred the beauty of the solitary bath we could have otherwise enjoyed completely. We naturally did not go up to the men's pool, but rather to the one for the women and children. I did fear that there might be trouble if I overstepped their hospitality towards me in this way. I disrobed completely, got wet, and lathered up. The pool was all a-glitter with moonbeams that slithered across the surface like water bugs. I dove from a rock and swam to the other side. I swam a couple of laps and finally got out of the water to dry myself.

Tapo could not contain his curiosity forever, and finally he asked me, "Why do you bathe nude?"

"This, my friend, is the way everybody dreams of bathing where I come from," I answered.

"But, aren't you ashamed?" he asked.

I was surprised at the turn of the conversation. He apparently could not hear as well as I, that everyone else was praying.

"No, why should I be ashamed?" I asked.

"Because God sees you!" he snapped back as if it had been the most obvious reason in the world. I had to admit that I had not thought of it in that way.

"I don't think he really cares that much how I bathe, as long as I bathe," I said.

"Well then, you don't know God!" which slammed shut that line of the conversation.

While we were standing on the rock discussing another problem, I heard someone say in a sing-song voice: "*Susulu i lo ta po*" (soo SOO loo ee lo tah poe), which was familiar to me from a line in a song then currently being sung in the village, meaning "That which shines at night." I suddenly realized that a chance moonbeam had picked out my brilliantly white bare bottom, the only part of me that was not sunburned almost as brown as the other residents in town.

By morning, and until the day I left the village, I was called by everyone, with a broad smile, "He who shines at night."

Chapter XXV
OUR SCHOOL *FIAFIA*

Our district, having lost its isolation so recently with the new road, still clung onto many of the traditional patterns that were disappearing in the bigger towns on the northern coast of the island. Easy transportation to Apia, and the movies, cut deeply into the historic demand for self-entertainment. Part of the project of the school, beyond the letters and numbers, was to teach them to be proud of their *fa'a Samoa*. It was also an opportunity to learn many of the old ways and to preserve them to pass on. It was Malaki and Linga, strongly supported by Patele, who decided therefore, that our school should hold a *fiafia* (FEE ah FEE ah, a festival). *Fiafia* is a good name for a good time. They would invite the students and teachers from the other two schools in the *Solulufinga* to our *fiafia* to be held over a weekend. This would show that the young people could carry on tradition and ceremony.

Every night after dinner for the two weeks before the date set upon, we met in the *Fale Palangi*. Linga, Malaki, and an elderly couple who coached them, had all the students in our school prepare traditional entertainment. They practiced dances that had not been seen for several years in our town. By the light of two pressure lamps, they sat on the floor going through the motions. They were weaving stories that in times past had been the basis of passing on to the young the cultural heritage and history of this proud race. Songs that had been unheard for so many years were new to this group. They were now being taught and practiced until they were heard almost continuously in one part of the village or another, and even out in the bush. Although I can not sing, I did join the dance practice. Linga kept us at the task she had set for us. We were learning something which that, without her drive, would surely have been forgotten in a very few years.

On the designated Friday afternoon, the students and teachers began to arrive by bus and truck. They were shown to the big guest *fale* right next to where I lived with Utai and Ponga, and they were made comfortable. The guest *fale* was normally the home of another *a'inga*, but they offered the biggest *fale* in the village for the weekend visitors. Linga had found a huge washtub and into it she poured the contents of several packages of orange flavored drink, and added buckets of stream water until it met with her taste. It was our welcoming refreshment.

One of the visiting groups complied with tradition by bringing with them an *ava* (kava) bush. *Ava* is a member of the pepper tree family. In ancient times virgins sat around the large ava bowl (tanoa) chewing on the root and spitting the salivated mush into the bowl where it was mixed with water, and served. Although we were planning to preserve many of the customs, we were all willing to forgo this one. The presentation of the ava bush was made by the donor standing outside the *fale*. He announced in a loud voice for the entire town to hear "Our group brought the ava root. It is the biggest ava root that we could find. It is the most expensive we have ever seen. It came from far up on the mountain where no one had ever been before." He continued to exaggerate the qualities of the gift with typical island eloquence.

The ava bush was then accepted by Malaki who praised it with even greater enthusiasm, not being able to thank the donating group enough. The root was then tossed unceremoniously out the back side of the *fale*. It was quietly replaced with some packaged powdered ava readily available in Apia. It was put into a bowl, and mixed with water according to custom, by the chief's virgin daughter. The coconut shell cups were then passed around in order of status position of the teachers and students, each letting a few drops onto the floor to please the spirits.

The formal greeting over, the visitors unpacked their suitcases and changed into their play clothes. The girls worked up teams for a "pasketpall" tournament and went at it with great energy. It is a game generally spurned by their brothers, who prefer to play it only if they can play with the girls. They rarely played it by themselves. Wearing their long *lavalavas* for modesty is a hindrance to their enthusiasm for the game.

The boys ran out into the main *malae* to choose teams for "lukapi," (LUH ka pee), which closely resembles the game of rugby from which it is derived. A regulation ball similar to an American football is used. Sometimes a "regulation" coconut is used in village games. Most players wore their *lavalava* at knee length, tied up at the waist. But no one wore shoes. The village crowd gathered here and sat on the *paepaes* of the surrounding *fales*, which made a good grandstand. They came to watch here because there was more chance of a big fight in lukapi, than in pasketpall. In between the small skirmishes that never really led to fighting, the boys played a great and energetic game. Good plays or good players were recognized by cheerleaders who, instead of leading organized cheers, danced a *siva* to gain more applause for the boys. The *siva* is a sort of hula that each person develops on their own to perform at any occasion. It is much appreciated by those watching and is sometimes better than the game. With all of these diversions, and the happy visitors all in a gay mood, the *fiafia* got off to a good start.

Friday evening everybody gathered in the main building for prayers and chow. The prayers followed the usual pattern by saying short prayers and responses. Considering that there was a mixture of many faiths, they all seem to have been included. It then came time for the presentation of the food. Those who were sitting nearest to the rear of the *fale* passed forward the several palm leaf baskets full of hot roasted food for the feast. One of the visiting young men was designated as Announcer. He went out onto the *paepae* to repeat in a loud clear voice each of the donations so that the entire village could hear it. Our town had supplied the food, and it was traditionally acknowledged in this way. A boy sitting among the baskets pointed to one of the host-donors, and that youth would say, "I have given three taros and two packages of fish." That would then be repeated to the Announcer as, "Lua Po has given three taros and two packages of fish." Outside in a loud clear voice the Announcer would repeat for all to hear, "Lua Po has given three taros and two packages of fish." Next, "Pepelo has given a large pot of cocoa, and a chicken," was heard from one end of the town to the other. And so it went. Donation after donation was recognized and accepted. It went much more quickly than it would seem. At the end of the long list of recognitions, the Announcer stated how grateful the guests were for the generosity of their hosts. He then returned to his place in the circle of people who were now dividing up the food and putting it on the woven palm leaf trays. These trays were then passed around, one tray for every two people. A grace was said, and with this as the end of the formality, we set to the task of eating the bounty spread before us.

The *Fale Palangi* was full to capacity as Patele addressed the nearly two hundred gathered students and teachers before him. He spoke of the pride he felt in the work we were all doing in going ahead and learning new ways, at the same time preserving the old ways. All of the teachers spoke in turn, including me. As I had to speak in what to them was a foreign language, I spoke slowly and clearly. I talked about how the other peoples of the world looked with longing at the South Pacific Islands that were at peace with their neighbors. I was glad that their own traditional system so far could take care of their own problems. I said that the word "Samoa" meant only "Paradise" in the minds of so many millions of people in other countries. I finished by saying that if the rest of the world would only follow some of the ways of the *fa'a Samoa*, we would be much better off. As a speech, it was mercifully short by their standards, but they seemed to appreciate my words of international jealousy. It was my only public address during my stay in the country.

We then went out to the *malae* where the rest of the townsfolk had gathered in a huge circle to watch the evening presentation. Each of the three schools of Patele's *Solulufinga* had prepared songs and dances to perform as their contribution. We were witnessing the budding of the cultural renaissance of Samoa. For "modern" youths, it would not have been so much effort to bring a battery operated machine to play dance music instead. They had left that life in Apia and for this weekend they were trying to recapture the magic of the past.

One of the other schools had practiced a stick dance that was a traditional series of military exercises of ancient times. They formed into several teams of four boys each. One pair of boys each had two short sticks. The other pair of boys each had a single long stick that they held with both hands. To the rhythm of a beaten *lali*, the boys attacked and backed off, parried and jabbed, bent and swayed, backwards and forwards, in and out, they struck at each other, or clashed their sticks together with swift jabs and swings. But each movement was to the sound of the *lali* and showed the results of thorough training. The clicks of the sticks as they hit each other sounded as one from this group of many. ("E Pluribus Unum") The strong shadows cast from the light of the pressure lamps danced in unison on the grass of the *malae*. The crowd was enthralled. They demanded another performance from the group, which readily complied. Everyone remembered that it was just such an encore of this stick dance that changed Samoan history.

The Kingdom of Tonga is a collection of low islands some 600 miles to the south of Samoa. It is populated with Polynesians also. Centuries ago a Tongan military expedition landed on the island of Upolu and defeated the Samoans. They became very demanding conquerors, and there seemed little hope of the Samoans escaping eventual slavery. One night, in order to entertain the Tongans, the Samoans invited them into the walled compound of the sacred *malae* where the temple stood. It was forbidden in all Polynesian cultures to bring fighting weapons into the sacred *malaes*. So, unarmed, the Tongans entered the compound to witness the dance. The Samoans performers entered with their stout sticks to perform their specialty dance. They formed their groups, and when the drummer started beating the *lali*, the dancers began their series of military movements that made up the stick dance.

The enemy was indeed pleased with the intricate and skillful motions of the teams. When the performance was over, they demanded a second chance to watch their newly conquered vassals entertain them. The *lali* sounded again. This time, the dancers spread themselves out further from the center until they were at the very edge of the seated Tongans. The performance went as before. Suddenly, upon a set signal from the drummer, the Samoans turned on their defenseless enemy and soundly beat them with their stout sticks, killing many of them. This ended the power of the Tongans. The expedition sailed home in defeat.

Tonga, though unsuccessful in its attempt at conquest, has never itself fallen under the power of another nation. They have built up a constitutional monarchy that is the model the other Polynesians looked towards to emulate in their own hopes for independence and stability. However, I have heard that Samoa (2005) has a form of a republic based on the Matai System.

With over a hundred visitors in town that night, there was little hope for peace and quiet. Many indeed were captured by the sporting urge to go fishing by torchlight. Others waded in shallows, which were well-lit by the bright moon reflecting off of the white sandy bottom. They were looking for such delicacies as octopus, crabs, sea cucumbers, or any other thing that they might chance upon. Some sat in the *fale* and sang or chatted, as students anywhere would do on a holiday weekend. A few went to play ukuleles and do a *siva* in the silvery sand. Many chose simply to pair off and stroll through the deep shadows of the town. During the time of tighter missionary oppression, all of these activities were forbidden. Anyone out walking at night was obligated to carry a lighted lantern. The missionary wardens were on patrol to see that no two lanterns went into the shadows together. If they did, or if the wardens caught two people without their lanterns lit, they would beat them or fine them for disobedience.

Saturday morning was devoted to the preparations of the great feast that was to come later in the day. For several days food had been collected from the plantations for the village to supply the needs of the guests. The guests on the other hand had brought their own items to share. Every *umu* in town was smoking as a sign that a vast amount of cooking was being done. Behind our *fale*, much of the activity was being carried on by Utai's family, because they wanted to show how much they could donate to the *fiafia*. One of the more interesting of the operations was the preparation of the big pig that Utai was giving.

Petelo had caught the biggest *pu'a'a* that the family had raised, and he led it from the village pig pen back to the cooking *fale*, where it was trussed up with the help of Lua Po. Once its feet were tied together, it was rolled over on its back squealing uncontrollably. Petelo took a sturdy timber and braced it under a heavy rock. He placed it over the pig's throat and stood with all his weight on the other end of the log, suffocating the struggling beast. The execution committed, the surgery began. All the hair had to be singed off with a flaming torch and, the carcass scrubbed free of all debris. Next he cut the anus free, and pulled the gut out far enough so that he could tie it into a knot. Then he cut the throat and severed all the tubes, pulled them out, and tied them with knots. Finally, he cut a larger square hole around the navel, likewise tying a knot, then pulled the entire viscera carefully out through this opening. Aromatic leaves were stuffed into the empty cavity and several red hot stones were shoved in and the carcass placed over the hot *umu*, covered over, and the roasting process began. The innards were picked over and separated. Selected parts of the intestines were cut free for special cooking. The lungs were kneaded into a flaming red mass and set aside for some designated *matai*. The rest of the intestines were taken back to the pig pen for the survivors to eat with gusto.

Around mid-day Petelo joined the other townsfolk gathering on the *malae* who were ready for the main presentation. The river had been crowded with young people taking a break from their labors. Everyone had been doing their share to make this *fiafia* the best possible.

Later, Patele Felise called me to the *Fale Palangi* where all of the notables were gathering. Someone had erected a flimsy archway with palm leaf decorations, through which were passing all the people from miles around who had come to see this mighty celebration. Patele stood tall on the steps, and with a speech, opened the ceremony to let the food presentation begin. The school bell rang and we waited, but not for long.

From both ends of the village, young people, all wearing their colorful school uniform *lavalavas*, came through the archway. They came in pairs carrying kettles suspended from poles, containing puddings made from taro or breadfruit. Teams of four boys each, carried platforms on their shoulders loaded with pyramids of roasted taros, breadfruit, ta'amu (ta' ah moo, a vegetable stalk), or bananas. Behind them came other teams with platforms of kegs of *pisupo*, cases of canned fish, roasted chickens, or bundles of baked fish. Behind these marched women carrying buckets of tea made from orange leaves, or beautiful cakes they had somehow baked in the *umus*. But most of the attention was paid to the men who brought in the roasted pigs. Heavy on their shoulders were the carrying poles from which hung the animals that had so recently been in the village pig pen. Each *pu'a'a* was decorated with red hibiscus blossoms. The flowers were stuck on the ribs of palm leaflets, to make them stand up. These had been jabbed into the crisp brown roasted skin. With all the other food, there were 300 taros, and 18 roasted pigs.

Properly presented in the loud clear voice of the Announcer, each of the foods was placed near the steps of the *Fale Palangi* for all to see. Patele Felise accepted all of the food in the name of the school and the organization, and thanked the village and the specific *matais* whose *a'ingas* had donated the tremendous amount of food. He then gave the order for the distribution to begin. The choice pieces went into the *Fale Palangi* where all of the dignitaries had gathered. The floor of the great room had been carpeted with a great number of fresh cut bright green banana leaves. Portions of the food from the kegs, the buckets, the pails, the baskets, and the platforms were piled in a long row down the middle of the room, along with loaves of bread and the cakes. Completely missing was any sign of fresh fruit, which would have added a great deal of contrasting color to the feast. In spite of the abundance of bananas, I never saw an islander eat a ripe yellow one. They prefer the wizened roasted green ones. Papayas, though they grow wild, are eaten green by the workers in the bush, but are never brought down to the town to ripen. I for one was literally starved for fruit, which could so easily have been tended right near every *fale* in the village.

Patele indicated that I sit down with him, along with a few others, and we began to eat by grabbing what we wanted. Instead of sitting down with us as I had expected, most of the village people present had brought palm-leaf baskets and were beginning to fill them up with everything they could get their hands on, within their allotted ration. Outside on the *malae*, men were butchering the pigs and tossing the almost-raw meat into heaps. These were then picked over by the basket bearers, each of whom took specific pre-designated pieces for their particular *a'inga*. Patele told me that the *pu'a'a* and the other foods had been only partially cooked to show that it had been put in the *umu*. The families that were now walking down the road loaded with their ration would have to cook it more in their own *umus*. Actually, their feast would be in their own *fales*, with none of the activity I had associated with the word "feast." We went on eating the things specially prepared for our small select group. By the time we had finished, there was no evidence of the ceremony that had immediately preceded the meal, except the tilting archway.

Lukipi and pasketpall were played strenuously throughout the afternoon as the heated tournaments continued. Quite a crowd had gathered to watch the boys' games, as the two visiting schools had well coached and practiced teams. It was not long before personal disputes raged into full-fledged fights. The crowd was becoming more and more pleased with the turn of events. Some members of the audience participated bodily if they thought their favorite player was being badly outnumbered. Eventually, the continued bickering on the field, while the game was still being played, developed into a free for all. The audience entered into the spirit of things by picking up small stones from the *paepaes* on which they were sitting, and tossed them into the foray. Several players were hit, and one was carried off of the field with a nasty gash over one eye. Someone had thoughtfully brought some sulfa powder in a bit of neatly folded newspaper. Three players in all needed first aid. This spectacle so unnerved me that I left to avoid having to see more. I tried to attend to the wounded as best I could while the others kept calling us all back. When I refused, Malaki came over and said that everything was all right. He added that there had never been a Samoan *fiafia* that had not ended in a big fight. "How do you think we earned the name 'The Irishmen of the Pacific'?" he asked.

The afternoon activities ended with the camaraderie restored among all the participants. Soon the bathing pool was full with the visitors, and many of the locals crowded around for a refreshing break. As the late afternoon shadows spread across the village, we all prepared for the evening's entertainment.

In the light of the pressure lamps placed around the *malae*, our own school Song and Dance Group was preparing to present their performances in the competition with the other schools. Our girls, dressed in our uniform of the navy blue *lavalava* and white blouses, entered and formed a chorus in front of the collapsing archway. Each had braided their hair and had large white flowers in it.

As a welcome to all those gathered, they sang the song for our school system, the *Solulufinga*, which began something like this: "*Solulufinga o le a susulu, susulu i lo ta po*," which meant, "The Haven for the Abandoned will shine tonight."

This is where the words "*Susulu i lo ta po*" came from, which I had heard while I was taking my bath in the pool that moonlit night, when I wasn't wearing my *lavalava*.

The girl's next offering seemed to be something of a love song and there were smooth actions of their bodies as they swayed with the rhythm.

Then the chorus line burst into a lusty number that required lots of body movement to tell the story. Feet zigzagged in the grass, knees bent up and down, hips swayed right and left, shoulders twisted fore and aft, while arms were flung thither and yon. It was a miracle that they all performed as one. We were so proud of the team effort and the amount of work they had put into this flashy number. After a bow to accept the wild applause gracefully, they performed an encore. They could not have done better. They took their places sitting on the ground. With this the archway suddenly disappeared into the darkness to the relief and laughter of all watching.

When it was quiet, our boys marched into the lamplight in uniform and formed a straight line and sat cross-legged on the grass, their hands in their laps. Their bare upper bodies were glistening with a fresh coating of oil. On their shoulders, they wore a fresh banana leaf that had been split down the middle rib far enough so that they could put it over their heads. Over each right ear was a big yellow flower.

The drummer began to beat on the *lali*. Every boy picked up the rhythm with his knees and held it. Then their shoulders picked up the beat, followed by their elbows, until all of their bodies were vibrating in unison. When they started this traditional *sasa, or* slap dance, they swayed to the left, they turned to the right, all of the time clapping, or waving, or sweeping the air with their arms extended to interpret the legend. Frequent slaps on their thighs, the stomach, or the chest, punctured the night air. Another loud snapping sound was made by a sharp downward movement of the upper arm, when the biceps slapped the side of their bare chests. I practiced long and hard before I could duplicate it. These sounds accentuated by contrast the smoothly flowing arcs made with their arms over their heads. Suddenly on a final beat of the *lali*, they all bent over, and we saw a row of bare backs almost level with the ground. Under hundreds of critical eyes of the townspeople and visitors, these boys had performed to perfection. The audience was completely enraptured at this show of their own culture. They demanded more and got more. Three times more they had to go through their routine. And each time more delighted with the appreciation they had drawn from the crowd.

Except for what may have happened during the Independence Celebrations when Samoa was granted its freedom from New Zealand on New Year's Day, 1962, the *fiafia* that I had just witnessed may have been one of the last community celebrations of this kind. A *fiafia* of this magnitude was just too expensive for most communities. I was so very fortunate to have had the opportunity to witness it.

A short time later one day in late June 1956, I was approached by a police officer in Apia who informed me that I must appear in town the following day. I was to find out from the New Zealand Department of Education that since I did not have a government-issued teaching certificate I must stop my "illegal teaching" and leave the island as soon as possible. They listened frigidly to my argument that our schools were trying to help the illiterate older youths and that it would be their only chance to learn for the changes coming to these islands. "No matter!" was the response I received. For the Board, their "policy" was more important than the reality of the ignorance they were willing to prolong. Apparently, their aim was to rid themselves of the annoying Priest who could not otherwise be put in his place. My hopes of staying in Samoa had just been cut down to four wonderful months. It was at that moment that I thought of the many things I had hoped to accomplish, and the few that had actually been achieved.

The following afternoon, when the bus arrived and I was closing down my class, I noticed a Palangi couple getting off the bus. This was most unusual, so I went over to investigate. I met Regg and Kathy Butcher, an Australian couple who were passengers on the banana boat that was in port. They had asked where they could go by bus to see some of the island and get back by evening to return to the ship. A Samoan had suggested that they take the Lefanga bus and go to the end of the line. There they would see some scenery and a few typical villages. He added that perhaps the Palangi teacher in Falese'ela might be there to show them around a bit. What luck for all of us.

The driver agreed to stay for about an hour, so we had enough time for a little tour. We went to my *fale,* and I asked Failili if she would make some orange leaf tea, then added that we would be back in a few minutes. That done, we started on our grand tour.

The first stop was to be the pigpen. I grabbed a bundle of weeds, walked over to Petelo's spot, hit his can a few whacks with the stick, and a couple of his pigs came trotting over, eager for any offering that might be forthcoming. Regg took some pictures. I tossed over the fresh greens, and I had a chance to scratch a large sow behind her ear, a sort of friendly good-bye to her as she eagerly devoured the weeds. She was "with litter," and Petelo had reluctantly offered to slaughter her for a final feast for me.

I had firmly declined. I liked the sweet pig and knew they needed her piglets for the future.

We then went off to check out the bathing pools. We saw a couple of women doing their washing in the lower pool. In the best of Polynesian hospitality, I asked if the visitors would like to take a bath. They politely declined, but thought it kind of me to offer. We admired the school *fale vau* in all its golden glory.

We returned to my *fale*, had a quick inspection of its contents and construction, and noted the cooking *fale*. I suggested that Regg and Kathy sit as comfortably as possible on the mats. Utai offered us a ceremonial welcome cup of kava from his large multi-legged, hand-carved, well seasoned, wooden *ava* bowl.

All this unusual activity was attracting a crowd of the neighbors gathering around staring in awe at the scene. Ponga and Utai were glowing with pride that they were gaining prestige at entertaining unexpected Palangi so lavishly. The onlookers were certain that we were celebrating a quick visit by the King and Queen of New Zealand. Everyone was enjoying the moment to the hilt. I suggested that they turn around and. with a regal Windsor smile give them the limp wave the Queen does as her carriage passes through the streets of London. It worked magic, and the village had something to talk about for the rest of their lives.

We relaxed with our hot orange leaf tea. Failili served some sliced cold taro, breadfruit, and some pieces of mango with coconut cream dip. My foreign guests had a chance to chat with Utai and Ponga, and all too soon our little party was completed. On our way to the bus, Regg offered me his card and insisted that when I got to Sydney that I give them a call. I promised I would, but said it might be months away. Soon they were gone, and the first guests we had ever had were on the way back to town, delighted with their native experience. The villagers went off in a dither, and things would never be quite the same again.

On my last day in Falese'ela, I had to board the creaking bus for Apia, waving back to a mass of weeping faces of my many friends and students. I boarded the plane for the flight to Fiji. It was the Fourth of July 1956, my own Independence Day.

Illustrations of the Islands of Samoa

Photo 53. The track around Savaii Island, Samoa

Photo 54. A taro patch.

PHOTO 55. THE FRAMING FOR THE ROOF OF A FALE ON TUTUILA ISLAND, AMERICAN SAMOA.

PHOTO 56. MOVING DAY FOR THE CURVED END SECTION OF A ROOF FROM ANOTHER FALE.

PHOTO 57. RUINS OF A FALE SHOWING FRAMING, ON SAVAII ISLAND.

PHOTO 58. A SAMOAN VILLAGE SCENE SHOWING SPOOLS OF MAT-MAKING MATERIAL
FOR WEAVING, AND COCOA BEANS DRYING IN THE SUN ON MAT IN FOREGROUND.

.PHOTO 59. L TO R: IOSEFA, HINA THE DRESSMAKER, AND LIKI WITH A BABY, SAVAII.

PHOTO 60. YOUNG MEN MAKING A SAMOAN VA'A, OR CANOE, SAVAII.

P 61. The Women's Committee cleaning the cemetery, Savaii.

Photo 62. An old man in an old va'a.

PHOTO 63 SAVAII VILLAGE BUILT ON LAVA FLOW INTO THE SEA.

PHOTO 64 THE ONLY TWO-STORY FALE I SAW ON SAVAII.

PHOTO 65 THE LONGEST FALE I SAW ON SAVAII.

PHOTO 66 MY FAVORITE HOUSE OF ALL WAS IN MY VILLAGE OF FALESE'ELA ON UPOLU ISLAND

PHOTO 67. THE AUTHOR'S SAMOAN FAMILY IN FALESE'ELA VILLAGE, UPOLU ISLAND.
BACK ROW: PONGA, UTAI, PETELO, FAILILI.
FRONT ROW: UNKNOWN, UNKNOWN, LUA PO, LUA AU, AND BABY NIKO.

PHOTO 68. AUTHOR ON HIS SLEEPING MATS INSIDE THE FALE
OF UTAI, FALESE'ELA VILLAGE, UPOLU.

PHOTO 69. THE VILLAGE ANNOUNCER DRESSED IN SAMOAN TAPA CLOTH.

PHOTO 70. BEATING THE LALI, FALES'ELA VILLAGE. IT IS TIME FOR PRAYERS.

PHOTO 71. GOING FORMAL TO A WEDDING, UPOLU ISLAND.

PHOTO 72 BRINGING THE WEDDING CAKE.

PHOTO 73. A SAMOAN BRIDE AND GROOM.

PHOTO 74. THE CATERED WEDDING RECEPTION.

PHOTO 75. A SAMOAN SHOWING A SIDE VIEW OF A PE'A
– HIS BODY TATTOO,
TUTUILA ISLAND, AMERICAN SAMOA.

PHOTO 76. CHILDREN PRACTICING THEIR SAMOAN SIVA, A DANCE, IN FALESE'ELA.

PHOTO 77. THE REAR VIEW OF THE PE'A.

PHOTO 78. PREPARING UTAI'S PU'A'A (PIG) FOR THE FIAFIA, A BIG PARTY, FALESE'ELA.

PHOTO 79 BUILDING THE ROOF ON THE GROUND.

PHOTO 80 THATCHING THE ROOF.

PHOTO 81 THE WHOLE COMMUNITY TURNS OUT TO RAISE THE ROOF,
EXCEPT ONE YOUNG MAN WHO IS LOSING HIS LAVALAVA.

PHOTO 82 MAUNGA, A PILLAR OF THE COMMUNITY,
HOLDING UP HER PART OF THE ROOF.

PHOTO 83 UTAI, MY LANDLORD AND MATEI.

PHOTO 84 WOMEN DOING THEIR LAUNDRY, SAVAII.

PHOTO 85 THE TA'AMU PLANT HAS AN EDIBLE STALK.

PHOTO 86 THE DELIGHTFUL MEN'S BATHING POOL, SAVAII.

PHOTO 87. BRINGING *PU'A'A* TO THE *FIAFIA*, FALESE'ELA VILLAGE, UPOLU.

PHOTO 88. SOME OF THE FOOD GIVEN TO THE FIAFIA, FALESE'ELA.

PHOTO 89 THREE IMPORTANT MATAI DRESSED IN FULL FORMAL REGALIA.

PHOTO 90 THE TOWN BAND DRESSED IN TAPA CLOTH
UNIFORMS.

PHOTO 91. THE GIRLS WERE OUR ONLY SAND-MOVING EQUIPMENT, FALESE'ELA.

PHOTO 92. THE BOYS WERE THE CARRIERS OF THE STONE AND THE BUILDERS
OF THE CAUSEWAY.